NEWMAN AND
HIS THEOLOGICAL METHOD

NEWMAN AND
HIS THEOLOGICAL METHOD

A Guide for the Theologian Today

BY

THOMAS J. NORRIS

LEIDEN
E. J. BRILL
1977

Nihil obstat:

JAMES DOLLARD
Censor Deputatus

Imprimatur:

† PETER BIRCH
Bishop of Ossory

25 March 1977

ISBN   90 04 04884 7

I consider that, gradually and in the course of ages, Catholic inquiry has taken certain definite shapes, and has thrown itself into the form of a science, with a method and phraseology of its own, under the intellectual handling of great minds, such as St. Athanasius, St. Augustine, and St. Thomas; and I feel no temptation at all to break in pieces the legacy of thought thus committed to us for these latter days.

John Henry Newman

TO MY
FATHER AND MOTHER

Who first taught me
The Good News of Christ

CONTENTS

PREFACE

During the Catholic period of his life Newman was reluctant to call himself a theologian.[1] The principal reason for such reluctance is to be found in his conviction that he was neither conversant with neo-scholastic theology nor the history of theology.[2] Two exceptions in the history of theology must be the fields of patristic[3] and Anglican theology.[4] In his years as an Anglican he attempted, with more success than any of his contemporaries, to create a new basis for Anglicanism in terms of his theology of the Via Media. Typical of this effort was his *Prophetical Office* which was written in 1837.[5] However, he gradually abandoned this position, having first reservations in 1839 and more serious doubts after 1841.

It is quite true that Newman was not a professional theologian if one means by this someone who is professionally engaged in the teaching of theology or is the head of a school of theology. Only for a short while in 1846 had he the idea, suggested by Wiseman, of founding a theological college for secular priests at Maryvale, an aspiration which he soon dropped as unrealistic.[6] In spite of all this it is still permissible to call him a theologian. He is a theologian 'sui generis' who, in his own words, "liked going his own way".[7]

---

[1] 1853-1875: Autobiographical Writings (1965) 299; LD XV 316f, XXI 212, XXIII 98, 205, XXIV 212f (important), XXVII 200f; Diff. II 293. See too the whole preface of my Newman-Lexikon (1975), 1039-44 (Theologie)

[2] LD XXIV 212f: ". . . really and truly I am not a theologian. A theologian is one who has mastered theology—who can say how many opinions there are on every point, what authors have taken which, and which is the best—who can discriminate exactly between proposition and proposition, argument and argument, who can pronounce which are safe, which allowable, which dangerous—who can trace the history of doctrines in successive centuries, and apply the principles of former times to the conditions of the present . . ." (1869).

[3] Patristics: J. Artz, Newman-Lexikon 590-3 (Kirchenväter), 638-9 (Library of Fathers), 79-80 (Athanasius-Ausgabe, engl.), and under the proper names of individual Fathers.

[4] Especially the "Caroline Divines" of the seventeenth century (see Newman-Lexikon 170).

[5] J. Artz, Newman-Lexikon 888-9 (Prophetical Office), 1129-31 (Via Media).

[6] Memorandym of May 10, 1878, in: Oratorian Papers 390. See also LD XI, 280f, XII 16 (1846/47).

[7] "Like St. Gregory Nazianzen I like going my own way". LD XXIV 213.

From a similar angle one may justifiably consider him a philosopher.[8]

Newman's manifold pastoral duties prevented him from devoting himself exclusively and full-time to systematic theological research. Indeed it was his keen sense of pastoral responsibility for his contemporaries and their situation which inspired him to write his principal works and to seek out new paths in theology.[9] In this way he has provided us with a thorough, closely-reasoned and personal starting-point for a new method of theological thought. For instance, his essay on doctrinal development introduced into the mainstream of dogmatic theology the category of the historical, just as the Catholic schools of Tübingen and Munich did for Germany.[10] His accent on the evolutive and historical quality of thought has resulted in a powerful stimulus for French theology, as B.-D. Dupuy has shown,[11] and has had its tangible effects on the Second Vatican Council. His was a direction of thought which transcended a merely deductive method. Thus Newman has touched on the modern problems of the historicity of truth and the sociological dimensions of knowledge.[12]

The apologetic of Newman also deserves a methodological analysis and evaluation. It starts out from man, paying special attention to the condition and situation of the unlearned, and then considers the reasons that justify the certitude of his faith. Furthermore, it sees assent as an independent act, certitude as a reflex assent, and reflection not as a verbal, formal and logical proof, but as a mental and implicit reasoning in which cumulated probabilities converge on certitude or proof as their limit.[13] The liberal rational-

---

[8] J. Artz, "Newman as a Philosopher", lecture at the Dublin International Newman Conference, June 1975, now in: International Philosophical Quarterly XVI (1976), 263-88. See also: "Newmans philosophische Leistung", in Newman-Studien X (in print).

[9] J. Artz, Newman-Lexikon 54-6 (Arbeitsweise Newmans), 835 (Pflicht, 1).

[10] See J. Artz, "Entwicklung und Auswirkung von Newmans Theorie der Dogmenentwicklung", in: Theologische Quartalschrift 148 (1968), 63-104, 167-198; and my introduction to my German edition of Newman's "Development" ("Über die Entwicklung der Glaubenslehre", 1969).

[11] B.-D. Dupuy, "L'influence de Newman sur la théologie catholique du développement dogmatique", in: Newman-Studien VI (1964), 143-66; and: "Newman's influence in France" in Red, 147-73.

[12] See J. Artz, "Newman as Philosopher", 284-7, and J. Artz, "Newmans philosophische Leistung", chap. 7 and 40.

[13] J. Artz, Der Folgerungssinn (illative sense) in Newmans Zustimmungslehre (Grammar of Assent), in: Newman-Studien II (1954), 219-45, 361-71. J. Artz, Der Ansatz der Newmanischen Glaubensbegründung, in:

ism of the time which rejected the certitude of faith stimulated
Newman to search for an epistemology which was not limited to an
abstract ideal of formal logical perfection but which took the
psychological facts and the concrete process of reasoning as its
basis. And so his epistemology began from the given possibilities
of the concrete individual in his concrete situation.

Sometimes one meets statements and passages in Newman
which seem to anticipate the phenomenological method more
according to M. Scheler's model of this method than E. Husserl's
model.[14] The anthropological starting-point which Karl Rahner
uses in his theology, as well as his rather Kantian-flavoured trans-
cendental method, are already present in Newman. In his *Grundkurs
des Glaubens* Rahner once refers explicitly to Newman: "There is
the fact of an 'illative sense', to use Cardinal Newman's word,
which is especially operative in any question requiring a definite
decision. Such a decision is a consequence of probabilities and
involves a certitude as well as an upright and responsible choice,
which is at once both knowledge and free action. In a paradoxical
way, the illative sense bestows scientific shape on questions which
in themselves are justly unscientific in shape. There is a first step of
reflection, which has to be distinguished from the step of reflection
in science (in the modern meaning of the word) simply because
life and living demand such a first step." It is this first step of
reflection which the opening section of Rahner's treatise on theological foundations considers.[15] This one instance shows how Newman
is present in the theological thought of today.

The few observations offered thus far may be enough to demonstrate that a special inquiry into Newman's theological method is
a pressing need. This method has not yet been adequately studied:

Newman-Studien IV (1960, 249-68. J. Artz, Newman-Lexikon, 339-44
(Folgerung), 344-6 (Folgerungssinn, illative sense), 400-4 (Gewissheit,
certitude), 513-4 (implizit-explizit), 1213-6 (Zustimmung, assent). J. Artz,
Wahrscheinlichkeit (Lexikon für Theologie und Kirche, X, 1965, 922),
Zustimmung (op. cit. X, 1420-1). J. Artz, Illative Sense (Historisches
Wörterbuch der Philosophie IV, 1976, 201-2, Implicit Reasoning (op. cit.
IV, 261-2).

[14] See above note for my philosophical studies on Newman, also my
inquiry "Newman und Kant" in: Newman-Studien VIII (1970), there 146f
and 151.—Max Scheler includes while Edmund Husserl excludes existence.
M. Scheler combines "Phenomenology "with "Philosophy of Value" (Wert-
philosophie), he criticises Kant's "Formalism in Ethics".

[15] Karl Rahner, Grundkurs des Glaubens, 1976, 22.

although many studies of Newman touch on it, none actually dwells upon it in an explicit manner. The subject of the present inquiry is not so much the content of Newman's thought as the structure and mode of his reasoning, his method.

A study like this has been necessary for a long time. Its value lies in its thoroughness, in the fact that it covers all spheres of theology. It not only analyses Newman's method but also focuses on the context of his time and its influence. It underlines the significance of Newman's thought for the present and the similarities between the two. A further merit of this inquiry must be seen in its highlighting of the connection between the development of Newman's method and the phases of his life, his own personal development.

The introduction of the author points out details of the subject-matter. Let me draw attention to a few aspects only. First, there is the accent on personalism, that inner relationship of all theological statements to the believing person. Next, the penetrating analysis of the concept of dogma throws light on the original statement of dogma and its essential and final formulation, its temporal conditioning and unchanging centre. Finally, this work clarifies the meaning of analogy for the perception of mysteries.

I am convinced that this unfolding of Newman's method will greatly contribute to the enrichment and development of modern theology.

JOHANNES ARTZ

Bonn,
December 3, 1976

INTRODUCTION

Cardinal Newman was born in 1801. He died in 1890, over eighty years ago. His name has not only survived the vicissitudes of time, but continues to grow in eminence. In fact, so great has been his influence in our day that he has been described as "the absent Council Father of the Vatican Council". One of the Fathers of that Council, Archbishop Robert Dwyer of Nevada, testified in these striking terms to the influence of Newman on the proceedings of the Council: "The Council might well be described as the flowering of the Cardinal's whole philosophy of religion".[1] The objective of this work has been an investigation of Newman's "philosophy of religion", my great concern being his method of understanding, teaching and transmitting the faith.

My one preoccupation, then, has been the method of Newman's theology, and not its content. I was anxious to get the answer to these questions: What is Newman doing when doing theology? Why is that activity theology? What does he discover in virtue of that activity? This study is an attempt at the discovery and articulation of the answers to these questions. In pursuit of Newman's theological method I had, of course, to probe his theological content. That probing put me in contact with a rich and profound theology. But all the while I kept on asking: What is happening here in Newman? What is he doing?

It is generally believed that Newman is an inexhaustible source for theses. The number of theses still being done on him continues to grow. And yet no one has actually studied his theological method as such. It is true, of course, that the topic has been touched at various tangents, but it has not received formal and explicit treatment. Content, and not method, has been the pursuit of nearly all Newman scholars. That so many studied, and continue to study, his theology is some indication of the splendour of that theology. But it follows immediately that, as method is the source and generator of content, an investigation of method in Newman's theology should be of immense interest and value. That method must be the key that opens the door to the riches and treasures of Newman's theology.

---

[1] Archbishop Dwyer, The National Catholic Press, December 3, 1967, 7.

My method of research entailed a careful and analytical reading of the Corpus Newmanianum, as the primary source. Shortly after commencing reading, I realised the wisdom of Professor Collins' advice: "First, at the outset it is better to assimilate a few basic themes in Newman than attempt a vast expedition through his writings ... In the second place, rather than run the risk of wild comparisons, it is safer for us to focus on Newman's own text studied for its own sake. We can accept the paradox that Newman's contemporary relevance lies precisely in being himself and inviting us to study his thought in its own shape and texture".[2] In the second place there were the writings of the various commentators, among whom the more recent, and the ones most relevant to the subject under study, were of principal interest to me. These secondary sources were of singular importance in helping me to context and situate Newman. Newman himself it was who said: "Every man is a son of his time, a product of his age". It was vital, then, to appreciate the character of his age and the problems of his time. Only within such a perspective could Newman's own work be apprehended and evaluated.

But there were problems. Newman was not a systematic thinker. He did not elaborate ordered systems. He wrote little except essays, discourses, sermons and letters. Works like An Essay on the Development of Christian Doctrine, the Apologia, and the Grammar of Assent are the exceptions that prove the rule. Almost every one of his works, then, has an eminently "situational" character, being written to meet a particular need, to answer a definite question, or to supply guidance to an individual or to a group of Christians.

The substance of my study, then, attempts a reconstruction of Newman's theological method. That method runs through all his theology. Newman lived in an age which has been called an "age of evidences", when, as he said, "love was cold".[3] Reason had been enthroned as the Messiah of the new age. The England of Newman's day not only professed faith in this new Messiah, but put that faith into practice in undertaking all her programmes, whether political, social, educational, or religious under allegedly enlightening guidance of "Reason". The scientists found the new philosophy stimu-

---

[2] J. Collins, Philosophical Readings in Cardinal Newman, Chicago. 1961, 27-8.
[3] OUS, 197.

lating, because it seemed to say that the destiny of mankind could be effectively planned and implemented purely in terms of science, in fact, their science.

It was inevitable that in such a rationalistic and scientific milieu Christianity would be subjected to a test of her scientific status. Did she give the real knowledge she claimed about God, and man, and God's plan for man? Could she exhibit the evidences for her doctrines as convincingly as, say, mathematicians and geologists exhibited theirs? In other words: is theology a science with a method of its own? The scientists, philosophers and many of the theologians answered these questions negatively. Christianity did not give certain knowledge about the "Unseen World". Its doctrines were but opinions. Her evidences could reach at best only a high probability and so unconditional acceptance of her dogmas of Faith, was dishonest and immoral. This mentality Newman described as Liberalism.

Our first chapter treats of Newman's diagnosis of the Liberal's attack on the principles of Revealed Religion. He pinpointed the root-cause of the attack: a method of positive science, valid in its own field, had been erected into a philosophical theory of mind and then applied inordinately to Christianity. Newman attempted, not only a refutation of this idea of investigation and method, but above all the provision of what he considered to be the correct methodology. His Essay in aid of a Grammar of Assent is his formal exposition of what he considered to be the true way of inferring, of proving and of verification, and of arriving at certitude. The work itself is his answer to the basic question: What am I doing when I am judging? Why is this particular activity judging? And in view of the quality of the answer given in the volume to these questions, it well deserves the praise lavished on it recently as "the masterpiece in the field of epistemology".

I next wished to see the formal structure of Newman's method in actual operation. An Essay on the Development of Christian Doctrine was precisely such an application, not as a mere theological exercise, but in a great and vital issue for himself: the claims of the Church of Rome to be the genuine heir to the Church of the Fathers. In the third chapter, then, I tried to observe the methodological operations of Newman as he tackled the problem, gathered the data, developed and refined an hypothesis of solution, and finally, verified his hypothesis. The chapter closed with a series of conclusions.

Still, theological method for Newman meant more than the application of a formal set of rules or directives, however sound or true. With dispassionate clarity he saw theology as the fruit of religion, and good theology as the product of religious love. This fact led me on, in Chapter IV, to draw out what Newman judged to be the very foundation of the whole theological enterprise and of a "personal Christianity". In short, Newman saw such foundations to consist of religious, moral and intellectual components. One's theology would inevitably reflect one's possession or lack of religious, moral and intellectual "conversion". Each conversion or interior operation opened up to the subject a "new world of meaning". "The foundation of our religious profession must be laid in the ground of our inner man".

The ground has now been well and truly cleared for all that is to follow. Newman has powerfully come to grips with the claims of the Liberals. He demands for theology a "Novum Organon" (Chapter I). Such an "Organum Investigandi" he formally outlines in the Grammar (Chapter II), and proceeds to show in operation in the Development (Chapter III). Finally, all method must be conceived of concretely, as the actual reflection of a concrete subject on the substance of Faith. The final four chapters follow on in logical sequence and embody the great principles established in the first four.

Chapter V illustrates Newman's method of doing fundamental theology, especially apologetics. It outlines his original manner of grounding the Christian Faith in history, and justifying its claim on our unconditional love and acceptance. As might be expected, he demanded a method alive both to the unique character of Christian Revelation, on the one hand, and to the particular situation of man, on the other.

In Chapter VI my concern was to highlight Newman's method of dealing with doctrines and dogmas. I show that he has been able to ground critically dogmas on a recurring operation of the mind, the act of judgement, which he personally appropriated. I claim for Newman's discovery of the act of judgment in the individual mind, and his underlining of its theological equivalent of doctrine in the mind of the Church, a real originality, perhaps, his greatest achievement as a philosopher and as a theologian. And as Newman's name is forever associated with the idea of doctrinal development, I deal with the development, permanence and historicity of dogma in his thought in the same chapter.

Newman excelled as a teacher of the Faith and as a prophet of God's word among God's people. Accordingly, in Chapter VII I try to break into the secret he had of making the thrilling mysteries of Christ's Kingdom, the "Unseen World", come alive for people. I show how Newman possessed an original style of shedding the light of the Christian mysteries on the human situation. By confronting the Word of God and the questions of man about man's existence, dignity and destiny, Newman succeeded in revealing to his contemporaries "the length and breadth, the heighth and depth of the mystery of Christ". For Newman theology is far more question than thesis. His method led to a real apprehension on the part of the faithful, of the centre and core of their faith, the person of Christ and his saving work in the Church.

In the eighth and concluding chapter I try to indicate the significance of Newman as a theologian for our own day, precisely in terms of the theological method he elaborated during his long life of service to the cause of Revealed Religion. He carefully diagnosed the influences on Christian Faith and theology in his own day: a reawakened interest in history, a yearning for a genuinely personal Christianity, and the positive sciences. His influence continues to grow. Among the many who profess their admiration for him as a theological thinker, I mention Fr. B. Lonergan, S.J., as an outstanding instance.

There is an interesting correspondence between the first four chapters of my thesis and the second four chapters. In general, the first four represent the foundations of method, while the second four constitute the edifice built up on these very foundations. Thus chapter two and chapter six are internally correlated, for, while the former articulates the role of judgement in human knowing, the latter underscores those faith-judgements in the Church, which we call dogmas. Chapter three on the Essay on the Development and chapter four on the conversion of the theologian, have their perfect complement in chapter five, which is on fundamental theology and apologetics. The eighth and final chapter shows how Newman has become an outstanding theologian for our time precisely because he was true to his own milieu, with its problems and aberrations, which milieu we considered in the first chapter.

What are my own conclusions about Newman? Shortly after he composed the Grammar he wrote to a friend that it was his considered view that "we need a Novum Organon for theology, and I shall be truly glad if I shall be found to have made any suggestion which will aid the formation of such a calculus".[4] My conclusion is that Newman has indeed aided the formation of a Novum Organon for theology. He would have rejoiced to have seen the extent of his contribution in this vital field in our own day.

To begin with, I have highlighted the fact that he has made a dynamic synthesis of classical deductive and modern inductive methodologies, that he has supplied theology with foundations that are at once interior, personal, religious and philosophical, and, finally, that in the illative sense he has provided a tool eminently adapted for scientific inquiry in a religion of historical incarnation, such as Christianity. Classical science could manage only the certain, the necessary and the universal. Newman worked out an original method of catering for the probable as well as the contingent and the particular.

Next, he has been able to critically ground a doctrinal Christianity as the only authentic form of Revelation in virtue of his self-appropriation of the act of judgement. Further, his method of disclosing the beautifully rich meaning of the Christian mysteries has both reinstated into the mainstream of Catholic theology the Patristic and Alexandrian style of theology, and has anticipated the insight of the First and Second Vatican Councils into the methods of dogmatic theology. As his own life was a great spiritual odyssey into the fullness of Catholic truth, in which he discovered "a new world, a world of overpowering interest",[5] in a similar way his theology displays a method of personally appropriating the unfathomable riches of Christ given us in the sources of faith in the living Church. And finally, he has indicated a method of dialectic, whereby counterpositions can be reduced to their presuppositions with a view to promoting reconciliation between clashing parties, and to leading people into new worlds of meaning. Finally, Newman saw that theology was being influenced in the fields of history, philosophy and science. In reply, he developed Christianity to meet an age of historical mindedness, scientific achievement, and philosophical sophistication. He well knew that the heart of man must be disposed to hear the Word of God in each age. Cor ad cor loquitur.

This introduction would not be complete without expressing my heartfelt gratitude to many. There was Fr. Latourelle, S.J., who

---

[4] Ward, II, 275.
[5] ECH, I, 23.

kindly accepted the direction of my reading and research. That acceptance was my fortune: he put at my disposal his time, energy, advice, patience and, above all, his theological mastery. The fact that I have come this far is due in great measure to his unfailing attention and encouragement. I express thanks, too, to Fr. C. S. Dessain, now called home to his eternal reward, and to the Fathers of the Oratory, Birmingham: from September to December 1972, I enjoyed the expert advice of the former and the hospitality of the latter. My gratitude is due also to my ecclesiastical superiors, my Bishop and Rector, who, each in his own way, made possible the preparation of this study. I am thankful to Sister Consilio, Kilkenny, for her generosity in typing the whole manuscript. Many more there are of whose assistance, in one way or another, I am deeply conscious. Let me but say that the writing of this work was, in the final analysis, a collaboration that made the writer: his prayer for them is that of John Henry Newman:

> "Thou canst make up to (them)
> All Thou takest from (them)
> And Thou wilt,
> For Thou wilt give (them) Thyself".

ABBREVIATIONS

Ap	Apologia pro vita sua, 1864, 1913
Ar	The Arians of the Fourth Century, 1833
Ath	Select Treatises of St. Athanasius, 1842-4
Cam	My Campaign in Ireland, 1896
Cons	On Consulting the Faithful, 1859
DA	Discussions and Arguments, 1878
Dev	An Essay on the Development of Christian Doctrine, 1845
Diff, I, II	Certain Difficulties felt by Anglicans in Catholic Teaching, 1850, 1876
DS	Denzinger-Schönmetzer. Ed. XXXIII
DTC	Dictionnaire de Théologie Catholique
ECH, I, II	Essays critical and Historical, 1873
GA	An Essay in aid of a Grammar of Assent, 1870
GA'	Grammar of Assent, Image Books Edition, 1955
Greg	Gregorianum, Rome
HS, I, II, III	Historical Sketches, 1872-76
Idea	The Idea of a University, 1889
ITQ	The Irish Theological Quarterly
Jfc	Lectures on the doctrine of Justification, 1874
LD	The Letters and Diaries, Volumes XI-, edited by C. S. Dessain, London, 1961-
LG	Loss and Gain: The Story of a Convert, 1848
Mir	Two Essays on Miracles, 1870
Mix	Discourses addressed to Mixed Congregations, 1849
Newman-Perrone	"The Newman Paper on Development", T. Lynch (editor), Gregorianum, 16 (1935), 403-44
NCE	The New Catholic Encyclopedia
OUS	Oxford University Sermons, 1843
PS, I-VIII	Parochial and Plain Sermons, 1869-70
PG	Migne, Greek
PL	Migne, Latin
PN, I, II	E. Sillem, The Philosophical Notebook, 1969-70
Prepos	Lectures on the Present Position of Catholics in England, 1857
Red	The Rediscovery of Newman, 1967
SD	Sermons bearing on Subjects of the Day, 1843
SN	Sermon Notes, 1913
TS	Theological Studies, Washington
TTE	Tracts Theological and Ecclesiastical, 1871
VM, I, II	The Via Media, 1891
VO	Verses on various Occasions, 1867
Ward, I, II	Life of John Henry Newman, London, 1912

CHAPTER ONE

THE PROBLEM OF METHOD IN NEWMAN AND HIS TIME

The Problematic of Newman's Contemporaries

The eighteenth and nineteenth centuries are recalled by historians and scholars as the age of Enlightenment. In the wake of the French Revolution, a host of new ideas, which had initially inspired the revolution, were quickly spread across Europe. These soon caught hold of the intelligentsia of the time, in whose minds and hearts, already aroused and eager for a change, they found a fertile receptacle. In the area of thought, religious and secular, reason was enthroned as the great gift and discovery of the time. Man, the world and their destiny would henceforth be regulated by reason and its counsels.

It is small wonder, then, that in this same century there comes to light the alleged antithesis and supposed opposition between the insights of reason and the claims of religion. The method of science seemed diametrically opposed to the spirit of the then current theology. Those who tried to bridge the gap between the two and found the effort exhausting or utterly beyond them, ended up either by admitting the incompatibility of the respective methods, or by opting for one to the exclusion of the other. Few there were who really got to the root of the alleged contrast and opposition. The roots of the matter were deep.

Newman, though a son of his time and a product of his age, was of the conviction that the root causes of the problem lay in the "unreal" theories which abounded about the nature of thinking itself, and in particular in the theory which led people to the view that philosophical thinking means nothing less, but also nothing more, than a process of formal demonstration. [1] Newman shows, for example, that the main source of confusion in philosophical controversies arises from the basic principles or assumptions on which each controversialist takes his stand, but which none explicitly states. In other words, the source of most disagreements is to be

---

[1] GA, 155-7; Dev 327-8.

found in the differences of basic principles which are ultimately metaphysical in character. [2]

It was clear, then, to Newman that for the debate between the partisans of science and the theologians to be constructive, investigation of human knowledge and understanding was necessary. It was no use continuing to reject the claims of science and the new mentality as rationalistic. It was Newman's conviction that only a painstaking study of the constitution of the mind and of human method could get to the root of the problem. The key to the solution of the debate, and the consequent delineation of the frontiers of scientific reason, philosophy and theology, would become clear upon establishing how a person comes to inquire and understand, verify and assent, reason and research, discover and believe. "Like Socrates, Newman has an extraordinary way of wrestling with the person who would judge him from the point of his own "prepared position", whether he agreed with it or not; if he succeeds in getting at this person, he either deflects his attention from his "prepared position" or makes him re-examine his reasons for accepting it or for presuming to use it to sit in judgement on him." [3]

A lifetime of reflection upon the profundities and "reality" of the Christian mysteries had taught Newman that the current attack of scientific reason on the method and procedures of theology was founded on an inadequate and partial view of human knowledge and decision. Accordingly, many of his works, like the *Apologia*, the *Grammar* and *The Development of Christian Doctrine*, were written to expose the weakness in the existing epistemology. Newman was convinced that the method propagated by the cultivated or scientific intellect of his time overlooked basic facts of history and experience which Newman wished to see incorporated once more in Theology and Philosophy. "Indeed his whole life was a battle against a rationalistic philosophy which professed to be empirical, but was the embodiment of an a priori theory doing violence to evident facts." [4]

To highlight the point in question we may give the outstanding example of William Froude, Newman's great friend and intimate. Newman saw "his dear Protestant friend" gradually drift from the Church under the influence of his growing appreciation of scien-

---

[2] E. Sillem, PN, I, 12.
[3] Ibid., 19.
[4] Ibid., 19.

tific methodology which, he thought, demanded in the theological field evidence and certitude that were not forthcoming. From his studies in physics, Froude had come to see the rigorous standards of evidence demanded by scientific investigation. On the 15th January, 1860, Froude had written to Newman: "I do heartily wish, (and I have heard others who think much as I do, express the same wish with equal heartiness) that you would really and fully work out this question—it is indeed one which you more than anybody else have been felt, by those who know you, to be competent to examine fully". [5] In this dramatic instance, Newman came face to face with the religious and practical consequences of the prevailing mentality on Christian Faith and Theology. Could the evidence for Christianity be exhibited to the same degree as the degree of evidence, for example, for the existence of America? If not, then how could one be sure?

In this instance another result of the prevailing and false view of investigation on methodology comes to light. Alleged difficulties in the area of religion were due solely to underlying, and often unknown, presumptions about scientific method. These problems, Newman felt, would be seen to be pseudo-problems as soon as the hidden reasons for the problem came to light. There was a tremendous need, then, to distinguish genuine from artificial problems in theology. But let us listen to Newman's own silver-lined prose.

> Half the controversies in the world are verbal ones; and could they be brought to a plain issue, they would be brought to a prompt termination. Parties engaged in them would then perceive, either that in substance they agreed together, or that their difference was one of first principles. This is the great object to be aimed at in the present age, though confessedly a very arduous one. We need not dispute, we need not prove—we need but define . . . when men understand what each other's meaning is, they see, for the most part, that controversy is either superfluous or hopeless.[6]

This passage very clearly shows how much he was aware of the crucial role played in our concrete living and individual lives by our way of thinking and deciding. And so we must now go on to describe the method of investigation which prevailed at Newman's time.

---

[5] Ibid., 245.
[6] OUS 200-1.

The Ideal of Investigation at Newman's Time

> The Authors to whom I refer wish to maintain that there are degrees
> of Assent, and that, as the reasons for a proposition are strong
> or weak, so is the assent ... but reasonings in concrete matters
> are never more than probabilities, and the probability in each
> conclusion which we draw is the measure of our assent to that
> conclusion. Such is what may be called the a priori method of
> regarding assent in its relation to inference. It condemns an uncon-
> ditional assent in concrete matters on what may be called the
> nature of the case. Assent cannot rise higher than its source: in-
> ference in such matters is at best conditional, therefore assent is
> conditional also.[7]

In this passage from the *Grammar of Assent*, which Newman wrote
in 1870, we have a limpid exposition of the investigation procedures followed by so many of Newman's contemporaries. It will
be useful to take a closer look at the implications of this method.

In the first place, it categorically claims that in concrete matters unconditional assent, or certitude of mind is unattainable.
The mind does not posses the faculty, or means, whereby it can
reach absolute and complete certitude. Probability, of a degree
strictly proportionate to the probability of the inference, is the best
that can be had. It follows that absolute and unconditional assent
is possible and scientifically legitimate only in the domain of demonstration. What is accepted unconditionally must have a corre-
sponding absolute proof. Assent and proof must be strictly and universally proportionate with regard to all conclusions or propositions.

Furthermore, the language of such a demonstrative proof is the
syllogism, or formal inference, of the Aristotelian type. Formal inference is the means and instrument of all demonstration. What
cannot be expressed in this medium can never be proven absolutely
and so remains permanently and irrevocably on the level of probability, great or little. Formal logic, then, becomes the measure and
means and test of all truth. As a corollary of this, finally, the champions of this method propose a methodic and positive doubt about
everything, pending its demonstration. [8]

For Newman, Locke exemplified, better than most others, the
spirit of this method. The only test of whether a man loves truth

---

[7] GA, 152-3.
[8] See Chapter IV.

is his acceptance or not of the principle of "not entertaining any proposition with greater assurance than the proofs it is built on will warrant". Locke's cultivation of this principle led him to "take a view of the human mind, in relation to inference and assent, which... seems theoretical and unreal". It is small wonder, then, that Newman should write: "Reasonings and convictions, which I deem natural and legitimate, he apparently would call irrational, enthusiastic, perverse, and immoral". [9]

The effect, which such a method and mentality would have on one's Faith and theology, would soon lead to methodic doubt, and doubt to scepticism, and scepticism to apostasy. Newman, alert to what was going on, saw the red light. The problem was sufficiently grave to merit a grave consideration, and radical enough to warrant, indeed demand, a radical treatment. Newman was convinced that the root of the problem lay in the false standards of investigation of the time.

Before we can appreciate, however, Newman's work on methodology, we must penetrate somewhat further into the mentality and ideal of method, which he had to confront, purify and deliver of its false presumptions. To this end, we shall devote some time in consideration of the historical genesis of Newman's own milieu.

The Historical Genesis of this Ideal

> During the course of the seventeenth and eighteenth centuries, philosophers had been engaged in a life and death dispute about the extent and limits of the certainty we are entitled to claim for the knowledge we ordinarily think we possess about ourselves and other things. Philosophy, had, in fact, been absorbed in controversies about the very origins and possibility of human knowledge and certitude. [10]

With Descartes a new epoch opened in the history of philosophy. [11] The great French philosopher and mathematician considered the thought of the past to be uncritical and that therefore its stand on the great questions of truth and objectivity, and their acquisition by the human person, was quite ungrounded. The basis and ground of all truth needed to be firmly stated and brought to light. Descartes sought, then, the original and fundamental ground

---

[9] GA, 155, 157.
[10] E. Sillem, PN, I, 25.
[11] F. Copleston, A History of Philosophy, Vol. IV, London, 1965, 149-152.

of all truth and certainty, an aboriginal principle, methodic and clear, which would henceforth be an incontrovertible and unquestionable justification and grounding of all truth.

This principle he located in his celebrated axiom: "Cogito ergo sum". The bridge to objectivity and truth is the person's awareness of his cognitional activity and concomitant and resulting certitude of his own existence. In this primary datum of human consciousness Descartes was sure he had the incontrovertible first principle on which to ground, critically and objectively, all truth.

Subsequent history, however, has clearly evidenced the failure of Descartes. Instead of gaining the methodic first principle, he had raised a greater problem than he had imagined. The epistemological problem has since occupied the forum in European thought. The bridging of the distance between mind and matter has plagued thinkers ever since. Their attempts may be classified into three groups: Rationalism, Empiricism and Idealism.

For Rationalism, the mind is more or less enclosed within the order of its own ideas, in virtue of which it conceives its own world as a projection of itself. It is a type of Idealism. Such a philosophy is exemplified in such great thinkers as Malebranche and Spinoza.

Empiricism, on the other hand, imprisons the mind within the order of sensations, derived from the outside, but which the mind is unable to penetrate, decipher and analyse fully. Newman encountered directly this brand of Rationalism in the writings of Hume and Locke. [12] It was the immediate and prevalent philosophy of the day. [13] "Towards the end of the eighteenth century and at the beginning of the nineteenth century, indeed during Newman's childhood, Kant made a supreme effort to close the gap between Idealism and Empiricism that had widened into a chasm, by making a synthesis of the two." [14]

However, his efforts did but open the gateway to the pure and absolute Idealism of Fichte, Schelling and Hegel. But neither Kant, nor any other leading philosopher of the day, considered that the whole conflict was due, in the long run, to unreal and false principles and presumptions with regard to the nature of human thought,

---

[12] Mir, 175; GA, 153-169; Dev, 327.

[13] J. M. Cameron, "Newman and the Empiricist Tradition", The Rediscovery of Newman, London, 1967, 76-96.

[14] E. Sillem, PN, I, 27.

which were assumed earlier, especially during and immediately after, the time of the early Rationalists, and which should never have been accepted. [15]

Although differing in character and overall orientation, these streams of thought had this much in common: "human reason is the measure of truth".[16] The England of Newman's day undertook her religious, educational, social and cultural engagements on the basis of this principle, that all thinking is reasoning, that is to say, conscious, scientific and methodical argument, and that as all men are equally well endowed by nature with the gift of Reason, these various orders could easily and almost automatically be reformed by state provision of equal opportunity for all. [17]

The Oxford University Sermons (1826-1844)

We are now at a stage where we can profitably proceed further into the study of Rationalism, or "Liberalism", as Newman preferred to call it. [18] The Oxford University Sermons, which stretch out over the great formative period of Newman's life between 1826-1843, have much to say on the theme of Liberalism. In these sermons, whose theme is the relation of Faith and Reason, we see Newman grappling with the "pretentious insinuations" of Liberalism. Although it was his conviction that the sermons had not the "method, completeness or scientific exactness in the use of language, which are necessary for a formal treatise", and were "written at intervals, and on accidental, not to say sudden, opportunities, and with no aid from Anglican, and no knowledge of Catholic theologians", [19] they are excellent sources in which we can study Newman's grasp of the implications of Liberalism in the domains of Religion, Faith and Theology.

In the rather lengthy preface prefixed by Newman to the third edition of the Sermons in 1871, he outlines the doctrine contained in the Sermons "in a categorical form, and, as far as possible, in the words used in the course of them". [20] At this stage of his life, Newman's thought had reached its apex in the *Gram-*

---

[15] GA, 157.
[16] E. Sillem, PN, I, 25.
[17] GA, 88-94; "The Tamworth Reading Room", DA, 254-305.
[18] Ap (1865 ed.), Note A, 491-502.
[19] OUS, vii, ix-x.
[20] Ibid., x.

mar of 1870, a fact which gives us extra trust in this summary of his earlier thought.

He begins by setting down the popular notions of Faith and Reason, in contrast with each other. "According to this popular sense, Faith is judging on weak grounds in religious matters, and Reason on strong grounds. Faith involves easiness, and Reason slowness, in accepting the claims of Religion; by Faith is meant a feeling or sentiment, by Reason an exercise of common sense; Faith is conversant with conjectures or presumptions, Reason with proofs." [21]

It is Newman's conviction that such a contrast of Faith and Reason, which tends to disparage implicitly the rational cogency and authenticity of Faith as unworthy of liberated and scientific Reason and contemporary man, is based in the final analysis, on unfounded assumptions and "pretentious axioms". Newman describes the "view" of human thinking, which underlies and supports this juxtaposition of Reason and Faith.

Reason is conceived by the Liberals as being explicit and conscious. Its model is the syllogism. Only logic is worthy of human Reason; only formal inference deserves the attention of the person who loves the truth. For the Liberals, Reason is a faculty of framing evidences, of expertise in logical argument, or again of acumen in irreverent deliberation of the secular mentality upon Religion. [22]

Against this artificially restricted view, Newman propounds "the large and true sense", which is in contrast with, but still expansive of, and co-ordinate with, the view of the Liberals. Besides explicit and logical reasoning, there is also implicit and natural inference; beyond a posteriori and evidential thinking, there exists the very genuine type of a priori thinking by anticipation and probability which leads the mind to a discovery of much that it would otherwise never know, and which enlarges the frontiers of human knowledge, and the province of possible knowledge, beyond all recognition. "There are two methods of reasoning—a priori, and a posteriori; from antecedent probabilities or verisimilitudes, and from evidence, of which the method of verisimilitude more naturally belongs to implicit reasoning, and the method of evidence to explicit." [23]

---

[21] Ibid., x-xi.
[22] Ibid., xiv-xv.
[23] Ibid., xiv, xii.

Thirdly, Newman contends that the ideal of Reasoning forwarded by the Liberals is unsound in itself, in that no matter how thorough or cogent an argument or syllogism is, there always remain principles or assumptions, on which the whole argument rests and which are ultimately unprovable. Newman puts this point in a passage of rare power and clarity. "However full and however precise our producible grounds may be, however systematic our method, however clear and tangible our evidence, yet when our argument is traced down to its simple elements, there must ever be something assumed ultimately, which is incapable of proof." [24]

Newman carefully analyses both the nature of reasoning and the nature of believing. He points out the falsity of so limiting reason as to make it an opponent of faith. Conversely, he stresses the fact that faith involves necessarily a definite use of reason. In other words, Newman roundly rejects a two-tier approach to faith and reason, which would put faith on one level and reason on a lower level never to meet. Such a separation easily produces false problems such as the classic conflict of fideistic religion and a religious science or philosophy. Newman ingeniously prevents such a clash by identifying the false grounds on which it is based, namely, the Liberals' principle that all reasoning worthy of the name is both conscious and explicit, and can be exhibited only in the syllogism. Newman masterfully displays the error of such a position by pointing out the existence of implicit, but real, reasoning which is complementary to explicit reasoning. [25] Avery Dulles is correct in considering the *Oxford University Sermons* as "perhaps the most useful analysis of the relationship between faith and reason for our time". [26]

Besides, Faith is genuinely a human act and operation and just what Liberalism could not allow it to be: an assent without doubt, or certitude, which is based on religious first principles; is implicit in its acts, and adopts the method of verisimilitude or antecedent probabilities, which converge on a focal point of certitude. If Reason is the faculty of gaining knowledge upon the grounds given, an act or process of Faith is an exercise of Reason, as being an instrument of independent knowledge concerning things external to us. [27]

---

[24] Ibid., 213.
[25] Ibid., xi-xii.
[26] A. Dulles, The Survival of Dogma, New York, 1973, 47.
[27] OUS, 207.

And finally, accuracy and truth are not acquired or reached independently of the mood or spiritual character of the person of the inquirer, as if human Reason was an absolutely mechanical or Platonic entity, totally beyond the region of the human passions and emotions. This point is central to all of Newman's thought, and shall occupy our attention at length later. "Faith is kept from abuse, for example, from falling into superstition, by a right moral state of mind, or such dispositions and tempers as religiousness, love of holiness and truth." [28]

Reasoning, then, may not be understood in an artificially restricted manner. It rather indicates "any process or act of the mind, by which, from knowing one thing, it advances on to know another; whether it be true or false reason, whether it proceed from antecedent probabilities, by demonstration, or on evidence. And in this general sense it includes of course Faith". [29] The act of faith involves this step from one vision of life to another vision, which is given to us in revelation. Of course such a step is taken not by the unaided reason but as a result of the workings of supernatural grace. In the light of this broad concept of reason Newman is justified in describing the ascent to belief as a process of reasoning, and the act of faith as a function of reasoning. In this way Newman convincingly shows that, while the term reason may frequently be employed in senses that are opposed to faith, there is a genuine sense in which one may speak of faith as an act of reason.

Newman is the pioneer of a remarkable insight which is still gaining ground: the derailing of human reason is responsible for many of today's most pressing problems. Eric Voegelin makes the point well: "We do not live in a post-Christian, or 'post-philosophical', or 'neo-pagan' age, or in the age of a 'new myth', or of 'utopianism', but plainly in a period of massive deculturation through the deformation of reason." [30] Newman clearly perceived the shape of that deformation as it appeared in the first half of the nineteenth century. Aware of the reductionism present in the popular and liberal understanding of reason, he tried mighti-

---

[28] Ibid., xvii.
[29] Ibid., 223.
[30] E. Voegelin, "The Gospel and Culture", Jesus and Man's Hope, Vol. II, Proceedings of the Pittsburgh Festival on the Gospels, Pittsburgh, 1971, 65.

ly both to diagnose its weakness and to propose an appropriate reformation. The outcome of this labour of almost twenty years was the volume, *Oxford University Sermons*.

Theological Method in the Liberal Theologians

We can outline, in brief, the standpoint of the Liberals in Theology. Their theological position might fairly be anticipated to reflect their view of human thought and philosophical method generally. This anticipation is confirmed on investigation.

An excellent exposition of the central tenets of the liberal theologians may be found in a note added by Newman in 1865 to the second edition of the Apologia. Part of that note is worth citing at this point of our considerations, as it serves to highlight, briefly and accurately, the viewpoint of the Liberals, whom Newman considered to be diametrically opposed, in spirit and in method, to the true or genuine mode of investigation demanded of the believer in the divinity of Christian revelation. Here we quote the first and most important five of the eighteen points made in the Note:

1. No religious tenet is important unless reason shows it to be so. Therefore, e.g., the doctrine of the Athanasian Creed is not to be insisted on, unless it tends to convert the soul, and the doctrine of the atonement is to be insisted on, if it does convert the soul.
2. No one can believe what he cannot understand. Therefore, e.g., there are no mysteries in religion.
3. No theological doctrine is anything more than an opinion which happens to be held by bodies of men.
   Therefore, e.g., no creed, as such, is necessary for salvation.
4. It is dishonest in a man to make an act of Faith in what he has not had brought home to him by actual proof.
   Therefore, e.g., the mass of men ought not to believe in the divine authority of the Bible.
5. It is immoral in a man to believe more than he can spontaneously receive as being congenial to his moral and mental nature.
   Therefore, e.g., a given individual is not bound to believe in eternal punishment.[31]

This is perhaps the most concise and brief account ever given by our author of the tenets and spirit of the liberal theology of the day. And Newman, who had spent his life in renewing and build-

---

[31] Ap (1865 ed.), 499.

ing up the Church, first the Anglican Church and then the incipient English Roman Catholic Church, detected in these "principles", the seeds of destruction of Christianity: the liberal movement nurtured within itself the seeds and germs of its own destruction. Besides, Newman realised, better than most of his contemporaries, the dominant role exercised by principles in the
growth or decay of any religious system. [32] It had ever been his
objective to prevent "the liberalisation of the Church", and now
he saw the Church threatened from within and without; already
some of her members were wavering in their allegiance. It was
a time for original and far seeing thought and activity. The Liberals needed to be combated on their own grounds and by their
own principles. [33] Newman would have to combat the two leading principles of the time, which constituted above all others the
very kernel and core of the liberal thought: firstly, that there can
be no truth in the Christian dogmas, as none can believe what
he cannot understand; and secondly, that certainty is attainable only by "demonstration" or by formally reasoned argumentation, and by this alone. [34] We now go on to consider Newman's
actual stand in the face of the contemporary liberal empiricism.

Newman's Stand against the Liberals

It is important to keep in mind that Newman was never engaged professionally in philosophy. He would not have let himself be considered a philosopher. He resolutely refused to enter,
at a professional level, the philosophy schools of the day. All
Newman's preoccupations lay in another direction, especially
that of theology and Christian education. Indirectly, however,
Newman did much philosophizing, and this because he was driven
to give much time, thought and attention to the perennial problems of the theologian. When we remember what we have just
seen in our efforts to determine the context of Newman and of
his service to the Faith, a service which flowed out into a literary production of some forty volumes, we readily appreciate
that it was inevitable for him to raise numerous issues in philosophy. The faith and supernatural vision by which Newman lived
and worked, demanded of him that he investigate the grounds

---

[32] Jfc, 312; Dev, 323-54; Prepos, 271-314.
[33] E. Sillem, PN, I, 241-50.
[34] Ibid., 60-6.

and basis of all thought, whether religious, theological or philosophical. Newman saw, besides, that many of the difficulties which prevent the access of people to the doorstep of the Faith, or are the occasion of others losing this great gift, were not strictly religious, but rather philosophical in character and origin. The instance of William Froude, which we have already seen, is a case in point.

Newman had two distinct, but correlated, ends in view in his opposition to the Liberalism of the day. Negatively, he hoped to remove the false theories current in regard to human method and thought, by pointing out the fallacious grounds, and seeming difficulties, on which they were built. But Newman, the artist, could never be content with pointing out the blackness and defects of the epoch; no, he hoped, positively, to outline a method, the immediate possession of all, which he would put at the disposal of all, the laity as well as the elite of the Church, a ready tool with which to detect fallacious argument and bring out the unconsciously possessed truth of their own genuine human method. [35]

It was Newman's firmly held conviction that the Liberalism of the day was an artificial problem. He felt that not even its supporters could, or did, live by it in all circumstances of life. It did violence to the universal, and universally accepted, laws of mankind. [36] The way to its removal Newman saw in the practical, spontaneous and natural methodology of thought and certitude, decision and action, which was the possession of all. However, this possession was implicit and latent. Newman took it on himself to bring it out into the clear light of day.

We have already seen, at some length, Newman's procedure in dealing with Liberalism in the context of the Oxford University Sermons, which cover almost twenty years preceding his entry into the Catholic Church. In these sermons he pointed out, tentatively but clearly, the types and scope of Reasoning proper to man. He contended that Reasoning may be implicit as well as explicit, consciously pursued but also unconsciously operative, anticipatory of answers which are reached largely in virtue of such anticipation, as well as strictly a posteriori or purely evidential.[37]

---

[35] This is the ultimate meaning of his principle, "Egotism is true modesty", GA, 379.

[36] GA, 169.

[37] OUS, "Implicit and Explicit Reasoning", 251-77.

We now propose to consider at greater length and with more system, Newman's thought on this latent methodology. His work in this direction culminated in the last period of his intellectual career (1858-1870) in the original and profound work, *A Grammar of Assent*. It is our hope here to establish the context of this highly original work, whose riches are not otherwise easily captured. We may then hope to outline the elements of methodology proposed therein.

Newman's "Personal Liberalism"

Philosophy is a personal witness. It is not an arbitrary statement of what ought to be, but a conscious turning to ourselves to discover the permanent and constantly recurring principles and operations, by which we continually judge and decide. Every person is the centre and origin of his own Weltanschauung. In his concrete thinking, a person is not led by some scientifically proposed law or axiom. "Philosophical thinking is an activity of a living person, arising from the action of the mind itself, forming and enlarging a person's mind in a way that befits the uniqueness of his personality, as, under the influence of the existent realities he apprehends, he puts an order and system of his own into his own thoughts." [38]

Indeed the whole of Newman's own life bore witness to the fact that thinking is an activity of the living person. He never wrote a formal treatise independently of all reference. Always he thought of the people for whom he was writing. In his vast literary output this unmistakeable personal quality is evident everywhere. He wrote little but letters, essays, sermons and discourses, and always for the needs of a definite group or individual. "Instead of thinking that he would be satisfied with the ideas or doctrines that a traditional school of philosophers defend as true in religion and metaphysics, and showing his readers how, or to what extent, he agrees with the views of his chosen masters, he thinks the other way round—that his readers can be certain of what he is certain, and he appeals to them to check the truth of what he puts forward as certain for themselves, from their experience." [39] In a word, Newman was proposing what has since been called rather accurately, a "method of phenomenological

---

[38] E. Sillem, PN, I, 5.
[39] Ibid., 4.

investigation". [40] By it he hoped to open up a ready, immediate and popular way of thinking and reasoning, to the layman as well as to the theologian.

Newman was quite aware that, however accurate and fruitful this method might be, its scientific explicitation or statement required a painstaking effort. This process consisted in the main of self-attention, whereby the person becomes critically aware of his own cognitional and ethical structures, and their operations. "We may gladly welcome", he writes, "such difficulties as there are in our mental constitution, and in the interaction of our faculties, if we are able to feel that He gave them to us, and He can overrule them for us. We may securely take them as they are, and use them as we find them." [41] By starting out from the order of what is, he was confident that the order of what ought to be could be arrived at and systematically stated. For Newman, as for the Existentialists, existence preceded essence. The great permanent and universally present "facts", or phenomena, of human psychology were the point of departure, and the means of verification for any theory or practice of science, natural or theological. Phenomena were the logic and "grammar" of life. And when Newman came to write his formal work on methodology, he very appropriately named it A Grammar of Assent, of which there will be more in our next Chapter.

The implications of this method are important. The person is no longer a mere function of impersonal Reason. On the contrary, he transcends the "Reasoning" of the Liberals. Again, ideas and realities separated from the individuals and persons, in which they live and move and have their existence, are not fully "real" or complete. Furthermore, Newman issues an invitation to all to discover for themselves their own dynamic and recurring modes and methods of operation, intellectual and moral. He is confident that this is the surest way to arrive at the truth and at reality. But more, philosophy (and theology as well, as we will have ample occasion to see later) has to do with the rapport existing between the person, and the persons and things he reflects on. Reflection leads to a closing of the gap that often unconsciously separates a

---

[40] J. Walgrave, "Newman's beschrijving en Verantwoording van het werkelijke Denken", Tijdschrift voor Philosophie, I (1939), 541-555; A. J. Boekraad, The Personal Conquest of Truth, Louvain, 1955, 138-140.

[41] GA, 344.

person and the real objects of his thought. "Realisation" by the
individual is a primary objective of philosophy and theology,
according to the mind of Newman. Finally, the process whereby
a person thinks and decides is not as simple or straightforward as
the Liberals would have all believe. "The process by which a man
reasons is as mysterious as the means whereby he remembers,"
Newman says somewhere.

As any process leads to a product, so this investigation proposed by Newman has resulted in what is called by Sillem, "Newman's doctrine of Personal Liberalism". [42] And as the method of
phenomenological investigation, which produced it, is the very
antithesis of the Liberal doctrine of logical demonstration, so also
is Newman's "Personal Liberalism" opposed to the "Rational-Em-
pirical Reasoning" of the Liberals of his day. However, to appreciate better the range and profundity of Newman's thought at
this point, we can draw out the salient aspects of his viewpoint
by considering the following points, which lie at the heart of his
approach. First, there is the mystery of each thing and of its place
relative to other things in the universe as a whole. Next, all human thinking is subject to growth and development, bound as
it is to time and the myriad objects and aspects of objects, which
vie with each other to gain its attention. Finally, it is therefore
pretentious and arbitrary to claim that logical demonstration is
the unique and only way to certitude about matters of facts: deductive reason, alone, is totally inadequate as a means of reaching certainty, and must be supplemented accordingly by a broader,
richer, more versatile and effective means.

A.   Concrete objects, persons or things all possessed a wealth of
meaning and interest for Newman. He who was acutely alive to
the riches stored, as it were secretly in the heart of natural things,
could not but consider as superficial any philosophy which pre-
sumed to manipulate them crudely with the tools of formal inference. From his own experience (and few people have ever possessed a self-awareness or knowledge equal to Newman's!) he
realised that one can consider something at length and still fail
to hit its kernel. "Thought is too keen and manifold, its sources
are too remote and hidden, its path too personal, delicate and circuitous, its subject-matter too various and intricate, to admit of

---

[42] PN, I, 67-148.

the trammels of any language, of whatever subtlety and of whatever compass."[43]

In the great sermon of 1843 on "The Theory of Development
in Religious Doctrine", which is the embryonic *Essay on the Development of Christian Doctrine*, Newman expresses this truth
in the context of revealed religion.

"As definitions are not intended to go beyond their subject,
but to be adequate to it, so the dogmatic statements of the Divine
Nature used in our confessions, however multiplied, cannot say
more than is implied in the original idea, considered in its completeness, without the risk of heresy. Creeds and dogmas live in
the one idea which they are designed to express, and which alone
is substantive; and are necessary only because the human mind
cannot reflect upon that idea except piecemeal, cannot use it in
its oneness and entireness, nor without resolving it into a series
of aspects and relations. And in matter of fact these expressions
are never equivalent to it; we are able indeed to define the creations of our minds, for they are what we make them and nothing
else; but it were as easy to create what is real as to define it."[44]
Mystery, then, envelopes the inner sanctuary of concrete realities,
natural as well as supernatural. The principle of mystery lies at
the root of a great portion of Newman's theological thought which
will occupy us later. [45]

B. "Growth is the only sign of life." As a being intrinsically
bound to history and space, the thought of man is necessarily
subject to growth and development. "In a higher world it is otherwise, but here below to live is to change, and to be perfect is to
have changed often." [46] Knowledge enjoyed a genuine type of
life, for is it not what is specifically peculiar to human life? Man
is a being of progress. He is born with nothing, as it were, achieved.
He sets out to increase and acquire, to grow and conquer. He is
developmental by nature; and his thought and thinking grow and
develop in a wonderful way.

Newman exemplified this growth in his own life, the record of
which we read in the *Apologia*, where he gives the "true key to
his whole life ... that living intelligence by which I write, and

---

[43] GA, 277.
[44] OUS, 331-2.
[45] Ar, 272-3.
[46] Dev, 40.

argue, and act". And from his phenomenological investigation of his own intellectual and spiritual odyssey, he possessed a vivid sense of the developmental nature of the human thinking of everyone. It was to this that Pope Paul VI referred in his eulogy of Newman on the occasion of the beatification of Blessed Dominic Barberi on 27 October 1963. Newman's journey was "the most toilsome, but also the greatest, the most meaningful, the most conclusive, that human thought ever travelled during the last century, indeed one might say during the modern era". [47]

C.   In fidelity to these two outstanding principles, Newman flatly denies the ability of abstract reasoning to give certitude about a truth, in the concrete. Abstract reasoning presupposes perfect and absolute definition of its elements, so that the process of inferential reduction should have an absolute right to our unconditional acceptance or assent. Such an absolute definition is possible only in the case of the creation of our minds and not in the case of what we find and encounter as uniquely and singularly and concretely existing, which is more easily created than defined. In the province of mathematics syllogistic reduction might work, but it is only operative and feasible in this field. Besides, it fails to take into account "all the conditions which really influence the behaviour of things in the concrete, existentialorder". [48]

We are now in a position to evaluate what Newman meant by "paper logic". For Newman, "it is the concrete being that reasons". "And then I felt altogether the force of the maxim of St. Ambrose: 'non in dialectica complacuit Deo salvum facere populum suum': I had a great dislike of paper logic. For myself, it was not logic that carried me on; as well one might say that the quicksilver in the barometer changes the weather. It is the concrete being that reasons; pass a number of years, and I find my mind in a new place; how? the whole man moves; paper logic is but the record of it." [49]

The theory of the Liberals did violence to the practice of humanity. Newman allows this practice to be revealed to all. What is arbitrary he knows will have to bow to what is, and what is supported by the common sense of all will have its way and its rights, and will prevail against arbitrarily selected axioms. "Let us take things as we find them: let us not attempt to distort them

---

[47] L'Osservatore Romano, 28 October 1963; AAS, 1963, 1025.
[48] E. Sillem, PN, I, 113.
[49] Ap, 285-6; see GA, 264.

into what they are not. True philosophy deals with facts. We cannot make facts. All our wishing cannot change them. We must use them." [50]

Newman's "Method of Converging Probabilities"

Negatively, then, Newman pointed out the defects in a purely syllogistic or rational conception of human thinking or investigation. However, he is all this time laying the basis of a solid alternative. This alternative, which was finally elaborated in the *Grammar* of 1870, he considered to be the method of converging probabilities. As all our considerations have hitherto been directed towards the *Grammar* (where we will find what Newman held and what he did not hold, in mature and more scientific form, about the genuine "Organum Investigandi"), we will now proceed to study the basis of this alternative. It is hoped that this study will help to situate the context of the *Grammar*, to reveal its more immediate roots and origins, and to advance our own personal grasp of its vital position in Newman's "view" of proper methodology, philosophical and theological. Newman himself would demand of us, his readers, that we verify his contentions from our own experience and in the intimacy of our own hearts. "He knows what has satisfied and satisfies himself; if it satisfies him, it is likely to satisfy others; if, as he believes and is sure, it is true, it will approve itself to others also, for there is but one truth." [51]

The central component of this basis is Newman's singular "view" of the true path to certainty and certitude. [52] In 1823 he came under the influence of the thought of the famous Anglican Divine, Bishop Butler of Durham. One of the principles, which he imbibed from Butler's *Analogy of Religion*, was that "Probability is the guide of life", a principle Newman confesses to be an "underlying principle of a great portion of (his) teaching". [53] Newman took this principle of Butler, but he purified it, especially in 1827 when he read John Keble's *The Christian Year*, from which he took a principle highly similar to the foregoing principle of Butler.

---

[50] OUS, 231.
[51] GA, 380.
[52] GA, 337-8, where Newman defines the terms, "certitude" and "certainty".
[53] Ap, 67-8.

On the second principle which I gained from Mr Keble, I could
say a great deal ... It runs through very much of what I have
written, and has gained for me many hard names. Butler teaches
us that probability is the guide of life. The danger of this doctrine
in the case of many minds, is its tendency to destroy in them absolute certainty, leading them to consider every conclusion as doubt-
ful, and resolving truth into an opinion, which it is safe to obey
or profess, but not possible to embrace with full internal assent ...
I considered that Mr Keble met this difficulty by ascribing the
firmness of the assent which we give to religious doctrine, not to
the probabilities which introduced it, but to the living power of
faith and love which accepted it.[54]

But still Newman was not satisfied. Both Butler and Keble,
he felt, were inadequate in their arguments for the logical cogency of Faith: their method "did not go to the root of the difficulty".
So Newman set out to complete and perfect what he saw as positive and correct in his masters.

"I tried to complete it by considerations of my own, which are
implied in my *University Sermons, Essay on Ecclesiastical Miracles* and *Essay on the Development of Doctrine*." [55] We have
now reached a vital juncture in what Newman thought to be the
true way of reaching certitude about practical and concrete issues in Theology, natural and Christian. From Butler and Keble,
Newman gained an insight into the role of probability, anticipation and the great human dispositions of love and goodness, in
helping it along the way to the goal of certainty. But they did
not go far enough. Newman set out to go further.

My argument is in outline as follows: that that absolute certitude
which we are able to possess, whether as to the truths of natural
Theology or as to the fact of Revelation, was the result of an assemblage of concurring and converging probabilities, and that, both
according to the constitution of the human mind and the will
of its Maker; that certitude was a habit of mind, that certainty
was a quality of propositions; that probabilities which did not
reach to logical certainty, might create a mental certitude; that
the certitude thus created might equal in measure and strength
the certitude which was created by the strictest scientific demonstration. And that to have such certitude might in given cases
and to given individuals be a plain duty, though not to others in
other circumstances.[56]

---

[54] Ibid., 78-9.
[55] Ibid., 80.
[56] Ibid., 80-1.

This quotation brings out the dominant theme of Newman's mind on proper methodology. Appearing at this stage of his life (1864), when he had behind him a great quantity of Theology, it casts light on all this work, and especially on the spirit, orientation and (what interests us) method adopted by its author. For this reason, it is worth our while to underline the salient points of Newman's position at the time (1864):

1. There exists the fact of the mind's certitude in the domain of religion and Faith.
2. Scientific demonstration, or logical proof of the scientific mathematical kind, is not the "way" to this certitude.
3. The human mind, on the will of its Maker and according to its own constitution, supplies a higher "way".
4. This "way" is an "assemblage of concurring and converging probabilities".
5. These probabilities manipulated by the mind's higher logic, lead to the absolute certitude of our assent to the truths of Natural Theology and the fact of Revelation.
6. This certitude might equal the vividness and power of the certitude that follows upon absolute proof.
7. A personal equation, or factor, of ethico-moral derivation, is involved in the ascent to assent.
8. As some probabilities sufficed to create certainty, it was plain that others were capable of generating a graduated scale of probabilities or opinion.
9. By way of corollary, Newman implies that we must always distinguish theory (which may be either opinion, apprehensive anticipation, antecedent probability, assumptions, verisimilitudes, etc.) from fact or truth, which is reached by lifting theory or hypothesis to the level of judgment.
10. This methodology led Newman to adopt an approach to Miracles in 1842 different from what he adopted in 1825-1826. In 1842 he saw that their credibility was to be judged "according to their greater or lesser probability, which was in some cases sufficient to create certitude about them", whereas in the earlier years he thought miracles could be "sharply divided into two classes, those which were to be received, and those which were to be rejected".[57]

Up to now we have been engaged in grasping the historical development and growth of our author's thought on method. Our considerations, however, have been focused, more or less, on the philosophical, rather than on the theological, side of Newman's

[57] Ibid., 82.

thought. And this is how we would have it. Our great and abiding objective is to detect and work out Newman's philosophy of method, which is permanently operative and decisive in this theology. Once we have grasped Newman's final stand on method in general, we expect to have at our disposal the tools with which to elaborate and draw out his theological method in its component aspects.

It is evident that the foregoing principles of Newman on method in philosophy will have a determining influence on his final state of mind, which is found essentially in the *Grammar*. There we will be able to view the operation of method in Newman's theology. However, Newman wrote already in 1844 that "it is evident what a special influence, such doctrine as this (i.e. converging probabilities) must exert upon the theological method of those who hold it. Arguments will come to be considered as suggestions and guides rather than logical proofs; and developments as the slow, spontaneous, ethical growth, not the scientific and compulsory results, of existing opinions". [58] In our forthcoming treatment of his method of explaining the Faith, we will be dealing at greater length with this topic.

---

[58] Dev, 336.

CHAPTER TWO

"A WAY OF INQUIRY OF MY OWN"

The Origin of the Grammar of Assent

In the December 1858 issue of "The Rambler", Newman was rather rudely awakened from any complacency he may have entertained in regard to the coherence and value of his already vast literary output, by an article written by the paper's editor, Richard Simpson.[1] Simpson lamented that "Newman gives us colossal fragments, but he does not usually construct a finished edifice. He is like Homer, from whom all the Greek philosophers took their texts, as St. Thomas culls the principles of his science from Scripture ... The judicial oblivion he has left us has found too faithful an echo among ourselves; and the consequence has been that Dr. Newman has almost ceased from literary production".[2] Newman felt that Simpson was right: he had given only "colossal fragments", not a "finished edifice".

At that time Newman had just returned from Dublin and his experiences there as first Rector of the Catholic University. During his rectorship (1854-1858), he delivered the series of discourses which now comprise the volume called *The Idea of a University*. The volume enjoyed an immediate success. Newman could but continue from Birmingham his work on behalf of Christian formation (he would prefer the term "formation" to "education"), which he had commenced in Dublin.

At this stage, too, the conviction was growing in his mind that the "signs of the times" all pointed to an inevitable conflict, which would impose on every man the necessity of having to choose for himself between two irreconcilable protagonists, the Catholic Church, on the one hand, and the secular Liberal world on the other. Anglicanism was a half-way house tending towards Catholicism. There was no time to be lost. Newman resolved to make ready the way leading to the true Church of Christ: the way must be

---

[1] E. Sillem, PN, I, 241-50.
[2] The Rambler, December, 1858.

made "popular, practical and personal", [3] must be made Every-man's Way.

In January 1859, just one month after Simpson's work Newman began the preparations of a work, which he entitled *Discursive Enquiries on Metaphysical Subjects*. The manuscript of this work, which is in the archives of the Oratory at Birmingham, shows clearly that Newman had in mind a work of great size and scope. He had in mind nothing less than his "Opus Magnum" for religious culture and philosophy. In the September of the same year, he began a new section, called "Formation of Mind".

On the 15th January 1860, Newman received a letter from his great friend William Froude, whose son, Hurrell, Newman had received into the Catholic Church. Froude confessed that, with his maturing appreciation of the rigorous standards of evidence demanded in scientific investigation, he was moving further and further into a scepticism and agnosticism. Newman could not stand by idly in the case of a "dear friend". This incident, perhaps more than any single event, decided and urged Newman on to a still greater dedication to his task. The same problem had arisen earlier (1858) in the case of J. M. Capes, the founder of "The Rambler". His problem was very like that of Froude. The teaching of the Church could, at its best, be only highly probable, for certainty was impossible and confined to the province of math-ematico-scientific demonstration. Capes was not satisfied with Newman's solution, and left the Church for a number of years. A recent author suggests that this discussion was the immediate genesis of the *Grammar*. [4] Still, it remains the opinion of many that Froude's letter is its most immediate single cause.

From 1859 onwards, Newman busied himself in the compara-tive quiet and tranquillity of the Birmingham Oratory, with his project, of which he expected so much. His dedication to the task had all the urgency of an emergency: he saw the Faith and ecclesial allegiance of many threatened, or, already destroyed, as in the case of William Froude. Worse still, the grounds on which Froude abandoned his Faith were spurious and quite "un-real". Scientific methodology is valid and correct, but in the prov-ince of science and technology, which is its own native land,

---

[3] Letter to Dr. Maynell, quoted in PN, I, 245.

[4] Joseph L. Altholz, The Liberal Catholic Movement in England, London, 1962, 73-5.

but once it is transported into all other provinces, it becomes dictatorial and usurps the rights of the broader, more human and more versatile "method of converging probabilities". More urgently still, the Catholics of the time, elite and rank-and-file alike, required a ready-reckoner in order "to render an account of that Faith that was in them"[5] to their aggressive, or simply sceptical and liberal, contemporaries. His *Discursive Enquiries on Metaphysical Subjects* never appeared in print. At a later date, possibly between 1864 and 1867, he decided to abandon the earlier work altogether. Instead he began a kind of theologico-philosophical scrapbook, which he joined to the earlier part, and called Sundries. What had happened?

After the appearance of his article "On Consulting the Faithful in matters of Doctrine",[6] Newman fell under a shadow. His orthodoxy was suspected by members of the Hierarchy. His subsequent projects for Catholic lay-education met with the active opposition of Cardinals Wiseman and Manning. Newman, who professed not only the rights of truth, but also the need for opportune truth in the Christian family, judged that his research would only aggravate an already tense environment. He reluctantly decided to abandon his Magnum Opus, but continued to work away, paper after paper, on his response to Froude's very definite and more restricted question. His objective was now narrowed and restricted. Still he could use much of the material he had already prepared. Only in 1866 did Newman discover a plan for his project.[7] He confesses that the work took a lot out of him. In 1870 he began to write in the silence and tranquillity of the Oratory's country residence at Rednal. After he had finished, he felt he had aged: "It is my last work", he wrote.[8]

Our itinerary of investigation has come to the stage of being the *Grammar's* context, "in which alone it can be understood".[9] We have come, not by the most direct route but by a circling or spiralling movement, as a mountaineer would ascend a difficult Alpine peak. We have gained the vantage point, from which it

---

[5] 1 Peter 3 : 15.
[6] The Rambler, July, 1859, 1-66.
[7] Ward, II, 245-6.
[8] Ward, II, 268.
[9] E. Sillem, PN, I, 58.

is hoped to conquer the heights of the *Grammar's* doctrine on
method. There are different possibilities open to a person who
wishes to get to know intimately a great factory. He can under-
take a rapid survey of the whole complex to gain a general idea
of the whole and then retrace his steps, studying each compart-
ment and machine in detail. Or he may start at the door to visit
systematically each and every item of the same factory. In our
imminent study of the *Grammar*, we will adopt the first procedure. Accordingly, we will first give a bird's eye view of the ground
covered by the *Grammar*, and then proceed piecemeal through
its teaching on methodology.

The Purpose of the Grammar: *"To describe the Organum Investigandi"*

In the December of 1880, Newman added an important note
to the *Grammar*. In it he has done us the courtesy of telling us
why he wrote, and what he intended to convey to his audience.
This explanatory note stands as a kind of summary, or overall
view, of this great work. And with it we set off. "Now, what do
I hold, and what do I not hold? The present volume supplies an
answer to this question. From the beginning to end it is full of
arguments, of which the scope is the truth of the Catholic religion".[10]
A little later he is even more precise in regard to the objective
he had in mind in writing: "I will add, that a main reason for edit-
ing this Essay on Assent, to which I am adding these words,
was, as far as I could, to describe the Organum Investigandi
which I thought the true one ... Religion has, as such, certain
definite belongings and surroundings, and it calls for what Aristotle would call a πεπαιδευμένος investigator, and a process of
investigation sui similis".[11]

It is clear at once that what Newman wishes to convey is the
true "process of investigation" or the proper "organum investigandi". And the province he has most especially in mind is the
religious and theological one, which requires a method "sui similis" and appropriate to its "definite belongings and surroundings". The goal of this method will be the justification of the

---

[10] GA', 383.
[11] Ibid., 387, 385-6.

"assent" of every believer, simple or cultivated, "to the truth
of the Catholic Religion". Here we detect his orientation towards
the specific opposition of the contemporary liberal spirit, personified in William Froude, which confined assent or certitude to
mathematics and straight science. And so "the essay begins with
refuting the fallacies of those who contend that we cannot believe what we cannot understand". It proceeds "to justify certitude as exercised upon an accumulation of proofs, short of demonstration separately".[12] We see once again his enduring preoccupation with the cardinal errors of the liberal theologians.

Again, the *Grammar* deals with method, not only in theory,
but also in practice. Accordingly, Newman not only expands the
great outlines and fundamental elements of method, but he also
applied this method. The *Grammar*, then, is a work on method-
in-practice, for Newman goes to the rounds of showing how he
would apply the principles of his Essay to the proof of Christianity's divine origin.[13] The *Grammar*, he writes, is an "argumentative work in defence of my Creed".

Newman, however, goes even further in this Note. In a passage of tremendous sweep of thought, depth of insight, and clarity of word and phrase, he gathers into a single "view" the rudimentary components of theological method, as they are presented in the *Grammar*. "There is a certain ethical character, one
and the same, a system of first principles, sentiments and tastes, a
mode of viewing the question and arguing, which is formally and
morally, naturally and divinely, the 'Organum Investigandi',
given us for gaining religions truth." [14]

This "Organum Investigandi" is composed of these elements:
assumptions and first principles, premises which enter into the
immediate ratiocinative process, ethico-personal dispositions, and
a mode of viewing and arranging the matter of the debate. In
fidelity to his procedure, Newman will study the Organum Investigandi in the course of the *Grammar*, by his method of Phenomenological Investigation. He will not enunciate mere characteristics or qualities of method, however important, he will be
concerned rather with the life and structure of our cognitional

---

[12] Ibid., 383.
[13] GA, 484.
[14] GA', 386.

and ethical nature, as it unfolds itself in our recurring and ordered cognitional and ethical operations. Secondly, Newman will
search for this permanent, recurring and dynamic structure in
his own consciousness. Thirdly, he will ask his reader to verify
for himself and from his own inner conscious experience the truth
of his assertions: foremost in Newman's mind is the need for
everybody, who would argue or debate on any subject whatever, to self-appropriate his own "naturally and divinely given
Organum Investigandi". Fourthly, this work of self-appropriation
completed, Newman will show how to employ systematically
this Organum Investigandi in gaining religious truth in theological
investigation; this is the stage of systematic application.[15] Fifthly,
Newman is aware that this new-found method will be by nature
sufficiently critical and grounded to be able to reveal the weak-
nesses, oppose the pretensions, and perfect what is of any worth,
in the counterpositions of the contemporary liberal theologians.[16]
If Newman has succeeded in this great undertaking (we have seen
the labour and pain it cost him!), then he has really overthrown
the "pretentious axioms" of the opponents of Catholic and Christian
belief, life and thought. It will be our hope to show how Newman
has done not only this, but has outlined a theological method
highly relevant to the spirit and needs of our time. At the end of
the *Grammar* he writes of the Christian faith:

> Some persons speak of it as if it were a thing of history, with only
> indirect bearings upon modern times; I cannot allow that it is a
> mere historical religion. Certainly it has its foundations in past
> glorious memories, but its power is in the present. It is no dreary
> matter of antiquarianism; we do not contemplate it in conclusions
> drawn from dumb documents plus dead events, but by faith exer-
> cised in ever-living objects and by the appropriation and use of
> ever recurring gifts.[17]

At this stage we consider, as useful, a graphic representation of
the contents, in logical order, of the *Grammar*, and then the addition of something by way of explanation.

---

[15] GA, 154, 168, 169, 172-4, 209.
[16] Ibid., 287-9.
[17] Ibid., 480.

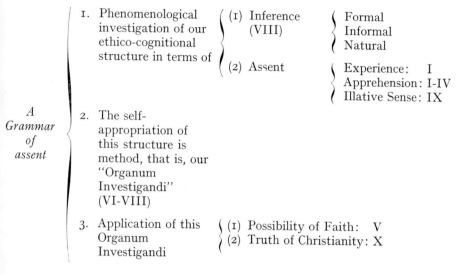

Assent and Apprehension

The *Grammar* has an abrupt opening, which sets the tone for much of the work. Newman does not follow a very rational plan or strict outline. The structure of the work is more pedagogical in tone and spirit than logical in its development. And Newman wished it to be like this. In fidelity to his principles, he felt that a person stumbles across the truth, discovering a point here, a thread there, sometimes by design, but more often accidentally. Many are the roads that lead to the discovery of the whole truth. Newman kept these truths, which he used in his earlier works, in mind as he wrote the *Grammar*, a work designed in its turn to be an answer to a specific problem exemplified by William Froude. Having considered, at some length, the origin and context of the *Grammar*, such a procedure on Newman's part does not surprise. It is his characteristic procedure. Accordingly, he offers us a treatment of ethico-cognitional structure, not in formal outline, but in the context of the definite problem, posed by the liberals and personified in Froude.

The key to the *Grammar* is the grasp of the vital distinction between inference and assent. Formal inference was held up by the liberals as the unique and only way to achieve a certitude that was deserving of our acceptance. Scientific investigation is the only means of gaining truth. Newman contends that true

judgement or assent is another and more universal means. He
contrasts assent with inference. Inference does not require of necessity apprehension of the terms of propositions to which it assents. Secondly, the conclusion of an inference is always conditional, dependent as it is on premises. Assent, or judgement, on
the other hand, is just the opposite. It follows upon apprehension
and is unconditional. Unconditionality and apprehension of its
subject are what constitute certitude. This accounts for the di-
vision of the work into two parts, the first on assent and apprehension, and the second on assent and inference.

Newman uses a terminology of his own. Not being a philosopher by profession, he coined his own vocabulary for this work.
It is important, therefore to see how he defines his terms. Apprehension is the imposition of a sense on the terms of which propositions are composed. Apprehension, however, is not the identical same as understanding. Understanding is ambiguous. "It is
possible to apprehend without understanding." [18] Apprehension
may be defined as an intelligent appreciation of an object, upon
whose perception it follows. Again, apprehension may be real or
notional. Real apprehension has to do with the relation of concrete and individual things to the person. The totality of the object is present, intelligently perceived and considered by the
subject. This apprehension possesses a living force and vitality,
and affects the subject profoundly. Notional apprehension, on
the contrary, has to do with things as they are related to one
another. It does not deal with totalities but with aspects of
wholes, and is more abstract and theoretical. These two modes of
apprehension, so central to thought, may be systematically distinguished in terms of their quality of content, direction of attention, and the presence or absence of a sense of reality or value.[19]
With regard to quantity of content, real apprehension makes
the whole thing present to the person perceiving. The object,
in its totality, engages the imagination and impresses itself deeply on the memory. When it comes to direction of attention, there
is a notable difference between real and notional apprehension.
Real apprehension focuses on the thing in itself, and not on the
thing as an object related to other objects. Its full preoccupation

---

[18] Ibid., 7, 17.
[19] Here I am indebted to an unpublished article of Bernard Lonergan,
Blandyke Papers, No. 291, February, 1929, 195-216.

is with the object it now perceives. Notional apprehension, however, regards "things, not as they are in themselves, but mainly as they stand in relation to each other ... Instinctively, even though unconsciously, we are ever instituting comparisons between the manifold phenomena of the external world, as we meet with them, criticizing, referring to a standard, collecting, analyzing them. Nay, as if by one and the same action, as soon as we perceived them, we perceive that they are like each other or unlike, or rather both alike and unlike at once. We apprehend spontaneously, even before we set about apprehending, that man is like man, yet unlike; and unlike a horse, a tree, a mountain or a monument, yet in some, though not the same respects, like each of them ... We are ever grouping and discriminating, measuring and sounding, forming cross classes and cross divisions, and thereby rising from particulars to generals, that is from images to notions".[20] Finally, with regard to the presence and absence of reality or value, real apprehension is an encounter between the object perceived and the perceiver. There is no diluting, no attenuation of the reality being apprehended. There is a real collision between the person and the concrete particular object that engages his attention. Not only is the whole of the object present, not only is attention focused exclusively on it, but the object's impact on us is profound and powerful. Real apprehension is, then, the source of what inspires us most, impresses us most deeply in life, and spurs us furthest.

In the pages of the *Grammar* that deal with apprehension Newman illustrates the distinction between real and notional apprehension using instances taken from everyday life. He refers to the cloud of vagueness which normally surrounds and envelopes the ideas that commonly circulate concerning the famous people of any time. What we normally possess is a caricature of these people, dependent upon the notions and reports we have heard or read. But such an apprehension or knowledge of people bears very little resemblance to the real persons. It is merely a dim reflection of their true personalities. Thus the events of the day, as well as the characters who figure prominently in them, lose their individuality and their distinctiveness. In this way we miss the real person for a notion, the individual person of flesh and blood for a caricature. This explains how surprised we are upon meet-

[20] GA, 28.

ing in person some famous celebrity with whom our only previous acquaintance was on a television screen. How ashamed, how amused we are since coming into possession of the real facts concerning him! Encounter with him transformed the notional into the real, the abstract into the concrete, the vague into the distinct, and the general into the particular.

The distinction between real and notional apprehension which Newman has been illustrating in the case of persons, might equally be illustrated in the case of all our ideas. A text in the *Grammar* does this admirably: "'Man' is no longer what he really is, an individual presented to us by our senses, but as we read him in the light of those comparisons and contrasts which we have made him suggest to us. He is attenuated into an aspect, or relegated to his place in a classification. Thus his appellation is made to suggest, not the real being which he is in this or that specimen of himself, but a definition. If I might use a harsh metaphor, I should say he is made the logarithm of his true self, and in that shape is worked with the ease and satisfaction of logarithms".[21] Real apprehension denotes for Newman the perception of wholes, that are vividly represented to us in the present, or vividly portrayed by memory from the past. The person, in other words, grasps the unity-identity-whole by means of experiential categories. Notional apprehension is of things among themselves, or rather of things in relation to one another. It perceives in terms of explanatory, or scientific, categories.

Apprehension and Theology

We can appreciate readily how important Newman considered this distinction to be. As we have already seen, he traced most of the contemporary difficulties, and problems in faith and theology to the "unreal" notions that then abounded in regard to the nature of knowledge. As Michael Novak puts it:

> In his *Grammar of Assent*, Newman strove hard to delineate the great psychological-intellectual difference between "notional assents" and truly self-committing "real assents", trying to capture ways of knowing, and living, selfinvolving ways. The problem of Creeds with their increasingly scientized expressions, capable of glib repetition and even more glib mental assent, and the slow economy of living growth in understanding, plagued his thinking incessantly.[22]

---

[21] Ibid., 28-9.
[22] M. Novak, Newman on Nicea, TS, 21 (1960), 444-53.

Newman sought to unite, in harmonious equilibrium, the notional clarity of dogma with the intensity of the Christian experience. Such a balance he considered to be the ideal condition of the faith. The notional and the real are distinct but complementary. He well realised that both the notional and the real were fraught with their appropriate dangers. The attempt of the theologian to establish notional clarity runs the risk of ending up in rationalism. Real apprehension on its own tends to produce a devotion that is narrow and easily degenerates into fanaticism or superstition. "The proposition that there is one Personal and Present God may be held either as a theological truth, or as a religious fact or reality. The notion and the reality assented to are represented by one and the same proposition but serve as distinct interpretations of it. When the proposition is apprehended for the purposes of proof, analysis, comparison, and the like intellectual exercises, it is used as the expression of a notion; when for the purpose of devotion, it is the image of a reality. Theology, properly and directly, deals with notional apprehension; religion, with imaginative." The distinction between religion and theology turns on the difference bteween fact and notion, better, things-to-us and things-to-things. The former is the experimental and personal order, while the latter is the scientific and abstract order.

It is important to remember, however, that, while theology and religion are distinct, they are not separable. Newman writes: "Not as if there were in fact, or could be, any line of demarcation or party-wall between these two modes of assent, the religious and the theological. As intellect is common to all men as well as imagination, every religious man is to a certain extent a theologian, and no theology can start or thrive without the initiative and abiding presence of religion". Newman illustrates the interdependence of the two by comparing them with the relationship obtaining between the scientific terminology of medicine and the shocking facts of disease which constitute its subject-matter. "Pathology and medicine, in the interests of medicine, and as a protection to the practitioner, veil the shocking realities of disease and physical suffering under a notional phraseology, under the abstract terms of debility, distress, irritability, paroxysm, and a host of Greek and Latin words. The arts of medicine and surgery are necessarily experimental; but for writing and con-

versing on these subjects they require to be stripped of the association of the facts from which they are derived." [23] Today Newman might formulate the distinction as comparable to that which
exists between economics and business, or between biology and
health therapy. In this way he lays a scientific basis for the exact
distinction between kerygmatic, biblical or "betende Theologie",
on the one hand, and scientific, speculative or systematic theology,
on the other. We shall have occasion to say more about this later.
For the present it is enough to merely take note of it in passing.

The mental act of assent, whether it be given consequent to
real or notional apprehension, is always unconditional and absolute. It is an act of the mind, without conditions or clauses. "In
either mode of apprehension, be it real or be it notional, the assent preserves its essential characteristic of being unconditional.
The assent of a Stoic to the 'Justum et tenacem, etc.', may be as
genuine an assent, as absolute and entire, as little admitting of
degree or variation, as distinct from an act of inference, as the assent of a Christian to the history of Our Lord's Passion in the
Gospel." [24]

However, if the act of assent, be it notional or real, is essentially and intrinsically perfect and absolute, notional and real
apprehension still have an influence on the quality or liveliness
of the assent. As the apprehension is real, so is the assent to it
real, more lively and vivid. As the apprehension is notional, so
is the assent to it notional.

Whereas apprehension is a necessary prerequisite of assent, inference may exist without any apprehension. Inference, however,
is normally accompanied by notional apprehension. Real apprehension is not enjoyed by inference, whose very structure mir-
rors the notional grasp of the mutual relations of things in Notional Assent.

At this point, Newman makes reference to his Tamworth Reading-Room Articles. The great theme of these brilliant and witty essays is that religion, contrary to the expectations of the
Government, is not sufficiently taught and presented by literature or science alone. Notions, ideas and abstractions, however
well chosen, well put, or ingeniously directed, do not secure a
real and deep Christian formation of the person. It is only vivid,

---

[23] GA, 115-6, 95, 20.
[24] Ibid., 36, 88-94; DA, 254-305.

direct and lively contact with the sacred that ensures real apprehension and, consequently, real assent, with all its vividness and
power in the life of the individual. Newman could not but see in
the Government's idea the logical expression of the rationalism
then prevailing. He was too much of a realist to be misled by bad
education theory, too richly experienced in the personal and painful ascent to the fullness of truth to be convinced that moral and
intellectual formations of individual, society, and Church could
be secured by an impersonal and vague educational programme.

Although he distinguished sharply notional and real assent,
he did not view them as opposed, the one to the other, but on the
contrary, he saw them as complementary. Real assent gives depth,
but not breadth of vision, while notional assent is broad but
superficial. Real assent is the principle of stability, permanence
and endurance in knowledge and truth, while notional is the principle of advancement, progress and development.[25]

Assent and Inference

Assent and inference, which occupy the second half of the book,
are treated at greater length than apprehension and assent. The
upshot of the first half was to show the indispensable role of apprehension in coming to assent, true judgement or certitude. To
highlight this importance and indispensability, he contrasted assent and inference, for contrast is luminous. However, apprehension of itself does not bring one to certitude. A necessary step is
not always the only step necessary. Assent requires as well that
apprehension be lifted by a process of ratiocination to the level
of certitude. And as he clarified the role of apprehension in cognitional structure by contrasting it with inference in the first half
of the *Grammar* so now he uses inference, in its various forms,
to bring into clear relief, "the real and necessary method" of lifting apprehension to the level of assent or unconditionality.

"As apprehension is a concomitant, so inference is ordinarily
the antecedent of assent ... but neither apprehension nor inference interferes with the unconditional character of the assent,
viewed in itself. The circumstances of the act, however necessary to it, do not enter into the act." [26] Newman's tentative theory
of cognitional structure, then, is a process involving three dis-

---

[25] GA, 32.
[26] GA, 150.

tinct and connected steps: first, apprehension of experience,
then ratiocination, which concludes, finally, in certitude or judgement. The process may be graphically represented as follows:

$$(I)\ Experience \rightarrow (II)\ Apprehension \begin{cases} Real \\ \\ Notional \end{cases} \xrightarrow{\ \ (III)\ \ } \begin{array}{l} Ratiocina\text{-} \\ tive\ Process \\ leading\ to \\ \downarrow \\ Assent \\ (IV) \end{array}$$

A difficulty, however, comes to light at once. On Newman's
own definition, the conclusion of an inferential or ratiocinative
process is relative, conditional and probable. Assent is just the
opposite, being absolute, unconditional, and certain. How, then,
can the transition be made from an inferential conclusion which
is relative and precedes assent, to assent which is absolute? That
is the question which he tackles all through the latter half of his
work, and is the occasion of the most profound and original part
of his thought.

In answering the question, Newman adopts a procedure we
might have anticipated. In terms of a phenomenological investigation of his own experience, he lays bare the common feeling
and practice of mankind who achieve, possess, and live by certitudes in many things and situations which concern them personally and vitally. Certitude is genuine and proper, moral and just,
for "treating the subject then, not according to a priori fitness,
but according to the facts of human nature, as they are found in
the concrete action of life, I find numberless cases in which we
do not assent at all, none in which assent is evidently conditional
and many ... in which it is unconditional".[27]

Having shown that assent is really absolute, certain and unconditional, Newman proceeds to ascertain "how it comes to pass
that a conditional act leads to an unconditional".[28] This task led
him into a detailed consideration of the great types of inference,
the formal, informal and natural, in each of which he clearly demonstrates the conditional character of the conclusion. How, then,
can such a conclusion attain the status of assent? From a phenomenological investigation, Newman determines the existence
of certain assent and conditional inference, which is propaedeutic

---

[27] Ibid., 168-9.
[28] Ibid., 252; Chapter VIII, 252-335.

to assent. But how is the passage constructed? By what faculty of the mind is conditionality converted into unconditionality? Newman answers in terms of the Illative Sense. The Illative Sense is a process resembling the mathematical process of taking the limit. But we must go back and pick up, at greater length and detail, Newman's mind on the nature, operation and limits of the various types of inference. This study is indispensable for a better grasp of Newman's methodology in general, and his application of it in Theology, which is our immediate objective.

The model of a formal inference is the syllogism. The propositions are carefully weighed, their terms are accurately defined, and the interdependence and logical consecutiveness of the propositions is considered with mathematical precision. Newman explains his thought in this remarkable passage: "Let then our symbols be words ... Let language have a monopoly of thought; and thought go for only so much as it can show itself to be worth in language. Let every prompting of the intellect be ignored, every momentum of argument be disowned ... Let the authority of nature, commonsense, experience, genius, go for nothing. Ratiocination, thus restricted and put into grooves, is what I have called inference, and the science, which is its regulating principle is logic".[29] Newman is far from a total rejection of syllogism. His contention is that it is limited and restricted, a formalistic structure, logically derived, but incapable of dealing with the great, human and broad issues of life and thought. By means of the formal inference, a geometrical rigour can be imposed upon its subject matter. However, not without a price! And the price is the artificial suspension of assent, or methodic doubt, even in instances where commonsense, the voice of nature, and experience are all unanimous in their approval of unconditional acceptance. But more: reality is narrowed down into a manageable size, which can fit the stereotype and safe procedure of the syllogism. Its propositions are abstract, notional and conditional so that "it does not hold a proposition for its own sake, but as dependent upon others, and those others it entertains for the sake of the conclusion. Thus it is practically far more concerned with the comparison of propositions than with the propositions themselves".[30] This means the loss of the "real" and the "full" for the sake of the

---

[29] GA, 256.
[30] Ibid., 257.

"notional". Formal inference enjoys competence only in the narrow field of the notional and abstract, and is usable only in the province of mathematics and the positive sciences. Furthermore, to contend that every assent must be scientifically demonstrable, or actually demonstrated before its unconditional acceptance, is firstly, to condemn the firmly held assents of the multitude, secondly, to restrict lawful certitude to an elite, which has had the benefit of a thorough education, thirdly, to find oneself at odds with what is, in practice and in fact, the existing order of things, and fourthly, it involves the relegation of the mind to a state of impotence.

In concrete matters, then, formal inference does not really prove, or, what is the same, demonstrate. And since "in this world of sense we have to do with things, far more than with notions",[31] we must look elsewhere for the ratiocinative operations which lead to assent. And as we are guided by our principles, known or unknown to us, and live by certitude in many things, the syllogism is unable to deal with either. It is neither the test of truth, nor the adequate basis of assent. A modern writer seems to express Newman's viewpoint very well: "A logical structure, no matter how perfect, seems to take man away from his own self as truth-seeking, as intimately concerned with the truth for himself, the truth as interior illumination, as a principle of vital growth; and this alienation seems to increase as his logical exploration advances".[32]

Newman proceeds to an investigation of the informal inference. It "is a multiform and intricate process of ratiocination, necessary for our reaching him as a concrete fact, compared with the rude operation of syllogistic treatment" and it is the "only real reasoning in concrete matters", for it brings us to certainty. He explains the nature of this type of inference as a "cumulation of probabilities, independent of each other, arising out of the nature and circumstances of the particular case which is under review; probabilities too fine to avail separately, too subtle and circuitous to be convertible into syllogisms, too numerous and various for such conversion, even were they convertible".[33] He clarifies still

---

[31] Ibid., 270.
[32] N. D. O'Donoghue, "Is there a Christian Sense ?", Irish Theological Quarterly, 37 (1970), 4.
[33] GA, 281.

further by naming three outstanding characteristics of this inferential species: it does not supersede the logical form of inference, but it is carried out in the realities and intricacies of life; next, as a process, it is more or less implicit, in that the mind is not aware of (and even if it were, is unable to expose adequately) all the motives which carry it along; and finally, as an inferential process, it does not go one step towards removing the universal conditionality of inferential conclusion.[34]

Newman practises what he is preaching in giving us three instances of this type of ratiocination, which belong respectively to past, present, and future. The example referring to the present, which is representative of the other two, is perhaps better known than the others, and for that reason we shall consider it here. It is the famous proof, by which he argues to the certainty of the proposition that Great Britain is an island. He explains that, although we give to that proposition our absolute assent, and are quite happy in doing so, the strict logical arguments we can produce in its favour are far from commensurate with our over-powering certitude about it. There are reasons for accepting, and for legitimate acceptance of an absolute and unconditional degree, which do not admit of strict and complete analysis, and still less, of demonstrative proof.

The reasoning process is more implicit than explicit, natural than designed. Fr. Harper in "The Month" [35] attacks the very conception of informal inference: "either my inference is formally valid or it is not. If it be formally valid, it is ipso facto moulded by logical law; if it is not it is no inference at all". But Newman shows that informal inference is the rule, and formal an afterthought, an attempt at analysis and systematisation of the ordinary procedure!

> Our reasoning ordinarily presents itself to our mind as a single act, not a process or series of acts. We apprehend the antecedent and then apprehend the consequent, without explicit recognition of the medium connecting the two, as if by a sort of direct association of the first thought with the second. We proceed by a sort of instinctive perception from premise to conclusion ... We perceive external objects, and remember past events, without knowing how we do so; and in like manner we reason without effort and

---

[34] Ibid., 284-6.
[35] June, 1870, 688.

intention, or any necessary consciousness of the path which the
mind takes in passing from antecedent to conclusion.[36]

As an example, he offers the cryptic proposition: "We shall
have a European war, for Greece is audaciously defying Turkey".[37]
Such a prediction is an inference in Newman's eyes. And more:
he contends that with it we ought to be satisfied, as it is the natural means, providentially provided, for coming to our conclusions, and ultimately to our certainties.

This procedure is also greatly dependent upon the moral structure of the person. It is a moral, as much as an intellectual, process. And so our criterion of truth is not so much the manipulation of propositions, but the intellectual and moral character of
the person maintaining them. This explains why for Newman
most people are distrustful of logic and its workings. Pascal's
brilliant description of Christianity in the *Pensées* convinces by
its overall and cumulative power, not by the logic of its mere
wording.[38]

The natural inference closely resembles the informal. It follows the same pattern in operation, enjoys an even wider versatility of competence, and is capable of entering and manipulat-
ing more complex issues and questions. It is exemplified especially in the uneducated, who know nothing of intellectual aids,
and in men of genius, who care nothing about them. Because it
is so much a part of a person, being natural, unstudied, and to
that extent unsystematic, it is less protected than the formal before the assaults of emotion, passion and prejudice. It is therefore
more dependent on the moral factors for accuracy of operation
than the informal is. It has a "success on the whole sufficient to
show that there is a method in it, though it be implicit".[39] It involves the whole man, body and soul, intellect and will, mind and
heart. Newton's perception of mathematical laws and Napoleon's
strategy in military matters are instances of this type of inference.
It enjoys a singular relevance in the sphere of religion and theology, where formal inference is incapable of dealing with the concrete
questions and issues proposed, and where informal inference is

---

[36] GA, 252-3.
[37] Ibid., 296.
[38] Ibid., 304, 295, 300-4.
[39] Ibid., 324.

sometimes cumbersome. It is the logic of the living mind, "far higher, wider, more certain, subtler than logical inference".

The Illative Sense: Its Centrality in Newman

The conclusions of natural as of informal inference are conditional and probable. Certainty has still to be reached. Newman focuses on the leap from probability to certainty, and on how such a leap is made. His question is: If logic and formal reasoning are both inadequate in explanation of how the mind reaches the unconditional, except in the case of abstract science, then how do we reach the truth in concrete matter and in the myriad contingencies that make up our daily existence? For the simple fact is that we do possess certitude of mind in regard to many issues: "Earnestly maintaining ... the certainty of knowledge, I think it enough to appeal to the common voice of mankind in proof of it".[40]

Newman's preoccupation at this juncture is with the power by which the mind assents. Assent is absolute and unconditional, and so the instrument by which such a mental operation is performed must be capable of such an absolute function. "Certitude is not a passive impression made upon the mind from without by argumentative compulsion, but in all concrete questions (nay, even in abstract, for though the reasoning is abstract, the mind which judges of it is concrete) it is an active recognition of propositions as true." [41] It is the mind that is able to perform such a vital task, and not any calculus, however stricly articulated and stringently applied. Newman denies that the bridge between the probable and the certain, between the conditional and unconditional, may be built by the logic of words, the technical apparatus of formal deductions, or indeed by any single and easily objectifiable process of mind, devoid of complex motives and subtle influences.[42] "Science, working by itself, reaches truth in the abstract, and probability in the concrete; but what we aim at is truth in the concrete," Newman writes.

It is easy to notice here Newman's intellectualism. He insists that the mind is sovereign. It is not the pawn of its own works. It is their master as being already their source. His investigation, and subsequent discovery and articulation, of the mind's power

---

[40] Ibid., 337.
[41] Ibid., 337.
[42] Ibid., 344-5; 271-2.

of judging in the concrete is perhaps his most original achievement, his most far-reaching contribution to methodology. This achievement, I believe, has not, in general, been adequately appreciated in terms of its philosophical and methodological implications.

Newman gave a singular name to his singular discovery, the illative sense: "This power of judging about truth and error in concrete matters, I call the illative sense". Allowing for the flexibility of terminology employed by Newman, it is still possible to determine the exact meaning of this vital term. Newman correlates it strictly "with the soundness of the reasoning" in contrast with the truth of the conclusion for which we must have recourse to the truth of the premises.[43] He elaborates his treatment of this mental reality in terms of its sanction, or act, its nature and its range of operation. In this way he deals with its essential task in the structure of cognition, its actual working and operation, and finally the fields or subject-matters in which it functions.

With regard to the sanction of the illative sense, Newman summarizes its contribution in these brief but powerful words: "It determines what science cannot determine, the limit of converging probabilities, and the reasons sufficient for a proof".[44] It is the faculty that takes us into the domain of what is real and what is true. Just as an inferential "conclusion is but an opinion: it is not a thing which is, but which we are quite sure about",[45] the illative sense, by contrast, reaches the thing which is, and gives us sureness of mind in its respect. In a word, it is "the power of judging about truth and error in concrete matters".[46]

This sanction of the illative sense is of the highest significance. According to logic, which is the formal exhibition of all demonstrative science, the only certain conclusions are deductions from self-evident principles: theories, hypotheses and opinions may have any degree of probability, but they can never be certainties, for absolute verification is not possible. For Newman, however, the illative sense is just such an absolute verification, because it is able to establish the focal point of an otherwise inconclusive evidence, meeting a question in the spirit, though not in the letter,

[43] Ibid., 346, 353.
[44] Ibid., 346.
[45] DA, 293.
[46] GA, 346.

of rationality. It concludes a process, too complex for easy and complete articulation, too elusive and minute for adequate analysis, and too rich in its data for restricted methods. Thus in its very operation, it reveals the limits of strict science, as expressed in the syllogism, and supplements science by another method, necessary in life and thought, both sacred and secular.

Newman further elaborates on the nature of the illative sense by reference to Aristotle's faculty of practical moral judgement, phronesis.[47] In the *Nicomachean Ethics*, Aristotle devotes the whole of book VI to the treatment of practical judgement.[48] "He calls the faculty which guides the mind in matters of conduct, by the name of phronesis, or judgement. This is the directing, controlling, determining principle in such matters, personal and social. What it is to be virtuous, how we are to gain the just idea and standard of virtue, how we are to approximate in practice to our own standard, what is right and wrong in a particular case, for the answers in fullness and accuracy to these and similar questions, the philosopher refers to no code of laws, to no moral treatise, because no science of life, applicable to the case of an individual, has been or can be written. Such is Aristotle's doctrine, and it is undoubtedly true." [49] Newman, who read and wrote on the *Ethics*, *Rhetoric*, and *Poetics* of Aristotle more than on the *Metaphysics*, was simply fascinated by his discovery at this point. Attempting to find a more flexible model for concrete speculative inquiry, he saw in the Aristotelian use of phronesis in the ethical field implications he might articulate, develop and apply in the speculative field.

Aristotle had contrasted the function of phronesis with the function of scientific knowledge: "The body of scientific knowledge is the product of logical deduction from premises which are eternally valid; but art and practical wisdom deal with matters susceptible of change." [50] Newman, realising the inadequacies of Aristotelian syllogistic science in the concrete, contingent world of human experience and knowledge, and admiring the ingenuity of phronesis as the faculty of practical judgement in the moral sphere, now had an insight into what might be in

---

[47] Ibid., 347-150.
[48] Nicomachean Ethics, Book VI.
[49] GA, 347.
[50] Nicomachean Ethics, Book VI, 6.

the concrete speculative field, now governed by Baconian and Newtonian science. A footnote added to a later edition of the Grammar bears out this point: "Though Aristotle, in his *Nicomachean Ethics*, speaks of φρόνησις as the virtue of the δοξαστικὸν generally, and as being concerned generally with contingent matter (vi:4), or what I have called the concrete, and of its function being, as regards that matter, ἀληθεύειν τῷ καταφάναι ἢ ἀποφάναι (ibid. 3), he does not treat of it in that work in its general relation to truth and the affirmation of truth, but only as it bears upon τὰ πρακτά ".[51] But it was Newman's desire to transform Aristotle's teaching into a ready instrument for his theological purposes. The following quotation bears this out: "There is a faculty in the mind which I think I have called the inductive sense, which, when properly cultivated and used, answers to Aristotle's phronesis its province being, not virtue, but the 'inquisitio veri', which decides for us, beyond any technical rules, when, how, etc. to pass from inference to assent, and when and under what circumstances etc. etc. not".[52] This quotation displays both Newman's contact with the thought of Aristotle in this field, as well as his independence and originality in the manner in which he extended this thought into a speculative treatment of contingent questions, too elusive to be capable of "syllogistic treatment", too important to be left to such a treatment, even were it possible. Realizing that the evidences for faith are various, that the mystery of Christian revelation culminating in the incarnation, death and resurrection of the Word made flesh, are contingent in their historical expression, Newman saw in the inductive or illative sense an instrument capable of being employed in the handling of these all important questions: he had the clue to the provision of that new method he believed theology needed, while, on the negative side, he had the answer to the totalitarian claims of the scientists, who contended that everything true may be demonstrated, to the liberals, who reduced all proof to logical proof, and to the rationalist empiricists, who needed intellectual conversion.[53] Perhaps the following quotation is an

---

[51] GA', 277: "arrive at the truth in what it affirms or denies", Penguin Translation, London, 1953.
[52] Ward, II, 589.
[53] See Chapter IV.

adequate summary of the nature of the operation of the illative
sense:

> I have spoken of the illative sense in four respects—as a mental
> exercise, as it is found in fact, as to the process it uses, and as to
> its function and scope.
>
> First, as an exercise of mind, it is one and the same in all con-
> crete matters, though employed in them in different measures ...
>
> Secondly, it is in fact attached to definite subject-matters, so
> that a given individual may possess it in one department of thought,
> for instance, history, and not in another, for instance, philosophy.
>
> Thirdly, it proceeds, in coming to its conclusion, always in the
> same way, by a method of reasoning which I have considered as
> analogous to that mathematical calculus of modern times, which
> has so wonderfully extended the limits of abstract science.
>
> Fourthly, in no class of concrete reasonings, whether in experi-
> mental science, historical research, or theology, is there any ulti-
> mate test of truth and error in our inferences besides the trust-
> worthiness of the illative sense that gives them its sanction.[54]

Having considered the sanction and nature of the illative sense,
Newman concludes his treatment in terms of a study of its range.
"Its range then is commensurate with the actual range of our
intellect." [55] It is deployed in the whole field of particular, concrete and contingent issues and questions. " ... it is the instrument of induction from particulars, and determines what are general laws, and what conclusion cannot reach beyond bare probability." [56] Most important of all, it enables Newman to expand
the horizons of religious thought immeasurably, to enter areas
of data and evidence hitherto unmanageable, and so to greatly
enrich the domain of knowledge itself. It lends solid philosophical
foundations to the intricate process by which a person reaches
the truth. "It is by the strength, variety, or multiplicity of premises, which are only probable, not by well constructed sylo-
gisms; by objections overcome, by adverse theories neutralised,
by difficulties gradually clearing up, by exceptions proving the
rule, by unlooked-for correlations found for received truths, by
suspense and delay in the process issuing in triumphant reac-
tions-by all these ways, and many others, the practised and experienced mind is able to make a sure divination that a conclusion

---

[54] GA, 351-2.
[55] Ibid., 355.
[56] Ibid., 354.

is inevitable ... for a proof is the limit of probabilities." [57]

Newman was at pains to pay attention to the individual logic of truth. "Every one who reasons, is his own centre; and no expedient for attaining a common measure of minds can reverse this truth." [58] This put him at loggerheads with the philosophical and theological ascendancy of his own day. But history has judged his intuition and direction as both original and valid in our day.

> "Leaving the case to Time, who solves all doubt,
> By bringing Truth, her glorious daughter, out."

Newman liked to cite this couplet from Crabb. To mention but one example of an author, who in our time, defends a position identical to that of Newman, one could name a philosopher like Michael Polanyi. In his classical work, *Personal Knowledge: Towards a Post-Critical Philosophy*, Polanyi underlines the fact that "true discovery is not a strictly logical performance, and accordingly we may describe the obstacle to be overcome in solving a problem as a 'logical gap' and speak of the width of the logical gap as the measure of the ingenuity required for solving the problem. Illumination is then the leap by which the logical gap is crossed".[59] Newman, who contended that in all our reasoning in the concrete fields of history, ethics and theology there exists a logical gap ("for logic does not really prove"), bridged that gap in terms of the illative sense, the faculty of personal judgement which reaches the concrete existent. It is worthwhile comparing what Polanyi writes above with the following typical citation of Newman: "And reason never bids us be certain except on an absolute proof; and such a proof can never be furnished to us by the logic of words ... but then the question follows, is there any criterion of an act of inference, such as may be our warrant that certitude is rightly elicited in favour of the proposition inferred, since our warrant cannot, as I have said, be scientific? I have already said that the sole and final judgement on the validity of an inference in concrete matter is commited to a mental faculty, which I have called the illative sense".[60]

---

[57] Ibid., 314.
[58] Ibid., 338.
[59] M. Polanyi, Personal Knowledge: Towards a Post-Critical Philosophy, London, 1958, 123.
[60] GA, 338.

Bernard Lonergan has also followed Newman's path in his great study of human knowledge, *Insight*.[61]

Cognitional Structure and Method

What Newman is attacking is a false view of methodology. Newman does not reject reduction as such.[62] But what he does certainly reject is the fallacious claim that all reflection that merits the name, can be expressed only by the syllogism. What Newman gives us in the Grammar is the most general and universal type of inference, which is the common possession of all, is involved with the pulsing issues of daily Christian living, knows how to handle the evidence available, and issues forth in certitude, wherever this is possible. This formally valid, but radically simple type of inference, embraces all other types within itself.

Our very lives are a vocation to be what we are, for we are "emphatically self-made". In our lives, "this law of progress is carried out by means of the acquisition of knowledge, of which inference and assent are the immediate instruments".[63] Inference and Assent, then, are essential to our daily living and growth, psychical, moral and spiritual. In the *Grammar*, Newman is convinced that he has given us the profile of the genuine Organum Investigandi. It had ever been his contention that "we are not justified, in the case of concrete reasoning and especially of religious inquiry, in waiting till such logical demonstration is ours, but on the contrary are bound in conscience to seek truth and to look for certainty by modes of proof, which, when reduced to the shape of formal propositions, fail to satisfy the severe requisitions of science".[64]

The Illative Sense, which determines what science cannot determine, the limit of converging probabilities and inferential conclusions, and the reasons sufficient for a proof, is the faculty which concludes the cognitional process. Apprehensions, which follow upon experience, are manipulated into inference, which in turn is taken to the level of unconditionality when subjected to the illative sense, or faculty of judgement. Newman summa-

---

[61] B. Lonergan, Insight: A study of Human Understanding, New York, 1957, see Chapter VIII.
[62] B. Lonergan, Collection, London, 1967, 2.
[63] GA, 342.
[64] Ibid., 407.

rised his view of cognitional structure in an unfinished letter written to William Froude on 29 April, 1879, in which he made a last
effort to deflect the scientist from his "prepared positions". " ...
in first principles we agree together ... Thus you insist very strongly on knowledge mainly depending upon the experience of facts,
as if I denied it; whereas, as a general truth and when experience
is attainable, I hold it more fully than you. I say 'more fully',
because, whereas you hold that 'to select, square, and to fit together material which experience has supplied, is the very function of the intellect', I should not allow the intellect to select,
but only to estimate them. I am led to conclude that you grant
or rather hold two principles most important to my view of the
great matter ... first that there is a mental faculty which reasons in a far higher way than that of merely measuring the force
of conclusions by the force of premises: and next, that the mind
has the power of determining ethical questions, which serve as
major premises to syllogisms, without depending upon experience.
And now I add a third, which is as important as any: the gradual
process by which great conclusions are forced upon the mind,
and the confidence of their correctness which the mind feels from
the fact of that gradualness." [65]

Our considerations have come a long way. We have studied
Newman's general stand on method. But now he does us the courtesy of applying his method. And as the book is divided into
halves, the first dealing with "the connection existing between the
intellectual acts of assent and inference", so we find a double application. First, the findings in the half on apprehension and assent
are applied to the possibility of Faith and Dogmatic Theology
(Chapter V: "Apprehensive assents in Religious Matters"); and
secondly, the theory of assent and inference is applied to the justification and proof of Christianity (Chapter X). But there will
be more about this later. [66]

---

[65] Ward, II, 587, 589.
[66] The whole of Chapter V takes up the apologetic of Newman.

CHAPTER THREE

THE METHOD OF *AN ESSAY ON THE DEVELOPMENT OF CHRISTIAN DOCTRINE*

At the conclusion of chapter one, in which we considered Newman's early preoccupation with the issue of a correct method, we expressed the hope of soon studying the actual operation of method in his theology. That study, however, was postponed while in our second chapter we analysed the methodological content of the Grammar of Assent. This resulted in an accurate view of what Newman himself meant by method, and gave us a clue as to how he might tackle various theological problems. It is now high time that we actually consider his method in operation in the realm of theology. *An Essay on the development of Christian Doctrine* is a good instance of such operation, and of it Fr. Walgrave has written these weighty words: "Obviously, he (Newman) needs to justify his method and he does this chiefly in the Essay on Development".[1] And not only Fr. Walgrave, but Newman himself regarded the Essay as a typical expression of his theological method. "I had a way of inquiry of my own," he wrote in the *Apologia*, "which I state without defending. I instanced it afterwards in my Essay on Doctrinal Development ... My method of inquiry was to leap in medias res." [2]

Everything, then, points towards the Essay as a classical example of Newman's theological method at work, and to it we now turn our full attention. What follows can be outlined in this way:

I. The Problem of Doctrinal Development, and its Origin for Newman.
II. The Data for a Solution of the Problem.
III. Suggestion of a Solution: Hypothesis of Doctrinal Development.
IV. Attempt at Verification of Hypothesis.
V. Result: Certitude.
VI. Summary Conclusions.

---

[1] J. Walgrave, Newman the Theologian, 227.
[2] GA' 383; Ap, 178.

The Problem of Doctrinal Development and its Origin for Newman

In 1839 Newman was supremely conscious that his "opinions in religion were not gained, as the world said, from Roman sources, but were, on the contrary, the birth of my own mind and of the circumstances in which I had been placed".[3] Newman had been born into the Anglican Church, had grown to Christian maturity within her fold and once the Oxford Movement took up the task of preserving and developing the Anglican Church, Newman knew he had "a work to do in England".

The period between 1833 and 1839 was one of intense spiritual and intellectual activity for him. This intellectual endeavour brought him into contact with the Fathers once more. Although he had made their acquaintance earlier as an undergraduate in Oxford, he had temporarily lost interest in them under the influence of what he later detected as incipient liberalism: he was beginning to prefer intellectual accomplishment to moral excellence. Shaken out of this danger by his good friend, Hurrell Froude, Newman resumed his studies of the Fathers. He wrote: "In proportion as I moved out of the shadow of liberalism which had hung over my course, my early devotion towards the Fathers returned: and in the Long Vacation of 1828 I set out to read them chronologically, beginning with St. Ignatius and St. Justin". In 1830 he accepted a proposal to do a detailed research on the Council of Nicaea (325 A.D.), as it was dealt with by the Fathers and writers of the time. It was a momentous decision. "It was launching myself on an ocean with currents innumerable; and I was drifted back first to the ante-Nicene history, and then to the Church of Alexandria. The work at last appeared under the title of The Arians of the Fourth Century." However, the most far-reaching influence on Newman came from the great school of Alexandria, where the battle of Arianism was first fought. "Athanasius, the champion of the truth, was Bishop of Alexandria, and in his writings he refers to the great religious names of the earlier date, like Origen, Dionysius, and others who where the glory of its see, or of its school. The broad philosophy of Clement and Origen carried me away; the philosophy, not the theological doctrine."[4]

Although Newman admits that he did not know when exact-

---

[3] Ap, 192.
[4] Ibid., 116-7; 127-8.

ly he first learnt to consider Antiquity as the true exponent of the doctrines of Christianity and the basis of the Church of England, still it is quite true to say that he had been decisively influenced by his encounter with the school of Alexandria: he had discovered the Church already teaching, defending and proclaiming the Gospel in new formulae of doctrine and understanding, and he had discovered what theology should do in the service of the Gospel and under the guidance of ecclesiastical direction. "The mind of the believer would have to be docile to figure and fulfilment, to fact and to symbol, to rite and historic-eternal significance. Somewhere in the possibilities of the data lay the fulness of meaning; Revelation had not come to leave men once more in a morass of scepticism and conflict." [5] The school of Alexandria taught Newman that Christianity possessed dogmatic, hierarchical, sacramental and theological principles.[6] He saw there the Church in the full thrust and vitality of her youth and he saw her living by a certain doctrine, intellectually equipped to carry the battle to her heretical adversaries, and historically matured in the appreciation of her manifold responsibility. He saw that these qualities of the Alexandrian Church made her theologians and students devotees of a method which required love of truth, creativity, understanding and loyalty to tradition. The Alexandrian movement helped create an intellectual clarity, keenness, and dedication to honesty and meaning. The very non-believers themselves, as Origen confesses, inspired the breadth of his efforts by their questions. Perhaps the most powerful single principle which influenced Newman's thinking prior to his "great revolution of mind" in 1844, was the Sacramental Principle by which he meant the general, but very real, similarity between the great realities, "which fill eternity", and some of the phenomena of human life, activity and culture: nature was a parable and opened on grace; the poets were seers, the philosophers the prophets of the pagans, all leading up to "the fullness of time". Therefore the Anglican and "holy Church in her sacraments and her hierarchical appointments will remain, even to the end of the world, only a symbol of those heavenly facts which fill eternity".[7] In a word, Newman had come to recognize in Antiquity the true ex-

---

[5] M. Novak, Newman on Nicaea, TS, 21 (1960), 448.
[6] Ap, 150-7; Ar, 38-99.
[7] Ibid., 128-9.

ponent of orthodox Christianity and the support and bastion of Anglican claims: the Fathers are the apologists of the Anglican Church! [8]

A second outstanding principle which Newman was to draw out and employ in the intellectual and spiritual ferment of the Oxford Movement was the dogmatic principle, "the main principle of the Movement ... I have changed in many things: in this I have not. From the age of fifteen dogma has been the fundamental principle of my religion: I know no other religion; I cannot enter into the idea of any other sort of religion; religion, as a mere sentiment, is to me a dream and a mockery. As well can there be filial love without the fact of a Father, as devotion without the fact of a Supreme Being. What I held in 1816, I held in 1833, and I hold in 1864. Please God, I shall hold it to the end".[9]

A third dominant principle was his opposition to the Church of Rome, whose main offence lay in the honours she paid to the Saints and the Blessed Virgin. Her devotional practices and numerous of her doctrines were unfounded in Antiquity. They represented corruptions rather than developments, a perversion of the Church of the Fathers rather than a faithful continuance.[10]

After John Keble's famous sermon on July 14, 1833 from the University Pulpit of Oxford on National Apostasy, Newman knew that the work he had to do in England had started in earnest. He set out to "bring out in a substantive form, a living Church of England in a position proper to herself, and founded on distinct principles".[11] He based himself on the great theological principles he had culled from his studies of the Fathers, especially the Alexandrines, and his objective was to ground theologically the claims of the Church of England. In this frame of mind he worked feverishly from 1833 to 1839, although many people were concerned about the possible effects such radical investigation might have on his future ecclesial allegiance. This concern was not shared by Newman himself; on the contrary, he brought out many volumes designed to justify, nay heighten, the Anglican position. Among these works were *The Church of the Fathers*, *The Prophetical Office of the Church Viewed Relatively to Romanism*

---

[8] Diff, II, 23-5.
[9] Ap, 150.
[10] Ibid., 154.
[11] Ibid., 171.

and *Popular Protestantism*, *Essay on Justification*, and *University Sermons*, to mention the more important. Using the help of the great Anglican Divines of the eighteenth and nineteenth centuries, Newman was confident he had given a real basis to Anglicanism, and established a source of future prosperity and growth against the liberalism of the age. At the beginning of 1839, then, Newman possessed supreme confidence in the orthodoxy of Anglicanism and the untenable stand of the Church of Rome. The Anglican Church had steered her way between the Scylla of Roman deviation from Antiquity and the Charybdis of Protestant Liberalism. It was the Via Media where truth and virtue lay.

Still Newman was far from being a dogmatist in his certitude; such an attitude would would have been foreign to his spirit.[12] He was open to the controversy which existed between England and Rome. Indeed, he had written in an early number of the Tracts for the Times: "Considering the high gifts, and the strong claims of the Church of Rome and her dependencies on our admiration, reverence, love and gratitude, how could we withstand her, as we do, how could we refrain from being melted into tenderness and rushing into communion with her, but for the words of Truth, which bid us prefer itself to the whole world? 'He that loveth father or mother more than me, is not worthy of me'. How could we learn to be severe, and execute judgement, but for the warning of Moses against even a divinely-gifted teacher who would preach new gods, and the anathema of St. Paul even against Angles and Apostles who would bring in a new doctrine?"[13] Newman saw that the defenders of Anglicanism relied mainly on the argument from Antiquity, while Rome argued from her undeniable Catholicity. The former confidently referred themselselves to the Treatise of Vincent of Lerins on the "Quod semper, quod ubique, quod ab omnibus", as a patristic justification of the Anglican argument from Antiquity. We will have occasion shortly to see Newman's own view of the proper application of this criterion.

In an article in The British Magazine, entitled "Home Thoughts Abroad",[14] Newman presented the case for Rome with outstanding clarity and power. The article, which is in the form of a dialogue

[12] Idea, 210.
[13] "Records of the Church", Tract 24, 7, quoted in Dev, IX.
[14] Included in DA, 1-63.

between Newman and a Roman Catholic, sets out to give a fair and objective exposition of the Roman case, whose strength is often underestimated by Newman's friends. The body of the article turns, not upon Papal Supremacy, but upon the respective faiths of the two Churches, a point we might have anticipated, remembering that for Newman the Roman crime consisted in the promulgation of dogmas not contained in Revelation. However, he was convinced that England and Rome had each a point to clear up, the former Catholicity and the latter Antiquity. "One remark more about Antiquity and the Via Media. As time went on, without doubting the strength of the Anglican argument from Antiquity, I felt also that it was not merely our special plea, but our only one. Also I felt that the Via Media, which was to represent it, was to be a sort of remodelled and adapted Antiquity." [15]

As yet no doubt had crossed Newman's mind regarding the justice of the Anglican position. Still he was aware, indeed extraordinarily aware, as the last excerpt indicates, of the need England had of clearing up the issue of Catholicity and Rome had of clearing up the point of Antiquity. However, for one who professed that a thousand difficulties do not make one doubt, the issue of the Catholicity of the Anglican Church in no way damaged Newman's total allegiance and unreserved commitment to his Church. Certitude qua certitude, Newman insists, is simply unconditional.[16] Supremely confident in his position, Newman kept up the dynamic tenor of his life dedicated to transforming the Church he loved so well, far from any anticipation of the storm that was about to break all around him.

The first cloud appeared on the horizon in the course of the summer 1839. From June 13 until August 30, Newman read the history of the Monophysites. "I was absorbed in the doctrinal question ... It was during this course of reading that for the first time a doubt came upon me of the tenableness of Anglicanism. I recollect on the 30th July mentioning to a friend, whom I had accidentally met, how remarkable the history was; but by the end of August I was seriously alarmed." [17]

At this time Newman also read a study by Wiseman of the

---

[15] Ap, 209.
[16] F. Bacchus, "How to Read the Grammar of Assent", The Month, 2 (1924), 110.
[17] Ap, 210.

Donatist Controversy and Anglicanism, which appeared in the August number of the Dublin Review under the title, "The Anglican Claim". Wiseman made much of St. Augustine's famous indictment of the Donatists, on the score of their opinions not enjoying the support of the Catholic orbis terrarum, with the words: "Securus judicat orbis terrarum". "For a mere sentence, the words of St. Augustine struck me with a power which I never had felt from any words before ... they were like the 'Tolle, lege—Tolle, lege' of the child which converted St. Augustine himself. 'Securus judicat orbis terrarum'! By those great words of the ancient Father the theory of the Via Media was absolutely pulverized." [18] Down came his theory of the Via Media. He no longer had a positive theory and he confessed that he "was very nearly a pure Protestant".[19] He was forced painfully to fall back upon the three fundamental principles of belief, which we saw constituted the foundation, rock-like, of the buoyant theological grounding of the Anglican Theory in the numerous works that issued from his pen in rapid succession between 1831 and 1839. And we remember that the third of these principles was Anti-Romanism.

Newman's loss of certitude, then, in the tenableness of the Via Media did not automatically produce a certitude in the Roman position. On the contrary, he insisted still in his accusation that Rome succumbed to an unjustifiable development, or corruption, of the doctrine of the Church of the Fathers, and to serious devotional deviations in worship. Till Rome ceases to be what she practically was, a union between her and England was impossible. This was his mind from "the Autumn of 1839 to the Summer of 1841". It was a traumatic experience indeed for Newman. He determined, however, to be led by conscience and duty. "I had to determine its logical value, and bearing upon my duty," [20] he wrote. Still more was to come.

In 1839 Newman had published Tract 90, his famous and eventful study of the Thirty-nine Articles. He wished to ascertain the limit of the elasticity of the articles in the direction of Roman dogma, for he had come to appreciate that in the Roman position, three elements had to be distinguished, otherwise wild confusion resulted. Newman outlined these three elements thus: (a) Catho-

---

[18] Ibid., 213.
[19] Ibid., 216.
[20] Ibid., 224, 213.

lic teaching of Antiquity; (b) Formal Dogmas in later Councils, and (c) Popular beliefs and usages sanctioned by Rome. Now Newman expresses himself thus: "The main thesis, then, of my Essay [i.e., Tract 90] was this: the Articles do not oppose Catholic teaching: they but partially oppose Roman dogma; they for the most part oppose the dominant errors of Rome. And the problem was to draw the line as to what they allowed and what they condemned".[21]

The tract had an impact far beyond what Newman could have anticipated. He became a centre of controversy. His very name was a symbol of discussion and heated debate. After the shock of 1839 and its summer discoveries, Newman decided to continue with his investigation of the antiquity of the doctrine of the Articles. In 1840 he retired to the relative tranquillity of Littlemore, then nothing but a farmers' village a few miles from his beloved Oxford. Here he was to visit frequently until 1845. It is precisely this period between 1840-1845 which is of the highest interest to us, as it is the time in which Newman tries to resolve a problem at once historical and personal, theological and spiritual.

As a first stage in the reading he proposed himself in the investigation of the doctrine of the Articles, he set himself down to a translation of St. Athanasius. This was in 1841. "But, between July and November, I received three blows which broke me." [22]

Firstly, he discovered in his reading of the history of the Arians, as written by Athanasius, the very same phenomenon he had found in the history of the Monophysites. His words are eloquent: "I saw clearly, that in the history of Arianism, the pure Arians were the Protestants, the semi-Arians were the Anglicans, and that Rome now is what it was then. The truth lay, not with the Via Media, but with what was called 'the Extreme Party' ".

Next, just at this time the Bishops began to charge him with infidelity and lack of orthodoxy in connection with the Tract. This indicated to him an unwillingness on the part of the Bishops to see any possibility of doctrinal reconciliation with Rome on the basis of the thirty-nine Articles, the very constitution, as it were, of the Anglican Church.

Finally, as if all this were not enough, there came the affair of the Jerusalem Bishopric, which resulted in an Anglican Bishop

[21] Ibid., 177.
[22] Ibid., 235.

being installed in Jerusalem as a pastor of Protestants and Orthodox, indiscriminately. Newman could not reconcile this move
with the Bishop's condemnation of his Catholic interpretation
of the thirty-nine Articles. On November 11, 1841, Newman sent
a protest to his Bishop at Oxford. It brought him on to the beginning of the end.[23]

Data for a Solution of the Problem

We have already seen how Newman set out to grapple initially with the problem of Roman Dogma, and popular Romanist
error in devotion. Firstly, he retained the primordial principles
which he gained from his lengthy study of the Fathers and which
laid the foundations of the 1833-1839 Movement. These principles
were the sacramental, dogmatic and Anti-Romanism: this we
have already seen. Then he initiated a thorough research into the
full import of the doctrinal content of the thirty-nine Articles.
How far could Roman dogmas be acceptable to one who subscrib-
ed wholeheartedly to the Articles? That was the question and
the problem. Next, he continued his studies of the Fathers. We
have just seen his interest in St. Athanasius. But he read widely
at this time, as the Essay itself will clearly demonstrate. For example, he gave much time to the celebrated criterion of Vincent
of Lerins: "Quod semper, quod ubique, quod ab omnibus".

In addition, he began a study of the history of doctrinal statements by the Roman Church. He was to realise, for example, that
the Thirty-nine Articles were formulated before the Council of
Trent was ended and so could not have been intended as the very
antithesis of Catholic principles and dogmatic formulations.
How real, and how apparent, was the alleged opposition? This
was a very concrete issue and Newman searched about in his mind
for a way to harmonize the unquestionable growth evident everywhere in the Roman Creed, and the equally unquestionable normative value of Antiquity for all ages of Christianity. Finally,
there was his strict fidelity to the dictates of inner conscience.
We shall have occasion to consider this in depth later, but here it
is of primary importance. "I had no right, I had no leave, to act
against my conscience. That was a higher rule than any argument
about the Notes of the Church ... I could not make a mistake;

---

[23] Ibid., 235, 236, 241.

for what is a higher guide for us in speculation and practice, than that conscience of right and wrong, of truth and falsehood, those sentiments of what is decorous, consistent, and noble, which our Creator has made part of our original nature?" It is hardly possible to exaggerate the trust Newman showed at this vital juncture in the "Kindly Light" of God. He contended that obedience, even to an erring conscience, was the way to gain light. He felt that "anything might become a divine method of truth".[24]

Suggestion of a Solution: Hypothesis of Doctrinal Development

Newman, then, entered 1842 acutely aware of a problem, for which his eager mind eagerly sought an answer and a solution. As was his custom, he leaped "in medias res". All his intellectual energies and intuitive powers were alert and tensed. His mind was prepared and ready for the magnitude of the task, which confronted it.

The upshot of this concern, at once personal (for it had to do with his most intimate convictions, his most private secrets), theological (for it was concerned with the apparent incompatibility between growth and development of the doctrine of the Ancient Church, on the one hand, and perseverance and immutability of a divine revelation given once for all, on the other), religious (in that it involved essentially his future ecclesial allegiance), and social (as Newman was the undisputed leader and hero of the Oxford Movement), was the clear emergence of the hypothesis of a divinely guided process of doctrinal development and growth as the probable explanation of the problem which we have just considered. The *Apologia* gives us the circumstances in which the theory grew on him. Accordingly, we will first turn to the *Apologia*, before turning to the Essay itself and to the Oxford Sermon XV for a statement of this hypothesis.

He confesses that he "gave his mind" to this hypothesis, at the end of 1842, although the idea had been in his mind for a long time. Now, however, he saw it as a distinct theory which might perhaps solve his difficulty.

> In 1843 I began to consider it steadily; and the general view to which I came is stated thus in a letter to a friend of the date of July 14, 1844; it will be observed that, now as before, my issue

---

[24] Ibid., 248, 249, 299.

is still Faith versus Church. The kind of considerations which weigh with me are such as the following: 1. I am far more certain (according to the Fathers) that we are in a state of culpable separation, than that developments do not exist under the Gospel, and that the Roman developments are not the true ones. 2. I am far more certain, that our (modern) doctrines are wrong, than that the Roman (modern) doctrines are wrong. 3. Granting that the Roman (special) doctrines are not found drawn out in the early Church, yet I think there is sufficient trace of them in it, to recommend and prove them, on the hypothesis of the Church having a divine guidance, though not sufficient to prove them by itself. So that the question simply turns on the nature of the promise of the Spirit made to the Church. 4. The proof of the Roman (modern) doctrine is as strong (or stronger) in Antiquity, as that of certain doctrines which both we and Romans hold: e.g. there is more of evidence in Antiquity for the necessity of unity, than for the Apostolical Succession; for the supremacy of the See of Rome, than for the Presence in the Eucharist; for the practice of invocation, than for certain books in the present Canon of Scripture, etc., etc. 5. The analogy of the Old Testament and also of the New, leads to an acknowledgement of doctrinal developments.[25]

Most important of all, Newman saw it as an hypothesis which possessed a high antecedent probability and cogent verisimilitude. "I saw that the principle of development not only accounted for certain facts, but was in itself a remarkable philosophical phenomenon, giving a character to the whole course of Christian thought." [26] Already Newman saw that this theory was not haphazard and volatile, but enjoyed a convincing appearance in that it seemed to be the key to many and otherwise disparate facts and phenomena. In a word, it was a good hypothesis. "The fact of the operation from first to last of that principle of development is an argument in favour of the identity of Roman and Primitive Christianity." [27]

The first preliminary outline of the hypothesis is to be found in the last of the *University Sermons*, which is entitled "The Theory of Developments in Religious Doctrine", and which was preached on the Feast of the Purification, 1843. As it is an useful introduction to his general theory of doctrinal development, we turn to it now for a preliminary exposition of the hypothesis.

Taking as his text, "Mary kept all these things, and pondered

---

[25] Ibid., 289, 289-90.
[26] Newman was at pains to evaluate all the facts relevant to the problem.
[27] Ibid., 290, 291.

them in her heart" (Luke 2:19), he illustrates how Our Lady is "our pattern of Faith, both in the perception and in the study of Divine Truth", in that she not only believed, but also dwelt upon it, not only possessed but also used it, not only assented, but also developed it. She is, moreover, a symbol to us not only of the faith of the unlearned, but also of the doctors and theologians of the Church, "who have to investigate, and weigh, and define, as well as to profess the Gospel; to draw the line between truth and heresy; to anticipate or remedy the various aberrations of wrong reason".[28]

As Revelation sets before the human mind of the believers certain supernatural and thrilling truths, there is made a very vivid and lively impression of the sacred truth on the tender soul of loving faith. The believer cannot forget the great sight. The great idea takes hold of a thousand minds by its living force, so that the doctrine may rather be said to use the mind of Christians, than to be used by them. It becomes the secret life of millions of faithful souls.

Fired and aroused by such a lovely impression, the mind tries to give accurate utterance to the "blessed vision" that holds it spellbound. Clear, explicit formulation of the inward vision is not easy, however, and the process of formulating is, initially, more implicit than explicit. Even centuries might pass without an adequate formal expression of an aspect of the original idea, which had all along been the secret joy of millions of Christians.

Eventually, however, an explicit and formal statement of this powerful inner impression is achieved. The doctrine has developed; its development is nothing more nor less than the external utter- ing of the internal experience; it is a process of implicit reasoning, "a gradual development towards the expression of what had been present from the very beginning in experience, although implicit and unnoticed", as Fr. Schillebeeckx puts it.[29] In this way Newman explains how "the doctrine of the Double Procession was no Catho- lic Dogma in the first ages, though it was more or less clearly stated by individual Fathers; yet, if it is now to be received, as surely it must be, as part of the Creed, it was really held every- where from the beginning, and therefore, in a measure, held as a mere religious impression, and perhaps an unconscious one".[30]

---

[28] OUS, 313.
[29] E. Schillebeeckx, Revelation and Theology, London, 1967, 152.
[30] OUS, 323.

Doctrinal formulation, then, seems to be part of the inner life and dynamism of Christian Faith and experience. But the very curiosity of the believer's spirit, which has been the inspiration of the very developmental process, also demands the ordering and relating, the harmonizing and defending, of the body of explicit formulations so derived. This is theology, and it is a science with its own subject matter and principles, its own logic and academic rigour and thoroughness. Newman gives powerful expression to this truth as follows:

> The Apostle said to the Athenians: 'Whom you ignorantly worship, Him declare I unto you'; and the mind which is habituated to the thoughts of God, of Christ, and of the Holy Spirit, naturally turns, as I have said, with a devout curiosity to the contemplation of the object of its adoration, and begins to form statements concerning Him before it knows whither, or how far, it will be carried. One proposition necessarily leads to another, and a second to a third; then some limitation is required; some fresh evolutions from the original idea, which indeed can never be said to be entirely exhausted. This process is its development, and results in a series, or rather body, of dogmatic statements, till what was at first an impression on the Imagination has become a system or creed in the Reason.[31]

But, lastly, these several dogmas do not go beyond the original idea, the primordial object of Faith, and the core of Revelation. They "cannot say more than is implied in the original idea, considered in its completeness, without the risk of heresy ... And in matter of fact these expressions are never equivalent to it ... Catholic dogmas are, after all, but symbols of a Divine Fact, which, far from being compassed by those very propositions, would not be exhausted, nor fathomed, by a thousand".[32] In this way Newman envisages a permanence within growth, and identity within development, of the one "Divine Fact". And this is his Hypothesis of Development of Doctrine, which is to account for the alleged Roman corruption of the Deposit of Faith. This was 1843.

It was but a beginning. Newman was not concerned with the possibility of the existence of a divinely appointed framer or legitimate judge of these dogmatic inferences, nor with the question of such an authority being infallible. His preoccupation was with

---

[31] Ibid., 329.
[32] Ibid., 331-2.

the fact of development itself. Besides, he realized that the subject was vast, more deserving of a volume than a short sermon, and vital for him personally. He had a valuable insight, however, and he was going to push it to its limit as a possible solution of his dilemma. We are on the threshold of the *Essay on the Development of Christian Doctrine.*

It is true that "Newman simply takes it for granted that, if there is a revelation, if there is one revelation, if that revelation's maintained public availability even to the unlearned is guaranteed by divine providence, then there must be somewhere in the world today an authentic, adequate and authoritative embodiment and expression of that revelation. The question then becomes: how do I decide which amongst existing contenders is that embodiment of revelation? Newman proposes to answer this question by means of an appeal to history".[33] This is the key to the Essay and explains why its preoccupation is with the problem of continuity between primitive Christianity and the Roman Catholic Church. Newman had lost his way temporarily and so he sought a new "view" of Christian history. "When we have lost our way, we mount up to some eminence to look about us," we do not "plunge into the nearest thicket to find our bearings," Newman comments at this time.[34] The *Essay* is the expression of this view of the Christian centuries: perhaps it is not so unusual after all that its very last page should exult in the discovery of a "Blessed Vision of Peace".

His synthesis, expressed in the Via Media theory, had shown itself unworthy of further acceptance as a just solution of the apparent dialectic between Roman "corruptions" and Protestant "errors". But where the Via Media would not work, the theory of the *Development of Christian Doctrine* might. It was an anticipation of an answer and might aid in the actual discovery of the true answer and solution. "Some hypothesis, this or that, all parties, all controversialists, all historians must adopt, if they would treat of Christianity at all".[35]

One thing, however, badly needed to be done: the hypothesis of doctrinal (not theological) development needed to be improved. The Oxford sermon was but a general approach, and Newman

---

[33] N. Lash, Change in Focus, London, 1973, 87.
[34] LD, XI, 69; quoted in Lash, Ibid., 89.
[35] Dev, 91.

was quite aware that any theory or hypothesis had to be accurate and precise in order to be really effective in moving towards an accurate understanding and evaluation of the data. He therefore determined to write an *Essay on Doctrinal Development* in which he hoped to develop his hypothesis. And as we have seen how the Sermon hypothesis did not consider the issue of a developing authority, or the nature of such an authority (if it exists), we would be justified in expecting Newman to expand his theory precisely in the direction of these issues. "This much, however, might be gained from an Essay like the present (on the Development of Doctrine), an explanation of so many of the reputed corruptions, doctrinal and practical, of Rome, as might serve as a fair ground for trusting her in parallel cases where the investigation had not been pursued." [36]

Chapter two of the *Essay on Development* is entitled: The Antecedent Argument in behalf of Developments in Christian Doctrine, and it is divided into three sections:

(i)   Developments to be expected;
(ii) An infallible developing authority to be expected;
and (iii) The existing developments of doctrine the probable fulfilment of that Expectation.

(i) Developments to be Expected

Newman repeats, though briefly, the fundamental reasoning of the famous Oxford Sermon, locating the phenomenon of growth in the discursiveness of the human mind. However, he goes further in this instance. He notices that the whole Bible itself is developmental in its message, and moves from beginning to end in a climate of increasing and growing revelation. Its earlier stages are anticipations of its later; the Pentateuch anticipates the Prophets, and the Prophets anticipate, though dimly, the fulness of time in the New Testament. "The whole Bible, not its prophetical parts only, is written on the principle of development. As the Revelation proceeds, it is ever new, yet ever old." This fact had a profound influence on him and intimated the dynamic nature of God's Self-communication in Revelation. It was a powerful "analogy" and convinced him that "we may fairly conclude that Christian

---

[36] Ibid., 31-2.

doctrine admits of formal, legitimate, and true developments, that is, of developments contemplated by its Divine Author".[37]

(ii) An Infallible Developing Authority to be Expected

In proportion to the probability of authentic developments in Revelation, it is to be expected that such developments really be genuine, that is, that they be preserved free of corruptive influence. Revelation is a divine gift from Heaven, whereby God communicates Himself to man. Man, however, is the sinful, fallible and mendicant recipient of this divine Truth of Revelation. In his possession, it will not, and cannot, cease to be divine truth. This implies powerfully the need of a divinely appointed self-preservative, or principle of self-preservation, within Revelation itself. A Revelation is not given if there be no authority to decide what is given; Newman then identifies this principle of self-preservation in development as the "infallibility of the Church; for by infallibility I suppose is meant the power of deciding whether this, that, and a third, and any number of theological or ethical statements are true".[38] If developments there must be, then authentic they must be. But if authentic, then there must be a divinely appointed teaching and guiding component given within revelation as its very preservation against corruptions, or false developments.

(iii) The Existing Developments of Doctrine the Probable Fulfilment of that Expectation

Now in the history of Christianity there happens to be a large body of Doctrine usually called Catholic, which claims to be, not only the authentic developed contemporary expression of Christianity, but above all the product of an "infallible sanction", the existence of which in the Divine Dispensation is antecedently probable, as we have seen. The fact of Catholicism is accepted universally, by those within, as well as without, the Christian fold. It is a fact with well developed features, clearly outlined contours. It comes to all and sundry as an unit and body, coherently structured and harmoniously blended, and demands either total acceptance or complete rejection. He that is not for it, is against it.[39] "All these things being considered, ... few persons

---

[37] Ibid., 65, 74.
[38] Ibid., 75-92, 78-9.
[39] Ibid., 93-4.

will deny the very strong presumption wich exists, that, if there must be and are in fact developments in Christianity, the doctrines propounded by successive Popes and Councils, through so many ages, are they." [40] With a powerful flurry of eloquence, expressing his comprehension and "vision", Newman concludes the chapter by hazarding the opinion that modern Catholicism is both Ancient Alexandria and the genuine heir of the Ambrosian Church!

Undoubtedly, then, the Essay goes much further than the sermon in its nuancing of an hypothesis of doctrinal development. In spite of this marked improvement in the articulation of a theory of development, there are authors today who strongly contend that Newman does not offer a highly developed hypothesis of doctrinal development so much as the clearly stated fact of development in doctrine. This fact of development makes no pretensions to explain the process of doctrinal development in itself. It is simply professed by Newman as a "theory" alternative to the prevailing theories of "immutability" and "corruption".[41] This fact of development dovetails with the antecedent probability that there will be growth and development in divine truth communicated to this world. Newman feels that it is the best solution, being "the simplest, the most natural, the most persuasive".[42]

The contention that the Essay does not articulate a well-formed theory of doctrinal development, such as a present-day theologian might attempt, may be admitted. Newman is not formally and specifically attempting to explain the process of doctrinal development. This is definitely not his purpose. His aim was, as we have originally stated, to solve a problem posed by the apparent discontinuity between primitive Christianity and contemporary Roman Catholicism. "The weight of the historical analysis in the Essay should be on the side of the search for continuity, rather than on the recognition of discontinuities, in christian history." [43] In the end what conquered the mind and heart of Newman "was what he took to be historically given, the inescapable conclusion before a particular constellation of facts", that "the Roman Catholic communion of this day is the successor and representative of the Medieval Church, or that the Medieval Church is

---

[40] Ibid., 96.
[41] See N. Lash, ibid., 88-92.
[42] Dev, 92.
[43] N. Lash, ibid., 87.

the legitimate heir of the Nicene: ... On the whole, all parties will agree that, of all existing systems, the present communion of Rome is the nearest approximation in fact to the Church of the Fathers, possible though some may think it, to be nearer still to that Church on paper".[44] As an Anglican Newman saw the principal fault of Rome in the dogmas that she seemed to add to those of the primitive Church. This was his chief objection against Catholicism. And so he writes that the *Essay* "is not written to prove the truth of Catholicism ... but to answer an objection against Catholicism." [45] The heuristic anticipation of doctrinal development permits him to see in the Roman "additions", not "corruptions", but legitimate "growths", of the original Christian "idea". "For Newman, an argument from antecedent probability is not the imposition of a preconceived theory upon the evidence, but a more or less well-founded claim that it is reasonable to expect that, in a particular case, the data bear witness to one state of affairs rather than to another. In our own day, when we have become conscious of the impossibility of 'presuppositionless' historical interpretations, and when even philosophers of natural science speak of the 'theory-laden' nature of scientific data, the formal validity of such a methodology hardly requires demonstration." [46]

The Verification of the Hypothesis of Doctrinal Development

But probability is not certitude, and verisimilitude is not truth. His frame of mind at this vital juncture is nicely expressed in this passage from the Apologia: "To be certain is to know that one knows; what test had I, that I would not change again, after that I had become a Catholic? I had still apprehension of this, though I thought a time would come, when it would depart. However, some limit ought to be put to these vague misgivings; I must do my best and then leave it to a higher power to prosper it". In a word, Newman set out to verify his hypothesis, for he knew that he "was not near certitude yet".[47] Accordingly, his next chapter is significantly headed thus: Historical Argument in behalf of the Existing Developments.

---

[44] J. M. Cameron, "Newman and the Empiricist Tradition", Red, 92-3.
[45] LD, XII, 332.
[46] N. Lash, ibid., 89-90: Lash refers, in a footnote, to the similarity which Newman's idea of "antecedent probability" bears to both Bultmann's "Vorverständnis" and Husserl's "Horizont des Verständnisses".
[47] Ap, 318, 307.

In the derivation of his hypothesis we noticed that Newman observed the same critical approach as he just now demands in regard to its veracity and trustworthiness. "We may err grievously in the antecedent view we start with, and in that case, our conclusions will be wide of the truth; but that only shows that we had no right to assume a premiss which was untrustworthy, not that our reasoning was faulty." It is just such a critical attitude which he now brings to bear on his hypothesis: if it can bear up with critical reflections and investigation, it may be worthy of assent and acceptance.

As the event, which is the development, is also the interpretation of the prediction, so too the fact and existence of a body of doctrine, existing in the historic seats of Apostolical teaching and in the authoritative homes of immemorial tradition, would seem to be the just interpretation of the antecedent expectations. Newman argues that if a known course of events, or the history of a person such as Our Lord, is found to answer on the whole to prophetical text, it becomes fairly the right interpretation of that text, in spite of difficulties. He continues: "This rule of interpretation admits of an obvious application to the parallel cases of doctrinal passages, when a certain creed, which professes to have been derived from Revelation, comes recommended to us on strong antecedent ground".[48]

Indeed Newman uses the very word "verify" in this outstanding passage which well expresses his mind at this stage. "In all matters of human life, presumption verified by instances, is our ordinary instrument of proof, and, if the antecedent probability is great, it almost supersedes instances." [49] But only almost! There must be an exhibition of evidence prior to assent and judgement. The evidence must be accumulated and selected. Its cogency then must be determined, and its value assessed. It is his conscious and deliberate weighing of evidence which Newman calls "verification" or "proof". This is the final phase in his method and is fittingly the most important; yet Newman is not able to explain how this step is ultimately made. Seeing the problem of the apparent opposition between the Anglican claim to Antiquity and the Catholic insistence on Catholicity and development, he was led to investigate the data of the problem. This investigation of data has yielded

---

[48] Dev, 114, 105.
[49] Ibid., 113-4.

an hypothesis of doctrinal development which seems to explain and justify the Roman position. In order to remove all doubt and reach absolute certitude, he sets out to "verify", and "prove" his hypothesis.

Evidence and arguments accumulate. He derives them from all quarters and slowly allows them converge on an overwhelming question: "Do they verify and prove the hypothesis?" The only essential question for Newman is whether the recognized organ of teaching, the Church herself, acting through the Pope, or Councils, as the oracle of heaven, has ever contradicted her own enunciations. "If so, the hypothesis which I am advocating, is at once shattered." [50]

His "method of proof" is one of "converging evidence" in favour of his hypothesis. This method, he contends, is just as powerful a proof of the Apostolic origin of Roman dogmas as can be reached by the "quod semper, quod ubique, quod ab omnibus". "In such a method of proof there is, first, an imperfect, secondly, a growing evidence, thirdly, in consequence a delayed inference and judgement, fourthly, reasons producible to account for the delay".

It is impossible not to observe at once the obvious similarity to the method he was later to outline in the Grammar. Even the very wording is significant. For example, he speaks of "convergence of evidence" here, while "cumulation of probabilities" is more commonplace in the Grammar; of "delayed inference" here, and of "natural and informal inference" there.[51] It was, we remember, the anticipation of the method outlined in the Grammar being operative in the Development which made us turn our attention there in pursuit of his integral theological method. Our findings prove that our anticipation has not been in vain.

However, Newman is well aware that the method he proposed is not accepted by the majority of his contemporaries. These base themselves on Lord Bacon as their authority. Bacon propounds a method that contrasts with Newman's. And as opposition and contrast are luminous, we now turn to see how Newman dealt with Bacon's ideas, hoping that, in the process, we will be able to get a still clearer vision of Newman's idea of method in theology.

Bacon put forward the principle of "methodic doubt", just as

---

[50] Ibid., 121, 123.
[51] GA, 281-335.

Descartes had been doing across the channel in France. Nothing was to be held without proof; the only sign of real intelligence was to demand demonstration for every belief and opinion. Nothing was to be received on antecedent probability, or on its own verisimilitude. "He who is not practised in doubting," says Bacon "but forward in asserting and laying down such principles as he takes to be approved, granted and manifest, and, according to the established truth thereof, receives or rejects everything, as squaring with or proving contrary to them, is only fitted to mix and confound things with words, reason with madness, and the world with fable and fiction, but not to interpret the works of nature." [52]

Studying the *Grammar*, we saw how it was precisely the same problem which preoccupied Newman there: Is logical demonstration the only way to certitude? According to liberals, like Capes, Froude and their school, which uncritically accepted the scientific model as the only valid one, the answer could be in the affirmative only. We observed how Newman proved that there is another way, more "practical, popular and versatile": the method of converging probabilities and illative sense. Strict logical demonstration, he contended, is valid but within its own field of physics and the positive sciences, where its subject matter is neatly and arbitrarily reduced to an artificial size, and expressed in a language, which allows it to fit into the narrow moulds of syllogistic inference.

In consideration of Bacon in our present context, we are not surprised to find Newman making two comments fundamentally similar to the thematic of the *Grammar*. Firstly, he restricts the validity of the Baconian method to the field of "strict investigation, and that in the province of physics". Secondly, he points out immediately that in the greater issues of history, ethics, religion and theology, the method cannot be applied! He notices that Bacon seems to allow this restriction, and finds the same principle upheld in the well known maxims of Aristotle, that "it is much the same to admit the probabilities of a mathematician, and to look for demonstration from an orator". And even if Newman is prepared to admit that his alternative method is less exact and perfect, he vigorously maintains that God "may bless antecedent

---

[52] Quoted in Dev, 110.

probabilities in ethical inquiries, who blesses experience and induction in the art of medicine".[53]

In order to clarify his mind at this stage, Newman dedicated a special chapter to some instances of development, or apparent development, where dogmas have arisen which do not have an indisputably recognizable position in the primitive history of the Christian Church. Of the three he gives in illustration of his theological method, we shall consider the third one, namely, the Papal Supremacy.[54]

The doctrine is not found, in developed form, in the Ancient Church, and is certainly not drawn out there in the explicit form which it now enjoys. However, there is an antecedent probability that God, in revealing His inner mysteries of truth and life, should have provided a special and permanent charismatic guidance to teach authentically and interpret, defend and explain to sinful men and all generations, the mystery of His saving plan. Secondly, there is a growing, if meagre, evidence in the Post-Nicene Church in favour of the existence of such a primacy on the part of the Bishop of Rome. This, then, is roughly the hypothesis, or, as he calls it, the "presumption". "It has ... two parts, the antecedent probability of a Popedom, and the actual state of the Post-Nicene Church. The former of these reasons ... is the absolute need of a monarchical power in the Church, which is our ground for anticipating it ... Moreover, all this must be viewed in the light of the general probability ... that doctrine cannot but develop as time proceeds and need arises, and that its developments are parts of the Divine system, and that therefore it is lawful, or rather necessary, to interpret the words and deeds of the earlier Church by the determinate teaching of the latter." [55]

This is truly an ingenious solution. But is it true? That is the question. "It will be said that all this is a theory. Certainly it is: it is a theory to account for facts as they lie in the history, to account for so much being told us about the Papal authority in early times, and not more; a theory to reconcile what is and what is not recorded about it; and which is the principal point, a theory to connect the words and acts of the Ante-Nicene Church with the

---

[53] Ibid., 110, 113, 112.
[54] The other two are: 1. "Instances cursorily noted", 2. "Our Lord's Incarnation and the dignity of His Mother and all the saints".
[55] Dev, 154-55.

antecedent probability of a monarchical principle in the Divine Scheme, and that actual exemplification of it in the fourth century, which forms their presumptive interpretation." [56] In other words, Newman is satisfied that the hypothesis is good.

This means he has to begin to prove and verify his hypothesis. Starting with the evidence of Holy Scripture, whose witness to the Church's authority and structure must include already much, very much, that can be appreciated and grasped only with the passage of time, he moves on through the testimony of the Fathers, Pre-Nicene and Post-Nicene, who by their words and deeds evidence a powerful and convincing support of his theory. He is able to conclude that the clear evidence of the fourth century is proof of the historical continuation of Post-Nicene from the Pre-Nicene Church. The only question that remains is whether the Papal Supremacy of the fourth century is the logical continuation of the dim, though definite, outlines seen in the preceding centuries. It is this question alone which prevents Newman from arriving at an unconditional acceptance of his own hypothetical solution.[57] He must first resolve this vital issue before he can assent absolutely to the probability and versimilitude of his hypothesis. The moulds of his critical and scientific method are already set and all he needs to do is to apply them, and a definite judgement will be his.

The instance of the Papal Supremacy brings to mind the need of proving and verifying the broader issues, of which it is but an example, namely, the logical, as well as the historical, continuity and sequence between the early centuries of the Christian Church and the Roman Catholic Church. For it may be objected against his hypothesis of doctrinal development, and the method of verification so far outlined, that it does not remove the possibility of seeming growth being, in fact, subtle error, and of apparent developments concealing radical corruptions of the ancient Depositum Fidei. The objection is a legitimate one, and must be fairly met. But how?

Certain tests must be made in order to evaluate the strength of the hypothesis. And since the debate is between development and corruption, "the breaking up of life, preparatory to its termina-

---

[56] Ibid., 154.
[57] Ibid., 164-5.

tion",[58] the tests have to do with the authenticity of development, in general, and in the particular instance of Christian doctrine. The objective of his choice of qualities of a true development focuses on the penetrating and critical insight into the real nature and genuine character of authentic growth. Newman knows a priori that real development is such as allows the Church's present self-understanding and self-expression to be isomorphic with its scriptural roots. As an organic and living body of heavenly origin, the true Church of Christ must be the contemporary living realization, in time and space, of the Church of the Fathers. Rome claims to be such a Church. From the point of view of history, her claim is irrefutable. But can the same be said from the point of view or angle of doctrinal coherence? Or logical sequence? etc... ? [59]

First of all, Newman drew certain conclusions concerning what it seemed from the evidence of the Gospels the Church ought to be at any time of her history. He then had to examine "the behaviour of early Christian thinking and living", in other words, the problem of the development of theology, to see if he could find "the whole image" of the Church which he had formed from the Gospels reproduced in the Theology of the Fathers and the life story of the early Church. "Finally taking his stand on Antiquity, he had also to assure himself that the Church of Rome, about which he read in Patristic Theology, was indeed recognisable, as in 1839 he suspected for the first time it might be, in the Church of Rome as it existed in his day. He saw the whole vast problem in a nutshell; 'Was I, or was I not, a Monophysite?'" [60] The tests, then, would have to be profound and penetrating, able to detect powerfully the reliableness of doctrine, and capable of immediate revelation of any kind of falsity or corruption. Conscious of the qualities his tests would have to possess, he had recourse to an analogy, which is a leitmotiv in his theological method (as we shall have occasion to see later). The analogy he took was that of organic growth. His words are eloquent:

> Taking this analogy (viz., a body growing or decomposing) as a guide, I venture to set down seven notes of varying cogency,

---

[58] Ibid., 170.

[59] See N. Lash, "Dogmas and Doctrinal Progress", Doctrinal Development and Christian Unity, London, 1968, 3-33.

[60] PN, I, 115-6.

independence and applicability, to discriminate healthy developments of an idea from its state of corruption and decay, as follows:
There is no corruption if it retains one and the same type, the same
principles, the same organization; if its beginnings anticipate its
subsequent phases, and its later phenomena protect and subserve
its earlier; if it has a power of assimilation and revival, and a
vigorous action from first to last.[61]

In this way Newman derived trenchant tests and definitve criteria for his theory of development, and the second half of the
Essay is given over to an exposition of each of the seven criteria,
together with its application. Yet it is one of the most misunderstood parts of all Newman's work, although most critics agree
that his account of the seven criteria of genuine developments is,
in itself, a masterpiece of historical and philosophical analysis.

> In building up his induction of the seven "notes", Newman chooses
> to be guided, more or less, by the analogy of the life of ideas with
> that of organic nature. This comparison needs to be properly
> understood . . . The analogue, may be, as it were, an archetype,
> a symbol, which I use to gain access to a reality it represents for
> me, but of which my knowledge is only vague and indirect; in that
> case, I am taken up wholly by the figurative image. But I may also
> make use of the analogy for purposes of instruction only, and then
> its function is merely accessory. I myself possess a clear knowledge
> of the thing I wish to describe, but it is more or less remote from
> matter and inaccessible to the generality of man . . . This is what
> happens here. It is a procedure particularly adapted to Newman
> with his genius for "realization". His own attention remains fixed
> on the living mind as it manifests itself in its own effects, and he
> uses physical life as a remote but striking analogy to facilitate the
> description of the processes of the mind.[62]

These criteria he elaborately drew out and painstakingly applied to the actual state and situation of the Roman Church. He
writes at great length on the first note, "permanence of type",
but after that he speeds up, and the end of the work is obviously
hurried. Something had happened to Newman; he had come to
harbour after a stormy sea, and he was certain of the truth of his
hypothesis of development of doctrine. And he had come into the
calm waters of comforting certitude, not by the way of demonstrations or in virtue of the cogency of syllogism, but through a gra-

---

[61] Dev, 171.
[62] J. Walgrave, Newman the Theologian, 260, 261-2.

dual process by which the "great" conclusion was forced upon the mind. He felt full confidence in its correctness, all the deeper for the fact of that gradualness.[63]

Result: Certitude

We recall how Newman set out to resolve the dilemma of Antiquity and Roman Catholicism, upon the collapse of his Via Media (Section 1). On the way we saw him collect data relevant to the "great issue" (Section 2), and how this led to a possible hypothetical solution to the problem in terms of a divinely appointed teaching authority in the Church, which authority would preserve from error the historical and developmental processes of doctrinal growth in their ultimate determinations, which we call "doctrines" or "dogmas" (Section 3). However, theory is not yet fact, and hypothesis is not yet truth. This enjoined on Newman the necessity, vividly "realized", of "putting a limit to his doubts" about his theory and its validity. This was the stage of verification and application of the seven "notes" of genuine development to his hypothesis of development (Section 4).

The upshot of all his research, which cost him so dearly, was the emergence in his mind of an overpowering vision of the truth of the Roman position and claim. "When he (Newman) had got some way in the printing [of the Essay itself], he recognized in himself a conviction of the truth of the conclusions to which the discussion leads, so clear as to supersede further deliberation." [64] His mind, by its judgemental ability,[65] focused the converging evidence on the point where he felt conscious of the unconditional validity of the hypothesis as a solution of his problem. He writes: "All this time (1845) I was hard at my Essay on Doctrinal Development. As I advanced, my view so cleared that instead of speaking any more of 'the Roman Catholics', I boldly called them Catholics. Before I got to the end, I resolved to be received, and the book remains in the state in which it was then, unfinished".[66]

The fruits of his "investigation" were even richer. He noticed that "the principle of development not only accounted for certain facts, but was in itself a remarkable philosophical phenomenon,

---

[63] Ward, II, 589.
[64] Dev, XI.
[65] GA, 336-78; J. Walgrave, Newman the Theologian, 4.
[66] Ap, 325.

and gave a character to the whole course of Christian thought. It was discernible from the first years of Catholic teaching up to the present day, and gave that teaching a unity and individuality. It served as a sort of test, which the Anglican could not exhibit, that modern Rome was in truth ancient Antioch, Alexandria, and Constantinople, just as a mathematical curve has its own law and expression".[67] Secondly, as the divine Revelation existing in the social body of the Church must and, in fact, does develop, so too there is a dynamic aspect to the individual's religious faith, so that "there was no medium, in true philosophy, between Atheism and Catholicity, and that a perfectly consistent mind, under those circumstances in which it finds itself here below, must embrace either the one or the other".[68]

Summary Conclusions

As we saw at the outset of this chapter, Newman was highly conscious that the Development instanced "a way of inquiry of his own", and secondly, that this way of inquiry was but the application of the method masterfully expounded in the *Grammar*. Accordingly, we have been at pains to outline the method of the *Development*. It remains for us to state, as clearly as possible, the new insight into Newman's theological methodology which we have discovered by our labours.

A pattern has emerged. This pattern is a process of investigation which begins from the data relevant to the problem, and moves to a tentative solution of the problem, which is variously named, as an "antecedent probability", or, more generally, an "hypothesis". This hypothesis is in turn subjected to critical reflection in order to test its soundness and validity, and the result of this "verification" is a certitude of the mind that the hypothesis is the truth. Verification has qualitatively transformed theory into fact. The problem to be resolved lay in the alleged conflict between the Ante-Nicene teaching of the Christian Church of Antiquity on the one hand, and the modern developments, both historical and doctrinal, which are commonly called Roman Catholic, on the other. Leaping in medias res, Newman discovered an hypothetical solution in terms

---

[67] Ibid., 290-1.

[68] Ibid., 291; in the GA', Newman returns to the same idea on pages 383-9. In our fourth chapter we will have occasion to develop this theme in some detail.

of a divinely given and divinely guided principle of growth within the divine fact of Revelation itself, such as the Roman Catholic Church perennially claimed. Still one could not accept unconditionally and absolutely, a mere hypothesis, however cogent its verisimilitude. It needed to be verified both in terms of critical historical reflection, and of doctrinal consistency. The "seven notes" of authentic growth served as seven tests and trials of the hypothesis. The result was an unconditional acceptance or assent to the Roman Catholic doctrine as the legitimate development of the teaching of Antiquity.

And this process is dynamic. Later stages presuppose and complement earlier stages, and are in turn presupposed and complemented by final stages. One stage summons forth a second, which then proceeds to summon forth a third, and so on. Hypothesis and inquiry presuppose and complement the data and its problems. Verification and critical reflection presuppose and complement hypothesis. In a word, the process of investigation gradually and systematically builds itself up into an ordered structure. On the way it demonstrates a deliberateness and drive which shows that the dynamic structure itself is deeply rooted in the inquirer, being therefore a permanent exigency of the human spirit. All this will be clarified by the use of a diagram, which, though quite obviously inadequate to express fully a cognitional and ratiocinative process, is still of some considerable use in the present context.

$$\text{I.} \quad \begin{matrix} \text{Problem} \\ \text{and its} \\ \text{data} \end{matrix} \longrightarrow \text{II.} \quad \begin{matrix} \text{Hypothesis} \\ \\ \text{verification} \end{matrix} \longrightarrow \text{III.} \quad \text{Certitude}$$

Newman added, of course, a fourth stage to his dynamically operative structure, namely, decision. Decision is nothing more than the existential acceptance in one's life of the truth of which one is intellectually and rationally conscious. It is the moment of truth, in that it demands consistency between knowing and doing, between knowledge and life. It is the call to be authentic. In this instance of doctrinal growth, it demanded that he "resolve to be received" into the Roman Church.

Furthermore, our anticipation of the "Organum Investigandi" of the *Grammar* being operative in the *Development* has been fulfilled. The former work set forth the method which Newman judged to be, humanly and divinely, the way given by God to all men to arrive, according to the divine pleasure, at the fulness of truth.[69] We saw how that method envisaged a structure which moved from experience to apprehension, both real and notional, and on to assent, having used the tools of inference and Illative Sense on the way between apprehension and assent. We recall that, diagrammatically, the structure is as follows:

$$\text{I. Experience} \longrightarrow \text{II. Apprehension} \overset{\text{Illative Sense}}{\underset{\text{Inference}}{\longrightarrow}} \text{III. Assent}$$

The similarity between this "Organum Investigandi", and the dynamic structure of the method observed in the Development, is more than incidental. Indeed we do not hesitate to affirm an identity between both, for, in the first place, any seeming difficulties are terminological rather than real. Apprehension is the equivalent of hypothesis. If apprehension is defined by Newman as the mind's "imposition of a sense upon terms",[70] hypothesis is the grasp of an intelligibility or sense in an otherwise unintelligible mass of facts and data. Again, the Illative Sense is the sense actually used in the critical stage of the cognitional process, which occurs after understanding and before the unconditional is attained, and therefore is similar to verification. Verification for Newman entailed a systematic assembly of argumets, all arising from the nature of development in general, and of doctrinal development in particular, arguments (or "notes", as he called them) too numerous to be mentioned in their complete number, too subtle to be capable of perfect exhibition, and too fleeting to be individually grasped, but which converge together on the truth towards which the hypothesis of development tends.

Verification in *Development* was involved with the truth of a completely practical and popular issue - the truth of the Roman Church's claim to Apostolicity. But the faculty of judgement in concrete issues is the Illative Sense, and so the evidence is complete for the affirmation of equality between verification and Illative Sense. And thirdly, the *Development* is a work which comes twenty-five years before the *Grammar*, so that a difference of terminology is conceivable, and, in the case of Newman who never

---

[69] GA', 386-7.
[70] GA, 7.

enslaved himself rigidly to a static scientific jargon, altogether to be expected. To contend that the author of the *Grammar* should have used exactly the same terms as the author of the *Development* would be tantamount to a serious misconception of the man, Newman, who always kept his ear to the ground, wrote from the streaming abundance of his conscious flow, and kept in mind continually the personal and immediate destination of all his works. Variation in his language and terminology does not mean variation in interior vision and perception.

Another conclusion that comes to mind is that the *Development* is an expression of Newman's praxis of personal self-appropriation in Christ. The Development is no mere theological exercise, no mere philosophical discussion. On the contrary, we have been at pains to point out just how concerned Newman was to discover the course he ought to follow as a disciple of Christ, once his allegiance to the Anglican Church had been overthrown. His purpose in writing it at all was to discover the true Church of Christ where he could clearly hear the word of the Lord and his summons to discipleship. The *Development* presents us with the theological foundation for his personal self-appropriation of authenticity in Christ. It can be justifiably stated of Newman that all throughout his long life he longingly looked for ever greater closeness to Christ, the Kindly Light, who led him amid the encircling gloom. But we shall have occasion to develop this point of self-authenticity in Newman at some length, later.

Next, convinced that the fundamental problems of faith and theology arose from the false "prepared positions" [71] that abounded in regard to the nature of thinking and reasoning, Newman grounds every step he takes in the Development in his own personal mental activities. His theology is, therefore, critical and personal. We were pleased to discover that Fr. Walgrave, in his fine work, *Unfolding Revelation*, which has just been published, is of a like mind: "His (Newman's) basic idea of development is a faithful translation in general terms of something that he saw at work in his own experience and that he brought to light by efforts of personal reflection with no aid from without. If it is true that Husserl's programme of 'going back to the things themselves' is the very mark of a great philosopher, then Newman is to be considered

---

[71] Prepos, 277-91; OUS, 200-1.

as an outstanding genius in the history of human thought".[72] He was vividly aware that a theology not grounded in an adequate conception of the role of human understanding and cognitional process in human life, would soon become an inadequate and literally inhuman theology.[73]

In the sixth place, there is to be observed an explicit parallel between the method of the *Development,* and the positive scientific method. "I consider, then that the principle of concrete reasoning is parallel to the method of proof which is the foundation of modern mathematical science, as contained in the celebrated lemma with which Newton opens his *Principia.* We know that a regular polygon, inscribed in a circle, its sides being continually diminished, tends to become that circle, as its limit." [74] Indeed, Newman detects a striking similarity between the method employed in the *Development* and "that which is considered to constitute a sufficient proof of truths in physical science". [75] We have already had occasion to take note of Newman's insistence on this isomorphism, which exists between the structure of positive scientific thought and the structure of theological thought, in the famous unfinished letter to the scientist William Froude, which Newman wrote in Rome on April 29, 1879.[76] It was his great desire to incorporate in theological science the multiform data available from biblical, patristic, historical, liturgical, spiritual and theological sources. Positive science, with its empirical, statistical and historical induction, furnished him with the model he needed. Further, inductive science led to an hypothetical or probable explanation of its manifold data. We have seen how Newman's hypothesis of doctrinal development constituted just such a probable explanation of the multitudinous data of his religious experience. And finally, positive science set out to verify experimentally its hypothetical explanations. In a similar style, Newman wished to test the soundness of his insight, to turn his theory into facts, his probable solution into a certain one.[77]

But now it seems that we may have fallen into a vicious circle, in that we have shown how Newman's method in the Development

---

[72] J. Walgrave, Unfolding Revelation, London, 1972, 297.
[73] M. Novak, "Newman on Nicaea", TS, 21 (1960), 450.
[74] GA, 313.
[75] Dev, 122-3.
[76] Ward, II, 586-92.
[77] Ap, 325.

is the very method of the positive science then current, from which, we recall, the Liberals drew and substantiated their rationalistic principles. Indeed, shortly after the publication of the *Development*, this very accusation was levelled against Newman. "Since I wrote, I find the Essay on Development is accused of denying moral certainty and holding with Hermes we cannot get beyond probability in religious questions. This is far from my meaning." [78] What, then, did he mean?

The question is justified. In the *Grammar* he successfully demonstrated the conditional nature of all inference, which is the unique tool of the positive sciences. No type of inference, whether it be syllogism, formal inference, or natural inference could lead to absolute certainty on its own.[79] Greater or lesser probability was as much as could be expected, depending upon the cogency of the arguments and the strength of the premises exhibited. To equate theological method with the method of positive science, is surely to accept, at least in principle, that absolute certitude is not possible in theological investigation.

Newman was aware of the objection. But the objection is only apparent. Firstly, the method of the *Development* led, in fact, to certitude of mind and to certainty of proposition. Secondly, this certitude resulted from the mind's own power of judgement in confrontation with a bundle of arguments variously derived. It was not therefore the result of mere comparison of arguments or propositions, however powerful. Moral certitude is a state of mind, in all cases, however, produced by probable arguments, which admit of more or less, the measure of probability necessary for certainty varying with the individual mind.[80] This is in nucleus the position he will articulate so splendidly in the *Grammar* as the Illative Sense, which exists and operates as the mind's principle of judgement, and hence also of certitude. No amount of argument or reasons can produce certainty. It is the mind itself that reasons and gradually moves to the unconditional grasp of the truth of an apprehension or hypothesis. This mental grasp, by the mind's own faculty of judgement (in the *Development*), or by the Illative Sense (as in the *Grammar*), of absolute unconditionality, is mental certitude. The mathematical calculus of taking the

---

[78] LD, XI, 288-9.
[79] GA, 6, 150-1, 286.
[80] Ibid., 303-5.

limit, or the lemma of Newton, resembles for Newman the functioning of the mind's judgemental faculty, no less in the *Development* than in the *Grammar*.[81]

It follows that here must be some ground for the isomorphism of scientific thought and Newman's theological methodology. Newman locates such a ground in the human personality as a drive towards understanding and discovery.[82] This vital point is splendidly articulated in two documents we have already seen, namely, the letter to W. Froude in 1879, and the famous Note II added in 1880 to the *Grammar*.

All this allows us to make a further conclusion: Newman's method harmonizes both classical theological methodology, as exemplified for example in St. Thomas and the great Scholastics, and concrete, historical and scientific inductive method. Transposed and used in Theology, classical method demanded a deductive process, of logical strength, from the incontrovertible truths of Revelation, as exhibited in doctrine and dogma.[83] The dogmas became the premises of the syllogism, which was regarded as foolproof in getting out the correct answer. Newman's method broadens this method by his original contribution of a supplementary inductive method of converging probabilities and illative sense. The whole labyrinth of arguments and maze of evidence used in the *Development* is an outstanding example of this type of method. By joining this method to classical method, he has wonderfully broadened the horizons of theology and theological research. He has, in a word, supplied our age with a "Novum Organon Investigandi" which allows it to break through to a new way of working in theology—historically, personally, and experientially. Even if it were for this alone, Newman must surely qualify for the praise lavished on him recently as a "good prophet of what we are now witnessing!" [84]

We have now reached a stage where we can attempt an explanation of the position Newman takes up in the *Idea*, the work in which he gives an airing to his view of theological method, as explicit as it certainly is most surprising. There he contends that deduction only is the instrument of theology. He goes on to contrast

---

[81] Ibid., 313, 320-1.
[82] See Dev, 3-54.
[83] Idea, 222-7; 440-2.
[84] J. Guitton, The Church and the Laity, New York, 1964, 8.

theology and the physical sciences precisely in terms of their respective methods: "Theology retains the severe character of a science, advancing syllogistically from premises to conclusion".[85] This method of Physics is just the reverse of this.

To interpret these texts correctly, it is important to remember the context and intention of Newman in so writing. The context of his statements is a lecture comparing Christianity and its science, theology, with the method of Physical Science. The lecture was delivered in 1855 to the schol of medicine in the newly founded Catholic University at Dublin, of which he was then Rector. Aware that he is speaking, not as a private person, but in his offical capacity, he is eager to approach the question of method "from the ordinary standpoint of Catholic theology". His intention is to safeguard the supernatural origin of the Christian dogmas as the gracious gift of God, and not the ingenious discovery of man. As Fr. Walgrave very correctly remarks, apropos the subject, "Newman brings out forcibly that Revelation may be made more explicit, but never added to ... he does not, therefore, rule out that implicit and spontaneous growth which constitutes the development of doctrine".[86]

It can now be seen that Newman has developed something unique in both philosophy and theology. He has reduced the various models of inference and reasoning to one archetype of inference. He had always contended that "logic does not really prove",[87] and so cannot deal with the great concrete issues of life, temporal and eternal. He is not attacking reduction as such. "Some other type of formally valid inference (is necessary) that possesses both the radical simplicity and indefinite flexibility necessary to embrace all other types within itself"; such an inference is the "ultimate unity of the simple hypothetical argument". In fact, Fr. Lonergan is convinced that Newman has found the "permanent structure of method ... the same general process of experience, of hypothesis, and of verification; the structure of scientific knowledge is a constant and that methodical constant squares with the Thomist metaphysical constant of potency, form, and act".[88]

---

[85] Idea, 441.
[86] J. Walgrave, Newman the Theologian, 57.
[87] GA, 264.
[88] B. Lonergan, Collection, London, 1967, 2, 15, 150, 151: Lonergan develops his theory of knowledge in his great volume, Insight, New York-London, 1957.

And finally, because the *Development* is essentially a first instance in Newman's praxis of personal self-appropriation of authenticity in Christ, he was not totally aware of the full import of what
he was doing and saying. This is why the *Apologia* was required
later to give the historical self-appropriation of his authenticity in
Christ, and later again the *Grammar* as the theoretical and philosophical foundations of this authenticity in Christ.[89]

---

[89] GA', 382-9.

CHAPTER FOUR

THEOLOGY AND ITS METHODICAL FOUNDATIONS

Newman refused to accept the contemporary notions and procedures in theological method. So much has become clear from
our investigations in the opening three chapters, in which we focused
our attention on the actual model then used in inquiry. Newman
was convinced that his comtemporaries relied on a method that
was both "theoretical and unreal". They had borrowed from the
natural sciences, as these developed since the time of Descartes
and Newton, the mathematical model of reasoning. This they
isolated and enthroned as the one and only way of conducting
an inquiry. The method which they found useful and effective
in the natural sciences they made the absolute norm for all reasoning and investigation in any subject under the sun. Logic and
formal inference became the highroad to all truth and what they
achieved in the natural sciences they could and would achieve,
when used properly, in "moral subjects" like history and religion.
In a word, the method of the positive sciences which expressed
in the language of logic becomes the syllogism, had become for
many the very foundation and basis of all knowledge, truth,
morality, religion and theology. The genuine Christian, in the
Liberals' opinion, could use this method to understand revelation,
to defend its claims on our unconditional assent and to influence
the society about him in the interests of its Christian calling and
of the formations of its members.[1]

In the light of his principles, Newman considered the Liberal
standpoint a perfect fallacy. Worse still, it was tripping up many
of his own contemporaries like a snare hidden in the grass. It
demanded of him both a convincing refutation and the provision
of a sound alternative. This explains why Newman spent so much
of his long life in laying down what he identified as the true foundations of a "personal Christianity" and an authentic theology.
We recall, to take only one instance, the silent labours from 1859
onwards on a project for Christian formation and culture. It is

---

[1] E. Sillem, PN, 241-50.

time, then, to propose Newman's insights into the systematic foundations of the Christian faith, and so also of theology.

In 1864 when Newman was already nineteen years in the Roman Catholic Church he wrote these words, at once so autobiographical and revelatory: "I have always contended that obedience even to an erring conscience was the way to gain light, and that it mattered not where a man began so that he began on what came to hand, and in faith, and that anything might become a divine method of truth, that to the pure all things are pure, and have a self-correcting virtue and power of germinating".[2] From his own personal experience he was acutely aware of such a "divine method of truth". He had traced an itinerary all the way from the edges of agnosticism to that Blessed Vision of Peace he discovered in the Catholic Church, an itinerary which Pope Paul VI eulogised as being "the most toilsome but also the greatest, the most meaningful, the most conclusive, that human thought ever travelled during the last century, indeed one might say during the modern era".[3] Well did he realise that the light that led him on the way towards the fullness of peace and truth was not as simplistic and trite as a formal inference. Indeed, he is quick to point out that his own "divine method of truth" had little to do with formal logic. Quoting St. Ambrose's principle, "Non in dialectica complacuit Deo salvum facere populum suum", Newman elaborates a first vital insight into the process of concrete discovery: "I had a great dislike of paper logic. For myself it was not logic that carried me on; as well one might say that the quicksilver in the barometer changes the weather. It is the concrete being that reasons; pass a number of years, and I find my mind in a new place; how? the whole man moves; paper logic is but the record of it".[4] As a result of the personal appropriation of his own inner odyssey he saw, in increasingly clearer light, that the way to the truth was in a direction totally different to the one then held in esteem, namely, the method of explicit inference and systematic demonstration.

It is true that Newman compared his method composed o f experience, hypothesis, and verification in the *Essay on Develop*-*ment*, to Newton's method of taking the limit in mathematics . It is true, too, that he related his method of convergence of prob-

[2] Ap, 333.
[3] Pop e Paul VI, L'Osservatore Romano, October 28, 1963.
[4] Ap, 28 5.

ability, illative sense, and certitude, to the method so ably employed by the same mathematician.[5] However, all this was to underline what he considered the only proper way of arriving at certainty about any concrete fact.[6] The very parallelism of concrete reasoning and the method of proof, which is the foundation of modern mathematical science, is grounded in the human person whose access to knowledge is "more delicate, versatile, and elastic" than "the rude operation of syllogistic treatment". In this way he has masterfully transposed the whole discussion of method into the domain of the subject, to the point where all modern thought is focused. He could only conceive of method concretely, as the living, vibrant, and personal thought of the concrete person, who can never be the mere instrument or pawn of an abstract set of rules for inquiry and discovery. "Long before existentialism had broken through the closed essentialist conception of man as animal rationale Newman had achieved that shift of perspective which opens up (this) new understanding of man and man's history."[7]

In the final chapter of the *Apologia* he decisively expresses his mind in favour of a concrete, rather than theoretical, stance with regard to the foundations of a personal and living Christianity:

> I have no intention at all to deny that truth is the real object of our reason . . . but of reason as it acts in fact and concretely in fallen man. I know that even the unaided reason when correctly exercised, leads to a belief in God, in the immortality of the soul, and in a future retribution; but I am considering it actually and historically; and in this point of view, I do not think I am wrong in saying that its tendency is towards a simple unbelief in matters of religion. No truth, however sacred, can stand against it in the long run.[8]

In this text, which presents his position so delicately that its full import easily escapes the reader, Newman once more opts for the concrete subject and his actual mental operations. It is possible to notice as well his concern with the inevitable bias and prejudice which appear in their operation, and with the aberrations and

---

[5] GA, 313.

[6] GA, 281.

[7] GA, 264, 281; N. O'Donoghue, "Newman and the problem of privileged access to Truth", ITQ, 42 (1975), 247.

[8] Ap, 379-80. It is well worth the labour to compare Newman's thought here with the dogmatic constitution, Dei Filius, of Vatican I, DS 3004, 3026; and with B. Lonergan. "Natural Knowledge of God", Proceedings of the Catholic Theological Society of America, 23 (1968), 54-69.

errors that result. Unquestionably Newman is driving at an adequate personal interiority by way of antidote to what he calls,
in the same place, the "all-corroding, all-dissolving scepticism of
the intellect in religious matters".[9]

Already we have had occasion to consider carefully the plans
for Catholic education and thought which Newman conceived
and set to work on after his return from Dublin in 1858.[10] He
thought in terms of a work of broad dimension, an Opus Magnum,
part of whose task would be the laying down of a basis and foundation for Christian thought and action, broad enough to be
ecumenical, deep enough to meet the rising tide of infidelity, popular enough to meet the needs of both laity and clergy, and sound
enough to draw out the rich veins of ore still hidden in the treasury
of Revelation. That this subject had been one of special concern
to him we can detect from the tone of a letter written many years
previously, on January 28, 1836, to his great friend, Hurrell Froude.
In it Newman declares that Sir James Stephen had written to
him in connection with this very theme: "He (Stephen) wanted
from me a new philosophy. He wanted Christianity developed to
meet the age".[11] This "new philosophy" would have to provide
new foundations for Christian thought and life in the teeth of
an age which Newman regarded as largely given over to the principles of Liberalism, of which a primary one was the belief that
theology and its interests were adequately catered for by formal
demonstrative reasoning.[12]

In 1841 something happened which stimulated Newman towards a first statement of the foundations of Christianity. In that
year Sir Robert Peel, Prime Minister of England, and Lord Brougham, issued a new programme for popular, national education.
Underlying and inspiring the whole programme was the principle
that the Christian character of society "could be secured and
maintained in the mass of men . . . by acquaintance with literature
and physical science, and that, through the instrumentality of
Mechanics' Institutes and Reading Rooms".[13] There scarcely
could be a clearer statement of the view that Christian formation

---

[9] Ap, 379.
[10] See pp. 36-40.
[11] Quoted in J. Guitton, The Church and the Laity, New York, 1964, 6.
[12] My Campaign in Ireland, 394-6; Ap, 94, 380-1; GA, 252-64; 418-24.
[13] GA, 88; see apposite remarks of C. Dawson, "Newman and the Modern
World", The Tablet, August 5, 1972, 733-4.

was nothing more than mere passing intellectual acquaintance
with elements of Christian truth scattered here and there over the
face of science and literature.

Alerted to the danger Newman came on the scene with a series
of witty, brilliant letters addressed to the *Times*. He later collected
these letters under the title, "The Tamworth Reading-Room
Articles", and published them as article four in his volume, *Dis-
cussions and Arguments*.[14] Thomas Vargish considers this article
as among Newman's master-works [15]

Newman levels the accusation of fallacy against the formulators
of the new programme. Their fallacy is their aspiration to form the
masses by means of philosophy. "Do not attempt by philosophy
what once was done by religion. The ascendancy of faith may be
impracticable but the reign of knowledge is incomprehensible."[16]
Furthermore, science sets out from the phenomena of nature and
moves towards a conclusion about their Maker, it has "little of a
religious tendency; deductions have no power of persuasion".[17]
But to "subdue the reason and overcome the heart", something
greater than science is required. Such a requisite will have to be
commensurate with the nature of man himself, who "is not a
reasoning animal; he is a seeing, feeling, contemplating, acting
animal".

He continues:

> The heart is commonly reached, not through reason, but through
> the imagination, by means of direct impressions, by the testimony
> of facts and events, by history and description. Persons influence
> us, voices melt us, looks subdue us, deeds inflame us. Many a man
> will live and die upon a dogma; no man will die for a conclusion.
> A conclusion is but an opinion; it is not a thing which is, but which
> we are quite sure about.[18]

The issue here is ultimately a clash of two "antagonistic" approaches, the one based on logic or formal demonstration, the other
on the subject's interiority. Newman brilliantly contrasts the two
viewpoints: "Logic makes but a sorry rhetoric with the multitude;
first shoot round corners, and you may not despair of converting

---

[14] DA, 254-305.
[15] T. Vargish, Newman: the Contemplation of Mind, London, 1970, 27.
[16] DA, 292.
[17] DA, 293.
[18] DA, 293.

by a syllogism . . . Logicians are more set upon concluding rightly, than on drawing right conclusions. They cannot see the end for the process".[19] The way to the truth, in particular religious and Christian truth, is not the way of demonstration and orderly, step-by-step argumentaton. Rather, it will be, as it always has been, the way of inner and personal growth, at once more complex, more comprehensive and more comprehensible than the reductionist approach of abstract formal reasoning.

Bernard Lonergan believes that Newman provides here the basic statement in connection with the concreteness of method. He writes in words that sound as if in commentary on Newman's own: "Basically the issue is a transition from the abstract logic of classicism to the concreteness of method. On the former view what is basic is proof. On the latter view what is basic is conversion. Proof appeals to an abstraction named right reason. Conversion transforms the concrete individual to make him capable of grasping not merely conclusions but principles as well".[20]

The foundations of theological reflection, then, may not be reduced to the status of a formal and rigorous method that pretends to arrive at the truth independently of the person. Newman makes the point still clearer: "Life is not long enough for a religion of inferences; we shall never have done beginning, if we determine to begin with proof. We shall ever be laying our foundations; we shall turn theology into evidences, and divines into textuaries".[21] Once more Newman displays his impatience with any insinuation that the mind be made to fit into one of its own products and instruments such as the methodical processes of inference. Logical procedures are designed for man, not man for logical procedures. "But if we commence with scientific knowledge and argumentative proof, or lay any great stress upon it as the basis of personal Christianity, or attempt to make men moral and religious by libraries and museums, let us in consistency take chemists for our cooks, and minerologists for our masons."[22]

Newman was convinced of the fallacy of attempting to provide a "basis for personal Christianity" in terms of science and literature alone. That the Liberals should have adopted such foundations

---

[19] DA, 294.
[20] B. Lonergan, Method in Theology, London, 1972, 338.
[21] DA, 295.
[22] DA, 295-6.

was not very surprising, given their principle that reason existed
in each person with equal power and clarity, and so was capable
of leading every person to the conquest of the whole truth in
his concrete existence.[23] For the Liberals, all formation, both
human and Christian, was merely a matter of training the intellect; for Newman it was "the whole man" who either grows or
declines. "Quarry the granite rock with razors," he writes in the
Idea of a University, "or moor the vessel with a thread of silk;
then may you hope with such keen and delicate instruments as
human knowledge and human reason to contend against those
giants, the passion and pride of man."[24] Theology, like all thought,
is the living activity of the living person, such as he is, and so
it involves his horizon and outlook, his moral as well as his social
being.

In his study of the dynamic character of ascent towards truth
in the mind and in the heart of the person, Newman discovered
the decisive role played by moral and religious factors, as well
as by intellectual factors. The primary source of this insight was
his own personal history, which taught him a truth which, he
confesses, "is habitually in my thoughts, whenever they are turned
to the subject of mental or moral science . . . viz. that in these
provinces of inquiry egotism is true modesty".[25] A secondary
source of the same insight, however, was the people Newman
came to know in his own life. He gradually realised that there
were different types of personalities, and so also of groups, differ-
entiated one from another in terms of these very same intellectual, moral, and religious factors.

It was Newman's method in broaching an issue to subject it
to a phenomenological analysis: from a comprehensive observation of the person in action he proceeded to work out the actual
nature of his personality and the first principles that constituted
it. This ultimately means that "in persons and events, he discerned
types; in other words, he looked beyond the persons and the events
to what they signified. Hence, to understand his thought or his
actions a typological method must be used. We must see behind
the individuals the eternal attitudes of which, for Newman, those

---

[23] A. J. Boekraad, The Personal Conquest of Truth according to J. H.
Newman, Louvain, 1955, 213-303.

[24] Idea, 121.

[25] GA, 379.

individuals are the incarnation in the flux of time. Thus Newman recognised himself in Athanasius just as later he recognised the Anglican Church in the Semi-Arians and in the Donatists".[26]

I have attempted to follow this method of investigation in pursuit of the factors of interiority that are the basis of a personal Christianity according to Newman. The fruit of my inquiry has been the discovery and delineation of three pairs of antithetical types. Attempting to keep close to Newman's own terminology, those pairs may be enumerated as follows: the religious type and the rationalistic type; the morally consistent type and the morally inconsistent; and, finally, the truly intellectual type and the liberal. I may now set out to describe each pair in the hope of bringing to light the ultimate foundation of each pair and of learning how the members of each pair reached such contradictory "positions". I intend, then, to paint the portrait of each type of person in order that it might be seen in what he differs from his antagonistic type, how he is what he is and how the no-man's-land between the two might be crossed.

The Religious Person and the Rationalist

Newman often expressed the point that his own mind was the source of much of his thought and knowledge, but in no area so much as in that of religion.[27] In the *Apologia* he speaks of three vital occasions, or "conversions",[28] each of which occurred at a decisive point in the trajectory of his personal development and had far reaching consequences for his subsequent activity and thinking. I will briefly consider them, as they provide us with what Newman calls "the true key to his whole life".[29]

When he was only 15 years of age, he admits that "a great change of thought took place in me. I fell under the influences of a definite Creed, and received into my intellect impressions of dogma, which, through God's mercy, have never been effaced or obscured".[30] Though only a first experience of transcendence, it had a lasting effect on his then developing personality, and it made him "rest in the thought of two and two only supreme and

---

[26] J. Guitton, The Church and the Laity, 23.
[27] Ap, 181.
[28] "Conversion" is an important word in the Newman vocabulary.
[29] Ap, 47.
[30] Ap, 58; see C. S. Dessain, "Newman's First Conversion", Newman-Studien, III Folge, Nürnberg, 1957, 37-53.

luminously self-evident beings, myself and my Creator".[31] In the years that followed the outstanding effect of this conversion took on the shape of a yearning for a living contact with the living God.

From Thomas Scott, whose bold unworldliness, vigorous independence of mind, and faithful following of the truth wherever it led him, he admired deeply, Newman learned the proverb henceforth to be the motto of his whole life in its progressive growth: "Holiness before peace".[32] There is to be detected here a definite religious option of such a fundamental nature as to be an otherworldly falling in love. This is confirmed perhaps by another phenomenon, also dating from this time, namely, a growing awareness of a divine call to lead a single life.[33]

The second decisive occasion in his interior itinerary dates from 1827, when he noticed himself "beginning to prefer intellectual excellence to moral excellence". In such a preference he saw an "incipient liberalism" which he promptly rejected.[34] One can see how deeply the influence of his first conversion had filtered down into his moral and intellectual being.[35] It was little wonder, then, that during the strange illness that overtook him at Leonforte in Sicily, he repeated in delirium: "I have not sinned against the light". He had received a fated call to holiness.

The third and final stage in his religious development occurred in the context of deciding about the Catholic Church's claim to be the genuine heir to the Church of the Fathers, a Church which he so thoroughly admired. A. J. Boekraad would have everyone pause to consider the lapidary statement with which the *Development* concludes:

> And now, dear Reader, time is short, eternity is long. Put not from you what you have here found; regard it not as mere matter of present controversy; set not out resolved to refute it, and looking about for the best way of doing do . . . Time is short, eternity is long.[36]

This turning towards God is central to all Newman's thought, is the source of much that is deepest and best in him, and—what is

---

[31] Ap, 59.
[32] Ap, 61.
[33] Ap, 63-4.
[34] Ap, 72.
[35] See pp. 199-203.
[36] Dev, 445.

important for my present concern—the key to his theological activity. Sillem's conclusion is correct: "Newman's entire philosophy is enclosed between the two focal points of the self and of God",[37] so that his philosophy of the person is covered by the vast dome of faith and theology. One becomes like the people one admires, and so "Newman stands before us today as the representative of the theology of the Fathers, and of none more than St. Augustine, whose whole mind is revealed in his famous words from the Soliloquies: "God and my soul are what I long to know. What! Nothing else!? Nothing at all! O God, always one and the same, if I know myself I shall know Thee".[38]

The effect of religious conversion is far from being a vague awareness, a mere romantic attitude towards existence. On the contrary, it is thematized in terms of a special faculty of mind, conscience, which is a specific and integral operation of the human soul, and an endowment of human nature. In his *Letter to the Duke of Norfolk*, Newman gives an elegant definition of conscience, the listener and speaker in the "intercourse between himself and his Maker":

> It is a messenger from Him, who, both in nature and in grace, speaks to us behind a veil, and teaches us and rules us by his representatives. Conscience is the aboriginal Vicar of Christ, a prophet in its informations, a monarch in its peremptoriness, a priest in its blessings and anathemas, and, even though the eternal priesthood throughout the Church should cease to be, in it the sacerdotal principle would remain and would have a sway.[39]

Newman contended that conscience has two distinct, but related, functions, the one of moral sense, and the other of moral obligation. The former produces the science of morality, while the latter is specifically the theonomous aspect and reality of conscience, which bring us into God's presence as our judge, who looks into the infinite abyss of our existence.[40] It follows that this latter aspect is of primary importance in as much as it is the final inspiration and ultimate guide of the moral sense. "This relatedness of conscience is shown more clearly in the comprehensive experience we indicate when we speak of a 'good' or a 'bad' conscience . . .

---

[37] E. Sillem, PN, I, 123.
[38] Ibid., E. Sillem, 127; St. Augustine, Soliloquia, I, 2, 7; II, 1, 1.
[39] Diff, II, 248-9.
[40] GA, 102-3.

The clearest intimations are given by the bad, the sinful conscience. The experience of sin is not a mere sentiment of moral ugliness, but of an outrage and injury to love".[41] Sin is, then, the very antithesis of the total turning to God as to the focal point of personal existence, which is implied in religious conversion.

The religious man, Newman well knew from his own vivid inner journey, is one in whom conscience has been allowed to have full sway. He has listened to God and has acted accordingly. Walgrave puts it in a nutshell: "The 'ethos' of the religious man is, then, a resultant of his fidelity to conscience; a special experience of God, received in the soul with entire submission, gives rise to a complex of ethical and religious principles, which, of themselves, by the steady workings of implicit reasoning, develop within the mind a religious conception of the world".[42] The religiously converted person views everything in a new light, because he is now something new. All his apprehending, all his evaluating, all his reasoning, all his deciding and acting have become something new, simply because he is in a new state of existence. Thus, for example, religious love is the safeguard of faith, and preserves it from all corruptive deviation.[43]

In contrast, the lot of the non-religious rationalist is bound up in misfortune. The dictates of conscience being deadened and finally eliminated, the role of conscience gradually diminishes. Morality becomes a matter of rational behaviour alone. Reason, and not conscience, gains the ascendancy. While the full flowering and the unrestricted operation of conscience deepen gradually the awe we feel before the mystery of God's being and the mystery of our own being, the rationalist stunts, and eventually removes, this reality from his consciousness.

The religious person, however, lives sub conspectu Dei. His conscience not only guides him according as the Creator wishes, but it becomes his great teacher, and it provides him with a whole series of religious and moral principles.[44] The interiority fostered by growing fidelity to personal conscience has so transformed the religious person that he can also grasp, with a real apprehension, "principles" of natural theology and of morality. In this way

---

[41] J. Walgrave, Newman the Theologian, 151-2.
[42] J. Walgrave, Newman the Theologian, 156.
[43] US, 249-50.
[44] GA, 410-13; Prepos, 263.

some of the light inherent in the love that is the fruit of religious conversion begins to shine and illumine his moral and intellectual life.

Among the most outstanding of these principles of natural theology and morality are the providence of God, the nature of the thing, the analogy between all the works of God, natural and supernatural.[45] These are the most influential principles of conscience. However, there are others which might be named here: the primacy of conscience in the pursuit of all truth and in the perception of values; sin as the forbidden reality of life; goodness or badness as the ultimate quality of human actions; and the meaning and sense of life to be found in moral action, in holiness, rather than in a high state of culture.[46]

The Morally Consistent Person and the Morally Inconsistent Person

In the course of the *Oxford University Sermons*, which Avery Dulles considers to be the master treatment of the relationship and interpenetration of faith and reason,[47] Newman frequently touches the theme of the moral component in faith and theology. A quotation that is typical is the following:

> Is not this the error, the common and fatal error, of the world, to think itself a judge of Religious truth, without preparation of heart? 'I am the Good Shepherd, and know my sheep, and am known of mine'. 'He goeth before them, and the sheep follow Him, for they know His voice'. 'The pure in heart shall see God;' 'he that is spiritual judgeth all things'. 'The darkness comprehendeth it not'. Gross eyes see not, heavy ears hear not. But in the schools of the world the ways towards truth are considered high roads open to all men, however disposed, at all times. Truth is to be approached without homage. Everyone is considered on a level with his neighbour: or rather the powers of the intellect, acuteness, sagacity, subtleness, and depth, are thought the guides unto truth . . They will enter upon the most sacred points of Faith at the moment, at their pleasure . . . Is it wonderful that they so frequently end in becoming indifferentists, and conclude that Religious Truth is but a name, that all men are right and all wrong, from witnessing externally the multitude of sects and parties?[48]

---

[45] Dev, 111-2.
[46] PS, I, 227; Prepos, 262-3; GA, 412; Ap. 61.
[47] A. Dulles, The Survival of Dogma, 47.
[48] US, 198-9.

As with the religious element, Newman went through a personal process which deepened his moral interiority and being. In his case this process was largely contemporaneous with the gradual movement towards full religious conversion. There are two places in his works where we can clearly study his preoccupation with this fundamental issue. The first is in the introduction to the *Apologia*, the other in the *Grammar*, and together they throw much light on his view of the nature of moral interiority.

The treatment of the issue in the *Apologia* takes on a special significance when we remember the context in which the *Apologia* was written: his defence of himself and his follow-priests against the accusation of Charles Kingsley. That accusation ran: "Truth for its own sake had never been a virtue with the Roman clergy. Father Newman informs us that it need not, and, on the whole, ought not to be". This judgement, which Newman felt to be an open attack on his own honesty, occurred in the course of Kingsley's pamphlet, "What, then, does Dr. Newman Mean?" The very title of the pamphlet gave Newman his cue to a reply.

> My accuser asks: 'What, then, does Dr. Newman Mean?" It pointed in the very same direction as that into which my musings had turned me already: ... Yes, I said to myself, his very question is about my meaning: "What does Dr. Newman Mean?" He asks what I mean: not about my words, not about my arguments, not about my actions as his ultimate point, but about the living intelligence, by which I write and argue and act. He asks about my Mind, and its Beliefs and its sentiments.

It was the "ultimate point" and issue, and although Newman "shrank from both the task and the exposure which it (the reply) would entail", he did not turn his face away. "I must show what I am that it may be seen what I am not."[49] That inward commitment to all truth and value, which was the mainspring of his life, must be described in historical and personal categories.

In the *Grammar* he is still more explicit and decisive. The context is his treatment of the sanction of the personal faculty of judgement, the illative sense. If man's "progress is a living growth, not a mechanism, and its instruments are mental acts, not the formulas and contrivances of language", then such progress pre-

---

[49] Ap, 47: compare with what St. Augustine states as the motivation for his writing of the Confessions, Confessions, X, 3; PL 32; 659-868.

supposes a healthy inner life in the person: a sickly organism does not progress.

> My only business is to ascertain what I am, in order to put it to use ... What I have to ascertain is the laws under which I live. My first elementary lesson of duty is that of resignation to the laws of my nature, whatever they are; my first disobedience is to be impatient at what I am, and to indulge an ambitious aspiration after what I cannot be, to cherish a distrust of my powers, and to desire to change laws which are identical with myself.[50]

Newman is demanding here a basic self-acceptance, a communion with the concrete individual that I am, as a necessary condition of possibility of self-realisation. His conviction is that there is a fundamental reality of the person, of the concrete person, which must be accepted.

Once the person has accepted himself and the laws that are identical with his very being, he can begin to live and develop in the direction of his proper perfection. Newman writes elegantly:

> What is the peculiarity of our nature, in contrast with the inferior animals around us? It is that, though man cannot change what he is born with, he is a being of progress with relation to his perfection and characteristic good. Other beings are complete from their first existence in that line of excellence which is allotted to them; but man begins with nothing realised (to use the word), and he has to make capital for himself by the exercise of those faculties which are his natural inheritance. Thus he gradually advances to the fullness of his original destiny ... It is his gift to be the creator of his own sufficiency; and to be emphatically selfmade.[51]

There is, then, both a complacency and a concern, a resting in the self as well as a concern with the self.[52] The former effects a communion with the real self, while the latter perfects and "realises" the potential of the personal self as "a being of progress". It may be helpful at this stage to represent, by means of a diagram, the depth and significance of Newman's thinking on the subject of moral conversion.

---

[50] GA, 343, 340.

[51] GA, 341-2; see J. M. Cameron's interesting comments, "Newman and Empiricism", The Night Battle, London, 1962, 223.

[52] F. E. Crowe, "Complacency and Concern in the thought of St. Thomas," TS. 20 (1959), 342-377.

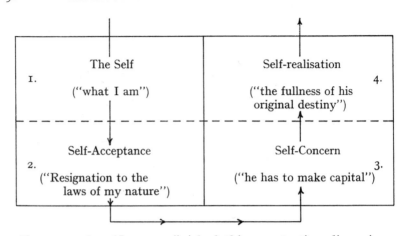

No sooner has Newman finished this penetrating digression on moral interiority than he proceeds to give the reason for his digression. Inference and assent are both central to this dynamic process of personal development, as being its "immediate instruments". But if these intellectual instruments do not enjoy the support and strength of moral interiority, or conversion, they will not function properly. They will operate to the detriment, rather than to the development, of the person. Newman explains: "If, then, the advancement of our nature, both in ourselves individually and as regards the human family, is to every one of us in his place a sacred duty, it follows that that duty is intimately bound up with the right use of these two main instruments of fulfilling it".[53] The agents of knowledge do not function in isolation, but are profoundly affected by the moral status of the person using them.

The ultimate grounding of this moral interiority is the will of Him who made man and so is responsible for his nature and person. "As the structure of the universe speaks to us of Him who made it, so the laws of the mind are the expression, not of mere constituted order, but of His will. I should be bound by them even were they not His laws; but since one of their functions is to tell me of Him, they throw a reflex light upon themselves, and, for resignation to my destiny, I substitute a cheerful concurrence in an overruling Providence."[54]

On the way towards self-realisation, the transcendently posited

---

[53] GA, 342.
[54] GA, 344.

nature of man must not succumb to the external pressure of society, custom, or habit. This is the origin of Newman's classic distinction between nature and culture, on the one hand, and between development and civilisation, on the other. In regard to the first pair, our nature is the internal core of the personality, comprising the first principles that govern much of our doing and thinking, while culture is the more external element, which supplies matter that is tested and evaluated if the internal core is developing authentically, but which easily tends to smother or thwart the true flowering of the self, if the self has left the way pointed out to it by "an overruling Providence". Civilisation is distinguished from development in that the latter designates the harmonious growth of the whole person, while civilisation generally is the flowering of a mere part or aspect, to the neglect of the whole.[55] "The progress of which man's nature is capable is a development, not a destruction, of its original state; it must subserve the elements from which it proceeds, in order to be a true development and not a perversion."[56]

Our study of Newman's insistence on high moral character as indispensable to the knowledge process, may be clarified somewhat by investigating, in the *Grammar*, the bearing of moral dispositions and ethical stances on all concrete processes of knowledge. In its very chapters on inference and on good judgement, the *Grammar* refers frequently and informatively to the contribution of one's moral status. In the section on informal inference, Newman contends that "we judge for ourselves, by our own light, and on our own principles; and our criterion of truth is not so much the manipulation of propositions, as the intellectual and moral character of the person maintaining them, and the ultimate silent effect of his arguments or conclusions upon our minds".[57] Earlier Newman had alluded to the "influence of moral motives in hindering assent to conclusions which are logically unimpeachable".[58] Newman proceeds to give no less than seven illustrations of concrete inferences in which the preponderance of moral factors is both undeniable and central to the outcome of the reasoning. "Truth there is, and attainable it is, but its rays stream in

---

[55] J. Walgrave, Newman the Theologian, 143-8.
[56] GA, 390; see Idea, 151-178; Dev, 44-5.
[57] GA, 295.
[58] GA, 162.

upon us through the medium of our moral as well as our intellectual being; and that, in consequence, that perception of its first principles which is natural to us is enfeebled, obstructed, perverted, by allurements of sense and supremacy of self, and, on on the other hand, quickened by aspirations after the supernatural." [59] Those who are morally inconsistent are hindered in their thinking. Any moral deviation erects a proportionate barrier against the perception of truth. The moral character and being that is the precondition of the personal discovery of truth consists in a certain love of all value, a rising above the self, which purifies inference and judgement, the instruments of progress. Newman is quite adamant that the great certitudes of our lives are reached "not ex opere operato, by a scientific necessity independent of ourselves, but by the action of our own minds, by our own individual perception of the truth in question, under a sense of duty to those conclusions and with an intellectual conscientiousness".[60] He felt, however, that such a conscientousness was not a commonplace, at least in its higher refinements: "in ordinary minds it (reason) is biased and degraded by passion, prejudice and self-interest".[61]

This analysis of the moral component in the acquisition of truth, the precondition of personal development, which Newman realised for himself in terms of the appropriation of his own interior odyssey, and which he then analysed in the persons and movements of the day, allowed him to apprehend clearly two "antagonistic" and contradictory types of moral personalities, the one morally consistent, the other morally opportunist and pragmatic. In the pages of the *Grammar*, he proposes, as examples of this antagonism, Pascal and Montaigne. Because "Montaigne was endowed with a good estate, health, leisure and an easy temper, literary tastes, and a sufficiency of books, he could afford thus to play with life, and the abysses into which it leads us".[62] The same clash of personality types is described, this time from a pastoral angle, in the opening discourse of the *Discourses to Mixed Congregations*.

---

[59] GA, 304.

[60] GA, 311; see pp. 207-8, where we have underlined the modernity of Newman's thought.

[61] GA, 324.

[62] GA, 304-5.

The case of Gibbon is particulary interesting. In the *Decline and Fall of the Roman Empire,* Gibbon suggested five causes in explanation of the fact of Christianity's survival under the relentless repression of the Empire, and its flowering immediately afterwards. The five causes were "the zeal of Christians inherited from the Jews, their doctrine of a future state, their claim to miraculous power, their virtues, and their ecclesiastical organization".[63] Newman comments in a direction we might have guessed. He notices that Gibbon has failed to consult the account the Christians themselves gave of the phenomenon. Newman asks: "Why did he not try the hypothesis of faith, hope, and charity?" And Newman answers: "Such thoughts are close upon him, and close upon the truth; but he cannot sympathize with them, he cannot believe in them, he cannot even enter into them, because he needs the due formation for such an exercise of mind".[64] In a word, Gibbon the man, and not Gibbon the historian, was at fault. Even as an historian, Gibbon is unable to do justice to the history of the rise and flowering of the Christian faith, because he lacks the moral formation appropriate to the intellectual labour involved.

The Authentic Intellectual and the Liberal

In our opening chapter we have seen how Newman was aware that most difficulties, in theology as in philosophy, could be traced, in the final analysis, to theoretical and unreal views on the nature of our thinking.[65] He believed it was our duty that we must look out "for modes of thought proper to our nature, and faithfully observe them in our intellectual exercises".[66] In our chapter on the Grammar we set out to portray the genuine features of what Newman considered to be the real "organum investigandi". Our present task, then, is to recall what we discovered there, and to relate it to our discussion of the intellectual component in theological foundations.

The Liberal position on the nature of our "intellectual exercises" contended that there is no adequate or legitimate way of attaining truth apart from demonstration. We can only be certain of those propositions which have been demonstrated. The Liberals

[63] Mix, 1-21.
[64] GA, 451, 456.
[65] See pp. 4-5.
[66] GA, 343.

vigorously defended the position that what cannot be reasoned with the clarity and cogency of a mathematical deduction is beyond the confines of proof and so cannot be known with certainty.[67] They were as clear as they were dogmatic.

It was this Liberal position that elicited Newman's response. That response began with the *Oxford University Sermons* and eventually bloomed into the *Grammar of Assent*. Newman considered the Liberal standpoint to be guilty of reductionism: "Ratiocination, thus restricted and put into grooves".[68] They had erected a scientific ideal of reasoning into a philosophical theory of mind, and so had done violence to facts, contradicted the commonsense voice of mankind which lives by many certitudes not logically demonstrated, and condemned as immoral the lives of many as based on unfounded certainties, and all this because they saw fit to treat the subject of our cognitional operations "according to a priori fitness", and not "according to the facts of human nature, as they are found in the concrete action of life".[69]

Newman was convinced that we not only possess certitudes in many areas of life, but also live by them, as being simply and absolutely true and unconditional. "His problem was to discover how one reaches this absolute in concrete judgement." [70] His solution is given in the pages of the *Grammar*. He shows that we come to know the really existent, the "thing which is",[71] in virtue of a process compounded of experience, apprehension, and the illative sense. The illative sense, or faculty of judgement in the concrete, reaches the unconditional. It transforms the hypothetical nature of apprehension and inference into certainty. It concludes the process of knowing by leading us to that which is true, simply and unconditionally. It terminates a process that represents the basic structure of all knowing, which is the "general process of experience, of hypothesis, and of verification".[72] Besides, it underlines the isomorphism of the general structure of the positive sciences with that of theology. In this way Newman has gone far towards disarming his Liberal opponents of their scientific method, which they so narrowly construed, but which Newman

---

[67] E. Sillem, PN, I, 62.

[68] GA, 256.

[69] GA, 168; see p. 4-5.

[70] F. E. Crowe, "Intuition", NCE, VII, 600.

[71] DA, 293.

[72] B. Lonergan, Collection, I, London, 1967, 150.

showed to be in harmony with theological procedures. This is the central point, in fact, of Newman's famous letter to the scientist, William Froude.[73]

With his penetrating insight into men, Newman saw people in opposing camps according as they upheld the Liberal view of knowledge, or the true and genuine one. In a man of William Froude's cast of mind he recognised the fundamental tenets of the liberal personality, while in a theologian like Paley he saw the theological counterpart of that personality. In Bishop Butler and in John Keble, however, Newman admired the genuine intellectual position of which he was the lifelong advocate.[74] Newman has written a short profile of the liberal theologian as personified in the Reverend Dr. Brownside, a fictitious Oxford University Preacher, who occurs as a character in Newman's novel, *Loss and Gain*.

> As a divine he seemed never to have had any difficulty in any subject; he was so clear or so shallow that he saw to the bottom of all his thoughts: or, since Dr. Johnson tells us that "all shallows are clear", we may perhaps distinghuish him by both epithets. Revelation to him, instead of being the abyss of God's counsels, with its dim outlines and broad shadows, was a flat, sunny plain, laid out with straight macadamised roads. Not, of course, that he denied the divine incomprehensibility itself, with certain heretics of old; but he maintained that in Revelation all that was mysterious had been left out, and nothing given us but what was practical, and directly concerned us.[75]

The Principles of Differentiation of each Pair

This dialectic of positions was consciously employed by Newman with a view to drawing out the ultimate implications of our fundamental religious attitude, our "moral state", and our intellectual theory and practice. What struck him was the contradictory positions on each of the three levels, the religious, the moral, and the intellectual. And so he could write: " ... at length two characters of mind are brought out into shape, and two standards and systems of thought, each logical, yet contradictory of each other, and only not antagonistic because they have no common

---

[73] Ward, Life, II, 586-9.
[74] GA, 418; Ap, 78-83; ECH, II, 421-53.
[75] Loss and Gain, 68.

ground on which they can conflict".[76] The religious man and the rationalist had no ground in common. They lived literally in two different worlds, the one filled with the reality of "two and only two luminous beings, the self and the Creator", the other with the barren self. In the same way, the deeply moral personality is guided by a standard that placed him in a world which had little to do with the pragmatic morality of the inconsistent person. Finally, the full implication of the liberal theory of knowledge reduced man to a world coextensive only with that which would be discovered by logical demonstration and mathematical reasoning, while the genuine intellectual person had a theory of knowledge comprehensive enough to reach and cover the great questions of life and religion.

And Newman saw the principle of differentiation of each pair, saw it with a keenness of vision that comes only from savouring the "infinite abyss of one's own existence", as this expresses itself in the lives of those who have made great interior journeys. This principle of differentiation was a conversion. It was more than a logical step. It was a qualitative jump, more than breadth of mind, or largeness of heart, or a deepening sincerity of religion. An inner, and indeed ontic reality, it changed one's meaning drastically, in that it turned the personality towards transcendent goodness, truth and value.

The morally good person has undergone the conversion involved in the decision to act, no longer according to his own pleasure and profit, but according to the objective demands of duty and value. This conversion results in the possession of a new criterion for decision and action. In his study of doctrinal development, *Unfolding Revelation*, Walgrave sums up the effect of moral conversion on one's quest for truth. "The attainment of truth in matters of ultimate concern and moral conduct is more than a question of brains, intellectual sagacity, and mental application. It is also a question of moral earnestness, fidelity to the voice of conscience, right conduct, openness with respect to all the intimations of truth that present themselves in one's daily intercourse with things and persons." [77]

Finally, the truly intellectual person has the asset of having a true idea of the knowledge process and of the logic of personal

---

[76] GA, 304.
[77] GA, 313; J. Walgrave, Unfolding Revelation, 295.

discovery. He is no longer hemmed in by "theoretical and unreal" views of knowing, as is the exponent of the epistemology of the Liberals. As a result he can deal with greater portions of reality, and will not cut himself off from the vast domain of the "unseen world" out of deference to a false epistemology. He will not a-bandon the content of revelation as mythical or impossible of attainment because he has "the true view" of how we arrive at certitude.

The Practical Priority of Religious Conversion over Moral and Intellectual Conversion

It is Newman's considered position that religious conversion normally and practically precedes the other two. The genuinely religious person grounds his whole life on the vision provided by the inner light of conscience, the organ of relationship between the creature and his Creator.[78] The principles which issue forth contemporaneously with that interior reversal that we call re-ligious conversion, actually help us to be morally integral, and guide us towards the discovery of the real nature of our mental operations. Furthermore, since religious conversion orientates the whole personality to the God of all and utter value—and Newman is naturally led to see God under the aspect of the tran-scendental moral attributes of His ineffable Being—it necessarily inspires one to live out all values in daily existence. Neither does the influence of religious conversion evaporate in the domain of rational and intellectual considerations. On the contrary, it steadies us, both religiously and morally, truthfully to search for the truth. "Intellect is helpless", he wrote "because ungovern-able and self-destructive, unless it be regulated by a moral rule and revealed truth." [79]

Because conversion, and not proof, is basic to Newman's idea of theological foundations, he puts forward a principle that is antagonistic to the dominant thrust of European thinking after Descartes. While the latter counselled methodic doubt, Newman recommended methodic faith. "Of the two," he writes in the *Grammar*, "I would rather have to maintain that we ought to be-

---

[78] Ap, 376-7; Diff, II, 247.
[79] HS, III, 49.

gin with believing everything that is offered to our acceptance, than that it is our duty to doubt of everything. This, indeed, seems the true way to learning. In that case, we soon discover and discard what is contradictory; and error having always some portion of truth in it, and the truth having a reality which error has not, we may expect that when there is an honest purpose and fair talents, we shall somehow make our way forward, the error falling off from the mind and the truth developing and occupying it! Thus it is that the Catholic religion is reached, as we see, by inquirers from all points of the compass, as if it mattered not where a man began so that he has an eye and a heart for the truth".[80] Such a heart, such an eye for the truth, is the essential provision of religious conversion.

It is fair, then, to conclude this section with the contention that, for Newman, the basis of all theology and of "personal Christianity", is interior, personal and dynamic. That basis is religious, moral and intellectual conversion, with the emphasis on the first one as the existential ground of the other two. "If a religious mind were educated in, and sincerely attached to, some form of heathenism or heresy, and then were brought under the light of truth, it would be drawn off from error into the truth, not by losing what it had, but gaining what it had not ... True conversion is ever of a positive, not a negative character." [81] The priority of religious conversion resides in its ability to dispose the intellect and moral being of the inquirer gradually and cumulatively to acquire the elements that constitute the truth in its fullness.

The Influence of Conversion on Theology

It was Newman's belief that "the multitude of men are not consistent, logical, or thorough; they obey no law in the course of their religious view; ... and are set down at this or that point in the ascending or descending scale of thought, according as their knowledge of facts, prejudices, education, domestic ties, social position, and opportunities determine". Nevertheless, he was equally convinced that "there is a certain ethical character,

---

[80] GA, 371-2.
[81] DA, 200; see Newman's brilliant description of "Catholic Fullness", ECH, II, 231-3; compare with Vatican II, The Church, 13; Ecumenism, 2.

one and the same, a system of first principles, sentiments and tastes, a mode of viewing the question and of arguing, which is formally and normally, naturally and divinely, the organum investigandi given us for gaining religious truth and which would lead the mind by an infallible succession from atheism to Christianity, and from Christianity to Evangelical Religion, and from those to Catholicity".[82] These ideas of Newman were made explicit in response to Principal Fairbairn, who had made the point that Newman had restricted the defence of his creed to the proposition that it is the only possible alternative to atheism. Newman considered such an alternative to be an "abstract alternative", because in the concrete each person moved towards the truth in strict proportion to the extent of his inner conversion. If a person found himself in the "ascending scale of thought" it was because he possessed the right ethical character, the correct system of first principles that derive from religious conversion, and, finally the true mode of arguing and reasoning. In the absence of these he was set down either in the "descending scale of thought" or in a position of permanent fixation in error and prejudice.

That the discovery of this threefold foundation of theology should have been suggested to Newman through reflection on the development of his own insight and religious faith, need hardly come as a surprise. In the Apologia he stated his view of the harmonious development of religious faith in the individual, which at its apex means an act of faith in the Catholic Church. "As there is a law which acts upon the subject-matter of dogmatic theology, so is there a law in the matter of religious faith." [83] Religion for Newman has definite belongings and surroundings, and it demands a habit of thinking and a temper of character appropriate to such a context. If such foundations are actually provided, a person can reach, with the help of God's grace, the fullness of truth. He will be led on to assemble gradually the constitutive elements of the Catholic Faith. Newman summarizes his thought in this remarkable statement, provocative if taken in the abstract, but true if we remember Newman's insistence that conversion is indispensable to the theological process:

---

[82] GA, 386-7.
[83] Ap, 323.

> I was led on to examine more attentively what I doubt not was
> in my thoughts long before, viz. the concatenation of argument
> by which the mind ascends from its first to its final religious idea
> and I came to the conclusion there was no medium, in true philo-
> sophy, between Atheism and Catholicity, and that a perfectly
> consistent mind, under those circumstances in which it finds itself
> here below, must embrace either the one or the other.[84]

A parallel insight was that into the growth and development of
religious doctrine. The subjective development and subsequent
clarification of doctrine in the course of the centuries was for
Newman "a remarkable philosophical phenomenon, giving a
character to the whole course of Christian thought".[85] In later
editions of the *Essay on Development* he lists doctrinal development as one of the constitutive "principles" of Christianity.[86]

Because personal growth in faith is not the fruit of mere intellectual sagacity or brains, but is rather the fruit of personal conversion, Newman refuses to fit the argument for his becoming
a Catholic into a nutshell. This may be seen clearly in a letter he
wrote in 1846 in explanation of his refusal to serve up a schematic
summary of his reason for becoming a Catholic. He writes:

> It is unreasonable in anyone to object that the grounds a person
> gives for his conversion cannot be expressed in a formula, but
> require some little time and consideration to master; which seems
> to be your correspondent's complaint of my Volume (Development).
> If I could express them in a formula, they would not really be the
> more intelligible or comprehensible . . . You must consent to think
> —and you must exercise such resignation to the Divine Hand
> which leads you as to follow it any whither . . . Moral proofs are
> grown into, not learnt by heart.[87]

At this point it is possible to represent, using a diagram, Newman's thought on the methodical foundations of theology. It is
our hope that this diagram will both summarize, and clarify further, the originality and serviceableness of Newman's thought
on this vital subject.

---

[84] Ap, 322; see J. Walgrave, Newman the Theologian, 201-3; also J.
Guitton, The Church and the Laity.

[85] Ap, 322.

[86] Dev, 326.

[87] LD, XI, 109-110.

The Methodic Foundations of Theology

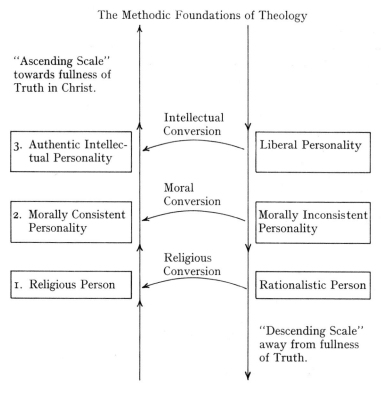

"Ascending Scale" towards fullness of Truth in Christ.

Intellectual Conversion

3. Authentic Intellectual Personality

Liberal Personality

Moral Conversion

2. Morally Consistent Personality

Morally Inconsistent Personality

Religious Conversion

1. Religious Person

Rationalistic Person

"Descending Scale" away from fullness of Truth.

It is time now to mention definite and particular influences of conversion in the domain of theology. To begin, religious conversion permits the person to grasp what Newman calls the great "system of Providence" by which one knows that all of God's works, natural and supernatural, are "in His hands". "It is God who teaches us all knowledge; and the way by which we acquire it is His way. He varies that way according to the subject matter; but whether He has set before us in our particular pursuit the way of observation or of experiment, of speculation or of research, of demonstration or of probability, whether we are inquiring into the system of the universe, or into the elements of matter and of life, or into the history of human society and past times, if we take the way proper to our subject-matter, we have His blessing upon us, and shall find, besides abundant matter for more opinion, the materials in due measure of proof and assent." [88]

---

[88] GA, 344.

From such a viewpoint, he is able to evaluate the phenomenon of growth in the world at large as a strong indication that the phenomenon of doctrinal development, as evident in the history of Catholic dogma, is not a corruption but a genuine growth. Religious conversion is again the source of the theological doctrine of analogy, whereby the lower orders of being are related to the higher on the basis of their being one Lord and Creator of all.[89] Another outstanding application of religious conversion is Newman's thesis that one cannot entertain, honestly and adequately, the evidence and arguments for Christianity without a prior acquisition of the appropriate dispositions that derive from religious conversion.[90] In a pastoral work, such as the *Discourses to Mixed Congregations*, he deploys in a pastoral way the reality of conversion.

Moral purification provided Newman with the means with which he felt equipped to penetrate into the men and movements of his day, as well as into the epic history of the Church. In the *Arians*, to take one instance, he is able to enter the history of the first great Christological Council with tools that fit him to give an explanatory account of the origins and development of the Arian heresy.[91] In Arius and Athanasius he detected the very incarnations of the morally inconsistent, and morally consistent, personalities, respectively. It allows him appreciate the complexity of doctrinal development, as is evident from a statement like the following: "Doctrines expand variously according to the mind, individual or social, into which they are received; and the peculiarities of the recipient are the regulating power, the law, the organisation, or, as it may be called, the form of the development".[92]

Intellectual conversion, finally, not only alerted him to the great strategy of his opponents, the Liberals, but it armed him for a lifelong combat with them. In his discourse, "A form of infidelity of the Day", he limpidly outlines their strategy in these striking terms that he puts on the lips of the typical Liberal: "You may have opinions in religion, you may have theories, you may have arguments, you may have probabilities; you may have anything but demonstration, and therefore you cannot have sci-

---

[89] Ap, 77-8; GA, 381-4.
[90] GA, 384f.
[91] Ar, 136, 219-36; TTS, 137-300.
[92] Dev, 178.

ence". Belief and unbelief are thus open and inveterate enemies
in the arena of history. The Liberals believed that "nothing can
be known about the unseen world." The result of this position
was "a feeling of absolute hatred for the dogmatic teacher".[93]

In the illative sense, Newman discovered a powerful weapon
which he deployed in the combat. This faculty of concrete judgement he found most relevant and serviceable, theologically speaking. It could lift theory to fact, opinion to certitude, it could transform probabilities into certainties. It enabled him to justify the
assent of faith in the simple believer, as in the *Grammar*;[94] to
deal with the phenomenon of a "consensus fidelium", and so of
the theological status of the laity, as in the famous article, "On
Consulting the Faithful in matters of Doctrine". Most important
of all, it provided him with the philosophical justification of his
"dogmatic principle" which he claimed to be central in Christianity. Furthermore, it extended beyond recognition the limits
of abstract science, because "it proceeds, in coming to its conclusion, always in the same way, by a method of reasoning, which
I have considered as analogous to that mathematical calculus
of modern times, which has so wonderfully extended the limits
of abstract science".[95] Thus it enables Newman to deal, effectively and theologically, with data otherwise and hitherto unmanageable.

---

[93] Idea, 387, 393, 390.
[94] GA, 346, 336-78.
[95] GA, 352.

CHAPTER FIVE

A GENERALIZED APOLOGETIC

Near the end of his life Newman wrote that "for thirty, forty, fifty years I have resisted to the best of my powers the spirit of liberalism in theology".[1] The onslaught of liberalism brought Newman to the task which is increasingly recognized as a fundamental duty of theology, namely, the task of justifying the Christian and Catholic faith. Not only did he consider himself called upon to give such an account of the faith: there was the curious fact that he needed the stimulus of circumstances to bring out what he held and what he did not hold, and the challenge of adversity to spur him on to the work of refutation and inquiry, an art in which he developed an incomparable skill. "What I have written, (he observed in his Journal on October, 14, 1874), has been for the most part what may be called official, works done in some office I held or engagement I had made—all my sermons are such, my *Lectures on the Prophetical Office*, on *Justification*, my Essays in the 'British Critic', and translations of St. Athanasius— or has been from some special call, or invitation, or necessity, or emergency, as my *Arians, Anglican Difficulties, Apologia* or *Tales*. The *Essay on Assent* is nearly the only exception. And I cannot write without such a stimulus. I feel myself going out of the way, or impertinent, and I write neither with spirit nor with point." [2] This means that the context of many of Newman's works demanded of him a dialogue between himself and the faith, on the one hand, and between himself and, on the other hand, Christians who thought and wrote in a contrary vein to his own. The providential circumstances that constituted the fabric of his life—the century he lived in, the friends he fell in with while in Oxford and later, the movements he encountered, the antagonists who opposed him as an Anglican and as a Catholic,—all combined to elicit from him a treatment of what is commonly called today fundamental theology. Nearer the end of his life he could write that he had written many "argumentative" works

[1] Cam, 395.
[2] Quoted Ward, II, 400.

in defence of his "creed": "I have published an 'Essay on Development of Doctrine', 'Theological Tracts', 'A letter to Pusey', 'A letter to the Duke of Norfolk', works all more or less controversial, all defences of the Catholic creed". If a present-day critic of Newman can speak of "the genius of his methodological insights", we may reasonably expect that such insight will be operative in his general apologetic. To the study of his labour in the field of fundamental theology we now direct our attention, hopeful of discovering and portraying his method.

The Argument for Christianity in the Grammar of Assent

Newman wrote the *Grammar* to describe the Organum Investigandi which he thought the true one. He hoped to outline in it a "popular, practical and personal" method of reflecting on the Christian Faith, and of justifying and defending its divine dignity and claim on our unconditional acceptance. Not content with a formal exhibition of his method in its pages, he also gave us an application of his method "to show how I would apply the principles of this essay to the proof of its (Christianity's) divine origin". In the final chapter of the essay he shows us his "method of arguments" [3] in operation. We now proceed to examine the argument.

His subject is Christianity. "It is a 'Revelatio Revelata'; it is a definite message from God to man distinctly conveyed by his chosen instruments, and to be received as such a message; and therefore to be positively acknowledged, embraced, and maintained as true, on the ground of its being divine, not as true on intrinsic grounds, not as probably true, or partially true, but as absolutely certain knowledge, certain in a sense in which nothing else can be certain, because it comes from Him who neither can deceive nor be deceived." [4] He is thinking, then, of Christianity as a revealed religion, and not primarily of its present day state and appearance on the stage of world history. It is the Christianity of the ante-Nicene period which is his theme and which he wishes to justify. He has already justified for himself the Roman Catholic interpretation and living out of this revelation of God through Christ Jesus in the Holy Spirit. That justification was the achievement of the *Essay on Development*. But now he wished

---

[3] GA, 484, 418.
[4] Ibid., 381-2.

to defend the very fact of a divine revelation and of Christianity's claim to be that very divine communication. In such a momentous subject, then, he had to apply the method formally outlined in the preceding chapters of the *Grammar*.

(a) *Christianity requires an appropriate Apologetic*

The subject of Christianity and the legitimacy of its claims on all men cannot adequately be considered within the field of the positive sciences. By its very nature it can only be treated at all within the broader fields of history, philosophy, theology and ethics. It is not to be expected, therefore, that it can adequately be dealt with by purely mathematical methods that apply and get results in the positive sciences. In particular, the formal inference, or the syllogism, will be inadequate to prove its claims. The syllogism has an insufficient methodological base to do justice to the depth and complexities of "so large, momentous, and sacred a subject".[5] As we saw earlier in chapter two, the syllogistic method is competent only within a well chosen series of data in a strictly defined field of study. It is unable to manage the great facts of life and history, of which Christianity is the most outstanding.[6]

Does this mean, in fact, that the Christian Revelation cannot be demonstrated scientifically? The syllogistic method was the weapon wielded by many theologians of the day, both liberal and High Church. Newman puts us beyond all shadow of doubt about the state of his mind on the matter raised by the question.

> I (do not) deny that demonstration is possible. Truth, certainly, as such, rests upon grounds intrinsically and objectively and abstractedly demonstrative, but it does not follow from this that the arguments producible in its favour are unanswerable and irresistible. These latter epithets are relative, and bear upon matters of fact; arguments in themselves ought to do what perhaps in the particular case they cannot do. The fact of revelation is in itself demonstrably true, but it is not therefore true irresistibly; else, how comes it to be resisted? There is a vast difference between what it is itself, and what it is to us.[7]

Among the theologians of the day who set out to give a "scien-

---

[5] Ibid., 379.
[6] Dev, 3-32; J. Walgrave, Newman the Theologian, 222.
[7] GA, 405.

tific demonstration" of Christianity, there was Paley. In his *The Evidences of Christianity* Paley tried to demonstrate the truthfulness of the Faith by employing the method of the syllogism. For his evidences, on which the syllogism is to be employed, he takes the "scriptural miracles". "This clearheaded and almost mathematical reasoner ... has such confidence in the strength of the testimony which he can produce in favour of the Christian miracles, that he only asks to be allowed to bring it into court." [8]

And Newman thought highly of the method of Paley: "I think Paley's argument clear, clever and powerful".[9] High praise indeed coming from a man like Newman! In spite of all that, however, he preferred a different "basis of argument" to prove the divinity of Christianity. Newman's principal criticism of Paley's method of argument was directed against the assumption that people in general were "reasoning animals". Paley's method was based on the principle, which Newman considered false, that the truth could be revealed to any individual in splendid independence of his own type of personality. "If I am asked to use Paley's argument for my own conversion, I say plainly I do not want to be converted by a smart syllogism; if I am asked to convert others by it, I say plainly I do not care to overcome their reason without touching their hearts. I wish to deal not with controversialists, but with inquirers." [10] This quotation gives us in a nutshell the reason why Newman rejected a method of argument, otherwise "clear, clever and powerful".

Such a discovery does not surprise us too much. In the last chapter we saw how Newman grounded all of theology on the interiority of the theologian. Such interiority, or "inwardness", we called conversion from its most obvious articulation which occurs in the life of the religious person. "Light is a quality of matter," Newman wrote, "as truth is of Christianity; but light is not recognised by the blind, and there are those who do not recognise truth, from the fault, not of truth, but of themselves". Paley's approach ignored this vital factor and even gave support to the case of the rationalistic liberals, who were prepared "to sit at home, instead of stirring themselves to inquire whether a revelation had been given; they expect its evidences to come to

---

[8] Ibid., 418-9.
[9] Ibid., 420.
[10] Ibid., 419-20; see VO, 74.

them without their trouble, they act, not as suppliants, but as judges ... and forget that revelation is a boon, not a debt on the part of the giver".[11]

(b) *The pre-conditions of an Apologetic*

(I) on the side of Subject Matter and
(II) on the side of the Apologist

A good method of apologetics, therefore, has two pre-conditions, the first on the side of its subject matter, the second on the side of the apologist. It will have to be able to deal with the complexity and profundity of a religion like Christianity, and secondly, it will have to be such as can cope with the state of soul of the apologist. In short, its method will have to take into account the special nature of Christianity and its evidences, as well as the peculiar nature of man. These will be its terms of reference. We can readily understand, then, why Newman felt "suspicious ... of scientific demonstrations in a question of concrete fact, in a discussion between fallible men".[12] The methods of the Evidential School are simply inadequate to fit the facts of Christianity, and were not designed to bring people to "recognise the truth and to "lay the foundation of our religious profession in the ground of our inner man". A recent commentator quite contends that "Newman lived at the end of the age of evidences, the age 'when love was cold', as he tells us ... The general tendency of his thought, with few qualifications and few backward glances, is the rejection of the supposedly coercive arguments from 'evidences', as they were propounded by such theologians as Paley, and of the demonstrative arguments of eighteenth-century natural theology. In their place he offers us 'inwardness' ".[13]

(c) *The Argument itself*

What, then, is the method which Newman proposes?

> For me, it is more congenial to my own judgement to attempt to prove Christianity in the same informal way in which I can prove for certain that I have been born into this world, and that I shall die out of it. It is pleasant to my own feelings to follow a theological writer, such as Amort, who has dedicated to the great

---

[11] Ibid., 405, 420; see VO, 60-74.
[12] Ibid., 405-6.
[13] J. M. Cameron, "Newman and the Empiricist Tradition", Red, 79.

Pope, Benedict XIV, what he calls "a new, modest and easy way of demonstrating the Catholic Religion". In this work he adopts the argument merely of greater probability. I prefer to rely on that of an accumulation of various probabilities. But we both hold (that is, I hold with him) that from probabilities we may construct legitimate proof, sufficient for certitude.[14]

We recall from our chapter on the *Grammar* how Newman treated the various forms of inference, of which he enumerated three, formal, informal and natural inference. In the section on informal inference, he actually gave the example, just mentioned, of how he would prove that he will die out of the world as he had been born into it. In the same place he also gave his famous argument for the proof of the proposition that "Great Britain is an island".[15] Besides the informal, there was the natural inference, which enjoyed great versatility in many different fields of activity and inquiry, especially in the field of religious inquiry.[16]

Newman proceeds to put his method into operation. He accumulates evidences, assembles arguments, and collects reasons, "too various for enumeration, too personal and deep for words, too powerful and concurrent for reversal".[17] These arguments begin with Old Testament prophecy, proceed to the coincident testimony of the two Testaments, and go on, finally, to the overwhelming argument derived from the witness borne to the divinity of Christianity by the bravery and heroism of the early martyrs, these being but a few "specimens, among the many which might be given, of the arguments adducible for Christianity".[18] Of course the combined force of these arguments varies from mind to mind, depending on each person's preparation of mind. They produce, however, a cumulative power, and a converging cogency, which tend towards the truth of the proposition "Christianity is God's message to us", as their limit. As with Pascal in his Pensées, which convinces by the number, consistency, and depth of its arguments, so it is with Newman in the *Grammar*.

---

[14] GA, 406.
[15] Ibid., 287-9.
[16] Ibid., 323-35. Newman gives the examples of Napoleon's military expertise, and of Newton's scientific ingenuity.
[17] Ibid., 484.
[18] Ibid., 484.

(d) *Some conclusions*

A number of conclusions are in order before we terminate consideration of Newman's method of apologetics. In the first place, Newman's method of argument brings in data from historical, personal, empirical, and statistical sources. In this way it enriches the collection of the "motiva credibilitatis" beyond recognition. In traditional apologetics, miracles were the sole arguments brought forward, but now this array, formidable in itself, Newman supplemented by a powerful influx of new materials.

Next, this allows the apologetic process to be both scientific, in the best sense of the term, and personal, at the same time. Newman makes the point very well: "In religious inquiry each of us can speak only for himself ... he brings together his reasons, and relies on them, because they are his own, and this is his primary evidence, and he has a second ground of evidence, in the testimony of those who agree with him".[19] In other words, apologetics, like philosophy, is a "personal witness".

In an age when Bacon's new ideal of science had greatly broadened the horizons of the positive sciences, Newman, who likewise sought a Novum Organon for theology, longed to see a similar creativity and originality among Christian thinkers. Wilfrid Ward writes in his life of the Cardinal "that ... the age of modern science was an age when Bacon's ideal of enlarging the knowledge of physical facts by careful induction had added greatly to the general knowledge of facts in the domain of history also. And such facts had their bearing on the a priori deductions of theologians".[20] Newman in effect had brought together both the classical deductive method and the modern inductive methodology. Next, all ratiocinative processes, like those of the informal and natural inferences, only yield probable conclusions. This point is developed with unmistakable clarity in the earlier pages of the *Grammar*. Apologetics, therefore, does not in itself and of itself produce certainty. Indirectly, however, it prepares the way for an "apologetical faith" in the Christian Message. But such certainty is the fruit of the mind's judgemental faculty, the illative sense, which lifts a conditional up to the level of the unconditional.

Fifthly, Newman's apologetical argumentative method has

---

[19] Ibid., 379-80; see DA, 366-7.
[20] Ward, I, 435-6.

been taken up by an outstanding present day theologian, Fr. B. Lonergan, S.J. In a paper which he delivered at the Journées d'études Mariales in Montreal in 1948, he took the subject of our Lady's assumption into Heaven, then undefined, and, among other aspects of the topic, he suggested "an outline of the argument from holy scripture for the assumption". The scriptural sources supply premises that are very broad and general, and are derived from the revelation of man's fall in Adam and his redemption in Christ. As in Adam all men died, so in Christ all men have come alive. From this scheme of things, he proceeds to investigate the role of our Lord and his Blessed Mother in the plan of salvation. Lonergan notices that "the more one thinks about it, the more numerous the aspects one considers, the fuller becomes the evidence and the greater its cogency".[21] The thrust of the argument is far from being syllogistic. In fact, a top-class theologian, Fr. F. E. Crowe, S.J., writes of it in these terms: ". . . it is remarkably like the process by which Newman would justify his judgement that Great Britain is an island".[22]

A similar procedure is seen in Newman's argumentative method in his famous *Letter to Pusey* on the subject of Our Lady's Immaculate Conception, which was written eleven years after Pius IX's definition of the dogma. It expressly sets out "to contribute to the accurate statement and the full exposition of the argument in question", the reason being that Newman feels a call on himself "to avow plainly what I do and what I do not hold about the Blessed Virgin".[23] In his controversy with Pusey, Newman agrees to accept the Fathers as his principal source and immediately goes on to ask: "What is the great rudimental teaching of antiquity from its earliest date concerning her? By 'rudimental teaching', I mean the prima facie view of her person and office, the broad outline laid down of her, the spirit under which she comes to us in the writings of the Fathers. She is the Second Eve".[24] From here Newman goes on to cite from St. Justin (120-165 A.D.), St. Irenaeus (120-200 A.D.) and Tertullian (160-240 A.D.), representative, respectively, of Palestine, Asia Minor and Gaul, and Africa and Rome. Their witness, which Newman

---

[21] B. Lonergan, Collection, I, 72, 75.
[22] Ibid., Preface, xxiii.
[23] Diff, II, 25.
[24] Ibid., 31.

corroborates by seven others, depicts Our Lady as being the "Second Eve" in the Christian people's view of her place in the economy of salvation. At this point he draws two inferences from the "rudimentary doctrine" itself. "The first relates to the sanctity of the Blessed Virgin; the second to her dignity." [25] We are struck at once by the striking resemblance of this inferential procedure of Newman to Fr. Lonergan's method of argument in the article just mentioned, and again, by the similarity of both to Newman's apologetic for the truth of the Christian Message.

Towards a Generalized Apologetic based on "First Principles"

We have seen, then, how Newman brings out the evidence for Christianity, accumulating various arguments, assembling them to converge on the topic under discussion, and allowing them to grow on the mind of the inquirer. We have also seen his vivid awareness of the sovereignty of the disposition of the subject himself. He well knows that any proof is relative to what he likes to call the "preparation of mind" of him for whom it is intended, and that it avails only if the latter is on the wavelength, as it were, of the apologist. He expresses himself on the matter in these terms: "It is not wonderful, then, that while I can prove Christianity divine to my own satisfaction, I shall not be able to force it upon anyone else ... in any inquiry about things in the concrete men differ from each other, not so much in the soundness of their reasoning as in the principles which govern its exercise, that those principles are of a personal character".[26]

Newman is adamant, then, that it is our "principles" which will ultimately come into play to determine whether or not a particular proof will be seriously entertained by an individual. This explains why he is careful, at the very outset of his "proof" of Christianity in the *Grammar*, to indicate the type of person with whom he is arguing. This typology he articulates in terms of two sets of "first principles", the first set of eighteen putting a person beyond the possibility of hearing his proof, and a second set constituting a person capable of hearing, and seriously responding to, his "method of argument".[27] In order to appreciate the role played by "first principles" in the justification of the

---

[25] Ibid., 44.
[26] GA, 407-8.
[27] Ibid., 410-11.

Faith, we now propose to pursue an inquiry into them in an attempt to discover their precise nature, operation and purpose.

First principles are "propositions with which we start in reasoning on any given subject-matter". They are "opinions which are held without proof as if self-evident".[28] They lie so deeply in the individual or in the community or society that they are generally undetected. But if undetected, they are powerful in their activity and influence on us. And there is "no man alive, but has some first principles", as there is no human group which is not, in the final analysis, grounded on some first principles.

Under the heading "Presumption" in the *Grammar*, Newman analyses some of them. The propositions "There are things existing external to ourselves", "There is a right and a wrong", "a true and a false", "nothing happens without a cause", are instances of first principles. Lecture six in his lectures, *The Present Position of Catholics in England,* is his magisterial treatment of the nature, operation and function of first principles in the individual person and in his society or community.[29] Together these principles form a structural pattern which constitutes their subject and acts as the directive influence in his thinking, affirming, decision making and action. To use a modern analogy taken from the field of biology, what chromosomes are to the inception, development and differentiation of animal life, first principles are to the life of the human being. Perhaps it is better to listen to the summary Newman himself offers:

> First principles are the means of proof, and are not themselves proved; they rule and are not ruled; they are sovereign on the one hand, irresponsible on the other: they are absolute monarchs, and if they are true, they act like the best and wisest fathers to us, but if they are false, they are the most cruel and baneful of tyrants. Yet, from the nature of our being, there they are, as I have said; there they must ever be . . . They are the conditions of our mental life; by them we form our view of events, of deeds, of persons, of lines of conduct, of aims, of moral qualities, of religions. They constitute the difference between man and man; they characterize him. As determined by his first principles, such is his religion, his creed, his worship, his political party, his character, except as far as adventitious circumstances interfere with their due and accurate development; they are, in short, the man.[30]

---

[28] Ibid., 57-8; Prepos, 279.
[29] GA, 57-70; Prepos, 271-314.
[30] Prepos, 283-4.

Because of their profound roots in our personalities, which explains their unconscious sway and secret influence with us, it is clear that they are not the fruit, at least initially, of our conscious intellectual, moral, or social efforts. They are an endowment, a heritage, not a personal acquisition. It follows that their main source is our own environment, in terms of its religious, social, moral, intellectual and cultural components. One's personal history is therefore largely constitutive of man, and no one can hope to understand himself or his society independently of where that society now stands, and of his milieu's set of first principles. And what applies to the community, applies all the more to that community in relation to its neighbouring and parental communities.

The implications of this fact of first principles being constitutive of the personality in the case of the individual person, and of a community in the case of the collectivity, are far reaching. For a start, it explains what we have already met, namely, Newman's principle of methodic faith. Against Descartes' methodic doubt, Newman proposed that the individual can only, and ought only, to start to reason from his existing standpoint. "If I may not assume," he wrote, "that I exist, and in a particular way, that is, with a particular mental constitution, I have nothing to speculate about, and had better let speculation alone. Such as I am, it is my all; this is my essential standpoint, and must be taken for granted." [31] It follows that the same fact imposes on each one the duty of being in communion with himself, and of rejecting the sin of separating from oneself. Precisely because our principles are embedded so deeply in our individual personalities, the only way of discovering these veritable and "absolute monarchs" of our being is through a healthy self-acceptance. "I cannot think, reflect, or judge about my being, without starting from the very point which I aim at concluding." [32] Thirdly, this demands at the same time that we set out from our necessary starting point of self-communion to discover what in our constitution is good, and to separate it from what is bad, and to promote the growth of the good. Being emphatically self-made,

---

[31] GA, 371-2, 340; see B. Lonergan's comment in his Method in Theology, London, 1972, 223-4.
[32] GA, 340.

we only gradually advance to the fullness of our original destiny through a "self-correcting process".[33]

The dint of life and experience, if honestly lived, may bring to light the principles which all along have been our secret masters. If they are false, we will be called upon to make the appropriate "self-correction". Furthermore Newman's thesis explodes the myth of the Enlightenment, which maintained that a man could study and pronounce on any subject under the sun, fairly, rationally, and intelligently, without presuppositions and without prejudgements. As our particular set of first principles makes us the kind of persons we are, it is simply dishonest to pretend they do not exist, and worse still to recognise their presence and then claim total immunity from them in concrete reasonings. Speaking of the defence of the Christian faith, Newman claims that the apologist's "true sobriety and modesty consists, not in claiming for his conclusions an acceptance or a scientific approval which is not to be found anywhere, but in stating what are personally his own grounds for his belief in Natural and Revealed Religion".[34]

We can conclude still further that Newman seems to have anticipated by a long time the emergence of the contemporary problem of interpretation. That problem is but the corollary to the discovery that every person in reasoning on the "subject of mental and moral science", is his own centre, and is not the mechanical instrument of a vague abstraction called reason. It has received excellent treatment at the hands of E. Betti, Fr. Lonergan, and H. G. Gadamer.[35]

Gadamer has come to the conclusion that history is an essential component of every individual and community. In the case of the Christian community, whose members are believers in the revelation of Jesus Christ, that history is what is commonly called Tradition. Gadamer writes:

> Properly speaking history does not belong to us but we belong to history. Long before we understand ourselves through introspective reflection, we already understand ourselves in a matter

---

[33] F. E. Crowe, "Intuition", NCE, VII, 600.

[34] GA, 380-1.

[35] E. Betti, Teoria generale della Interpretazione, Milan, 1955; B. Lonergan, Insight, London-New York, 1957; H. G. Gadamer, Wahrheit und Methode, Tübingen, 1960.

of course way in the family, the society, the nation of which we are members. The self-reflection of the individual is no more than a flickering within the streaming circle of historic life. Therefore the pre-judgements of an individual are not so much his own pre-judgements. They are rather the historical reality of his being.[36]

All this throws remarkable light on Newman's predilection for argument drawn from the history of Christianity in support of Christianity. The arguments he used in the *Grammar* were drawn very largely from the province of sacred history.[37] In history, Newman felt, the essential principles of the Christian Religion were to be seen. To justify Christianity he had only to collect and exhibit to good effect these first principles as they displayed themselves in the annals of that history. The self-understanding of the Christian community is called Tradition. In studying that tradition, he discovered it to be a "first principle" of Christianity, which argued a spiritual presence in Rome, which was nowhere else and which constituted a presumption that Rome was right.[38]

Sixthly, in terms of first principles Newman established a way of dealing effectively with conflicts and collisions between various Christian confessions and theological schools. As a particular set of first principles determine the reality of a person or a community, "all depends on which set of opinions you begin by assuming".[39] As a Catholic will have his first principles, so a Protestant will have his own, "and again when a Catholic is seriously wanting in this system of thought, we cannot be surprised if he leaves the Catholic Church, and then in due time gives up religion altogether",[40] Newman wrote in 1880. The truth of Catholicism therefore turned on the validity of its first principles. Its defence was a question of bringing to light the false first principles of conflicting Churches. The winning of the members of such Churches could be considerably promoted by bringing them to reflect fairly and honestly on their assumed principles. In this way, Newman outlined an extremely fruitful method of arriving at a "synthetic view" of apologetical procedure.

His great volume, *Lectures on the Present Position of Catholics*

---

[36] Quoted in J. Walgrave, Unfolding Revelation, London, 1972, 30.
[37] GA, 426-79.
[38] Dev, 326n; Ap, 290-1.
[39] Prepos, 290.
[40] GA', 387.

in England, is a good instance of his method in practice. The subject of the volume is his defence of the Catholic Church against the fanatical prejudice aroused against her by the popular Protestantism of the day. At the beginning of the last lecture he gives a resumé of the drift of his thinking.[41] Protestantism's opposition to the Catholic Church was grounded on her view of the Catholic Church, and this view was the fruit of Protestantism's own series of first principles. However, Protestantism was not aware of the operation of such "monarchs" and "masters". Newman asked of the exponents of the rival religion only a "recognition that Catholics have principles of their own", and then "a study of those principles, a fair representation, a refutation". Of these principles Newman was prepared all during his own lifetime to "render an account". We need only recall the *Essay on Development* and the *Apologia*, to mention a couple. But now he asks that Protestants do the same, namely, that they acknowledge that they have their first principles, then test their validity, and finally judge the strength or weakness of their "position" accordingly. A first principle that cannot be proven is an "assumption", "and the infliction of our own unproved First Principles on others" is bigotry, and a radical unwillingness to be reasonable is mere prejudice.[42] With prejudiced persons, debate is useless, for something more radical than argument is necessary to shake them out of their self-willed blindness. In fact, conversion is necessary to make them different, interiorly and inwardly.[43]

With honest inquirers, however, a method of argument bent on reaching a "synthetic view", is worthwhile. The long quote that follows well expresses our author's standpoint, in terms of advice to his brothers of the Oratory:

> Others... wish to think well of our doctrines and devotions, but stumble at them. When you meet with such, ask them whether they are not taking their own principles and opinions for granted ... Entreat them to consider how they know their existing opinions to be true ... If they say that penances are absurd or images superstitious or infallibility impossible, or sacraments mere charms, or a priesthood priestcraft, get them to put their ideas into shape and to tell you their reasons for them. Trace up their philosophy

---

[41] C. S. Dessain, John Henry Newman, London 1966, 99-101; Prepos, 365-71; see Ward, II, 57.

[42] Prepos, 297, 370-1, 292, 291.

[43] See Chapter IV.

for them, as you have traced up their tradition; the fault lies in the root; every step of it is easy but the first. Perhaps you will make them Catholics by this process; at least you will make them perceive what they believe and what they do not, and will teach them to be more tolerant of a Religion which unhappily they do not see their way to embrace.[44]

This "synthetic view" apologetic, which Newman is here proposing, is therefore to be conducted in a spirit of reconciliation between the Churches. As such it ought to be very relevant to ecumenical debate. In this connection it is worthwhile quoting something he wrote in 1880: "... there is a certain ethical character, one and the same, a system of first principles, sentiment and tastes, a mode of viewing the question and of arguing, which is formally, and normally, naturally and divinely, the organum investigandi given us for gaining religious truth, and which would lead the mind by an infallible succession from the rejection of atheism to theism and from theism to Christianity, and from Christianity to Evangelical Religion, and from these to Catholicity".[45] In fact, Newman had used a similar method, when still an Anglican, to ascertain the extent to which the teaching and doctrines of Rome were compatible with the thirty-nine articles; the experiment resulted in the writing of his famous *Tract Ninety*.

Antecedent Probability and Evidences

The outstanding achievement of the *Oxford University Sermons*, which stretched over the formative part of Newman's life, was their highlighting of two distinct, but complementary, types of reasoning. One was evidential in nature and tried to impose logical rigour on its subject matter. The other was of an a priori character, and sought to enlarge the horizon of knowledge by going beyond the limited province open to a posteriori procedures. Our author gives us this summary of the two types of ratiocination: "There are two methods of reasoning—a priori, and a posteriori; from antecedent probabilities or verisimilitudes, and from evidence, of which the method of verisimilitude more naturally belongs to implicit reasoning, and the method of evidence to explicit".[46] We have already considered in this chapter the "method

---

[44] Prepos, 314; see OUS, 200-1.
[45] GA', 387.
[46] OUS, Preface, xii.

of evidence", and so it remains to treat of the "method of verisimilitude".

Newman, however, did not consider the "method of antecedent probability" adequate of its own if one hoped to advance
to a defence or a "proof" of a theological position. An antecedent
probability, or "presumption", needed the support of evidences.
We must slightly refine, then, our objective in this section, and
speak not just of Newman's apologetic of antecedent probability,
but rather of his method of combining antecedent probability with
evidence. "In all matters of human life," he wrote, "presumption
verified by instances, is our ordinary instrument of proof, and, if the
antecedent probability is great, it almost supersedes instances," [47]
and so evidence also.

This method, however, is far from entirely novel to our investigation. We have met it already in our efforts to detect, and then
draw out, the method he employed to solve his crisis of ecclesial
allegiance in the *Essay on the Development of Christian Doctrine*.
However, our treatment of it there was necessarily cursory, as
our main purpose was the overall theological method, and not
merely the implicit apologetic in that method. We can reasonably hope, then, to find fruitful the present pursuit and elabora-
tion of the implicit apologetic. In fact, J. Walgrave intensifies
our hopes by writing: "When they (the method of antecedent
probability combined with evidences) supplement and reinforce
one another, we have the most conclusive possible proof".[48] Moreover, Newman is of the conviction that this method will be very
effective "in subjects which belong to moral proof, such, I mean,
as history, antiquities, political science, ethics, metaphysics,
and theology, which are pre-eminently such". In particular, theology and ethics give to the method under consideration a "weight
and cogency which it cannot have in experimental science".[49]
Antecedent probability, as a term, covers a series of hypothetical arguments, which include hypothesis, anticipation and hope,
and analogy. We now propose to consider each one individually,
outlining its formal structure. We hope in the source of our outline to highlight his apologetical methodology.

---

[47] Dev, 113-4.
[48] J. Walgrave, Newman the Theologian, London, 1960, 227.
[49] Dev, 112; GA, 379, speaks of "mental or moral science".

(a) *Hypothesis*

The outstanding instance of hypothesis being used to solve a problem is, of course, to be found in the pages of the *Essay on Development*. We dwelt on that work at length in our third chapter. We recall that after the shattering of the Via Media which he had laboured to develop and portray, Newman felt very nearly "a pure Protestant". He knew, though, that whatever the form of historical Christianity, "at least the Christianity of history is not Protestantism. If ever there were a safe truth, it is this".[50] But he was equally devoted at the same time to the "principle of anti-Romanism", which, with the dogmatic and sacramental principles, had constituted the bed-rock of the synthesis now pulverized beyond all hope of reconstruction. The dilemma was completed by the patent fact of Roman Catholicism and her claims to be both the historical and logical heir to the Church of the Fathers. But how could she be, when the very essence of her offence consisted in the corruptive developments she had allowed and accepted during the flow of history? That was the crux of the matter.

Newman suggested an hypothesis. In 1843 it received its first formulation in the last of the *Oxford University Sermons*, the title of which was "The Theory of Development in Religious Doctrine". Newman saw that its usefulness lay in its ability to account for a difficulty, the so-called "variations of Popery". By gradually refining the hypothesis of development he arrived at the position he splendidly articulated in the two opening chapters of the *Essay on Development*. This hypothesis was better than the earlier one used in the Oxford sermon, in that it covered the data of the problem more comprehensively, and made intelligible hitherto colliding phenomena. As a result, his hypothesis produced an ever greater antecedent probability that Rome's position was the true one. It supplied, in a word, an heuristic which Newman hoped could do in the theological area what the age-old "X" of algebra had been doing in the area of mathematics.

The second half of the *Essay* was devoted to an attempt to verify by an accumulation of evidences the antecedent probability of the hypothesis of ongoing doctrinal developments. We

---

[50] Dev, 7.

remember how successful Newman was in his verification.[51] In fact, he worked out in the same work the permanent structure of method, the general process of experience, hypothesis and verification. In virtue of this method he was able to handle, intelligently and effectively, a great range of otherwise unmanageable theological data. "As there were probabilities," he wrote, "which sufficed to create certitude, so there were other probabilities which were legitimately adapted to create opinion." His discovery of such a broad method accounted, for example, for the "main difference between my Essay on Miracles in 1826 and my Essay in 1842 ... that in 1826 I considered that miracles were sharply divided into two classes, those which were to be received, and those which were to be rejected; whereas in 1842 I saw that they were to be regarded according to their greater or less probability, which was in some cases sufficient to create certitude about them, in other cases only belief or opinion".[52] Between 1826 and 1842 Newman had learned how to deal with probability and hypothesis, a breakthrough nothing short of being epic.[53]

(b) *Anticipation and Hope*

The anticipation and the hope that are intended here have nothing in common with a begging of the question or a forcing of the issue, for such would gravely offend Newman's sense of "intellectual conscientiousness". But they have much in common with his method of analysing a situation or a subject in such a way as to produce in the one who analyses an overwhelming question, an outstanding need, or a genuine longing. "Moral proofs are grown into", he wrote. A question, a need, or a longing may have the effect of bringing about in an inquirer the dispositions necessary to weigh, honestly and fairly, the evidences and claims of a subject. It follows that this method of anticipation is intimately related to the quality of the inquirer's intellectual, moral and religious conversion. But more will be said about this later.

---

[51] Dev, Advertisement, XI; see his Tract, "Holy Scripture in its Relation to the Catholic Creed", in DA, 109-253: this Tract contains some of his best thought.

[52] Ap, 122, 123-4.

[53] See F. E. Crowe, "On the Method of Theology", TS, 23 (1962), 637-42.

The foregoing considerations can be made more concrete by an examination of a particular use of this apologetic method. We select an instance which is to be found in the final chapter of the *Grammar*, and has to do again with his defence of Christianity. He draws his argument for the Christian religion, this time not from the Christian Religion, but rather from the idea and nature of the world's historical religions. The actual derivation of his argument from this realm of natural religion is conducted through the following stages: first, a phenomenological investigation of the body of religions of history; next, an exposition of the findings of such an inquiry; and thirdly, the emergence of an anticipation of a supernatural revelation so strong as to constitute a powerful antecedent probability that it will be bestowed on humanity by the Creator.[54]

Newman first wants to exhibit the prima facie shape or form of the natural religions, to determine with all possible accuracy their nature and distinctive doctrines. He is careful not to impose the prototype of Christianity on the welter of world religions, "which have taken root in the many races of mankind, since the beginning of history, and before history, all over the earth".[55] He wants to let these religions speak for themselves. His own testimony is eloquent:

> It may be said, perhaps, that educated in Christianity, I merely judge of it by its own principles, but this is not the fact. For, in the first place, I have taken my idea of what a revelation must be, in good measure, from the actual religions of the world; and as to its ethics, the ideas with which I come to it are derived not simply from the Gospel, but prior to it from heathen moralists, whom Fathers of the Church and Ecclesiastical writers have imitated or sanctioned.[56]

The world religions exhibit a twofold aspect, the one gloomy and severe, the other hopeful and bright. In regard to the former aspect, religion "is founded in one way or other on the sense of sin". On this foundation are founded its rites, observances and doctrines. Carrying the burden of guilt and conscious of sin, the adherents of these religions devise these ways to alleviate their plight and win back the Deity's favour. This severe aspect of

---

[54] GA, 384-403.
[55] Ibid., 387.
[56] Ibid., 424-5.

Natural Religion is also its "most prominent aspect, because the multitude of men follow their own likings and wills, and not the decisions of their sense of right and wrong".

However, there is also a brighter side and then religion becomes a source of hope, a way of alleviating the human burden of guilt, and of advancing towards reconciliation with the Deity. But Newman wished to consider the gloomy aspect in the first place for the reason that he does "not recognize the religion of what is called civilisation, as having legitimately a part in the delineation of Natural Religion". The only civilisation worthy of the name in Newman's mind was that which resulted in the harmonious growth and uniform development of man's whole nature with all its faculties. The religion of civilisation had forfeited its rights to be regarded as such, in recognising indeed the moral sense, but ignoring the conscience, so that "the religion in which it issues has no sympathy either with the hopes and fears of the a-wakened soul, or with those frightful presentiments which are expressed in the worship and traditions of the heathen". But genuine natural religion was a blessing. Newman lists some of the blessings and qualities of the brighter side of religions. They include hope for the future, the recognition of the ultimate source of temporal blessings, the solace of prayer, the rite of sacrifice removing guilt and placating the offended Deity, and a dim foreshadowing of the doctrine of meritorious intercession. Implict in all these religious practices is the vivid awareness that "God Himself is Sanctity, Truth, and Love".[57]

The dominant fact that stands out among the findings of Newman's investigation is the connaturality of the idea of Revelation. In the religions of the world there is always the implicit recognition that the Deity addresssed might speak back in reply, and often the express request that He actually speak to man and set to work in order to alleviate the darkness and distress that weigh upon the world. Newman sees in this a further indication, of "how congenial the notion of revelation is to the human mind so that the expectation of it may truly be considered an integral part of Natural Religion".[58]

Finally, the result of this study of the history of religions and their common features is, first, a growing, and then a vivid anti-

---

[57] Ibid., 387; 395, 390, 391, 412.
[58] Ibid., 399.

cipation that a revelation will in fact be given. This anticipation
establishes a point of entry for a possible Revelation. Above all,
it produces in the mind and heart of the inquirer into the claims
of Christianity the "class of sentiments, intellectual and moral,
which constitute the formal preparation for entering upon what
are called the Evidences of Christianity". Newman lists ten of
these sentiments in this remarkable passage:

> a belief and a perception of the Divine Presence, a recognition of
> His attributes and an admiration of His Person viewed under
> them; a conviction of the worth of the soul and of the reality and
> momentousness of the unseen world, an understanding that, in
> proportion as we partake in our own persons of the attributes
> which we admire in Him, we are dear to Him; a consciousness on
> the contrary that we are far from partaking them, a consequent
> insight into our guilt and misery, an eager hope of reconciliation
> to Him, a desire to know and to love Him, and a sensitive looking-
> out in all that happens, whether in the course of nature or of human
> life, for tokens, if such there be, of His bestowing on us what we
> so greatly need.[59]

These sentiments, then, produce an antecedent probability
that a revelation will be given. More important still, they establish
preconditions for a revelation, and indicate some of the tests
that can be applied to verify a particular Revelation claiming to
be "the Voice of God to man". On the basis of them, the inquirer
can ask: "Which religion claiming to be the Revealed Religion
is truly such?", and can have some idea of what he is seeking.
On the strength of them, the apologist of Christianity can point
to Christianity as the "only one Religion in the world which tends
to fulfil the aspirations, needs, and foreshadowings of natural
faith and devotion", for already he has set up an antecedent
probability to which "it is difficult to put a limit to (its) legitimate
force".[60] The task of assembling the evidence and accumulating
it into arguments is now relatively easy. Furthermore, the hope
of convincing one's opponent, or of meeting the needs of the inquirer, is almost assured of success. As moral proofs are grown
into, rather than demonstrated, anticipation and hope have brought
low the mountains of pride and filled up valleys of human passion
and prejudice.

---

[59] Ibid., 412, 412-3.
[60] Ibid., 424, 418.

(c) *Analogy*

The study of Joseph Butler's *Analogy* provided Newman with an outstanding philosophical and theological implement: analogy. Henceforth Newman referred to the Anglican Bishop of Durham as the "great philosopher", and he employed frequently, in his apologetical works, the principle of analogy, though its primary value lay in its suitability for reflection on the mysteries of the faith, a topic on which we shall have much to say later. But here our concern is with the apologetical aspect of analogy, which Newman expressed in the words that "probability is the guide of life".

The ground of analogy was the theological fact that the Creator of nature is also the God of Revelation. God's operation in nature came from the God who revealed Himself in His Son, Jesus Christ. A similarity or correspondence between nature and grace was to be expected, if both were the work of the one Lord. Butler had "paralleled the difficulties of grace to the difficulties of nature". To those who refused to accept the profoundly mysterious doctrinal truths of Christianity, Butler pointed out that to be consistent they ought to reject nature as well, for it had its mysteries. Newman writes: "If we found it asserted in Butler's Analogy that there is no consistent standing or logical medium between the acceptance of the Gospel and the denial of a Moral Governor, for the same difficulties can be brought against both beliefs, and if they are fatal as against natural religion, should we not have understood what was meant?" [61]

Newman with typical insight observes that "Butler does not prove Christianity to be true by his famous argument, but he removes a great obstacle of a prima facie character to listening to the proofs of Christianity. It is like the trenches soldiers dig to shield them when they propose to storm a fort".[62] Its value in Butler's case, then, is mainly negative. And such is the main and primary use of analogy. However, Newman expanded the application of it to include a positive use, as well as the negative.

Two of his sermons exemplify Newman's negative use of analogy. They are to be found in the *Parochial and Plain Sermons*, and

---

[61] GA', 384.
[62] Ibid., 384-5.

have as their subjects the doctrine of the Blessed Trinity.[63] He has in mind the then current antipathy towards doctrinal Christianity, especially among those who could see little theological value in the revealed mysteries, and tended on account of their mysteriousness to reject them. Newman with great sagacity describes "some of the mysteries which are involved in our own nature", and concludes his description in these terms, which reliably suggest the thrust of his thought: "It is certain, then, that experience outstrips reason in its capacity for knowledge; why then should reason circumscribe faith, when it cannot compass sight?" [64] The believer in accepting God's Word is no more inconsistent than the non-believer who accepts nature with its endless unresolved mysteries. The believer, in fact, has the better case because he is such in virtue of the principle that justifies the confidence in nature of the non-believer.[65] The latter, however, fails to make the connection and detect his inconsistency.

However, "argument which tends to prove must be positive". If analogy is going to be capable of producing antecedent probability, Newman sees it must have a positive effect and force in addition to its valuable negative function. Such positive force Newman locates in its ability to bring together in support of the Christian faith arguments of natural and supernatural derivation. It was able to make nature and grace witness together to the truth of the Christian faith. What formerly appeared antagonistic and opposed, Newman succeeds in bringing into an alliance on the side of Revelation. For example, he notices that "the fact of Mediation so prominent in Scripture and in the world, as Butler illustrates it, is a positive argument that the God of Scripture is the God of the world". Immediately afterwards, he goes on to say that the argument from analogy had a decisive influence on his thinking in the *Apologia*.[66] Already in 1838 he could write of the usefulness of analogy in the realm of a generalised apologetic: "... the argument from analogy, which starts from the profession of being only of a negative character, ends with being positive,

---

[63] PS, IV, "The Mysteriousness of our Present Being", 282-94; VI, "The Mystery of the Holy Trinity", 343-61.

[64] PS, IV, 283, 285.

[65] K. Dick, Das Analogieprinzip, Newman Studien, V, Nürnberg, 1962, 84, 100.

[66] GA', 384, 385.

when drawn out into details; such being the difference between its abstract pretension and its actual and practical force".[67]

Our investigation of Newman's method of apologetics has come full circle. We have attempted to outline the main thrust of his highly nuanced apologetic, without neglecting in the process the many interesting ramifications and possible applications of his method. Aware of the divinely unique character of Christian Revelation, on the one hand, and of the irreducible individuality of each human being who might inquire into it or defend it, on the other, Newman, we contend, has outlined an original justification of Christianity, powerful yet elusive, popular yet genuinely scientific. As moral proofs are grown into, so Newman's apologetic prepares the heart for unreserved surrender, and the mind for unconditional assent, to the Gospel.

---

[67] DA, 153.

CHAPTER SIX

THE DOGMATIC PRINCIPLE AND DOCTRINES

The Dogmatic Principle

From the age of fifteen onwards Newman's destiny, social, intellectual, spiritual and religious, was guided by one outstanding principle, the principle of dogma. It dominated his mind, guided his decisions and impressed itself on his heart with invincible persuasion. His words are worth recalling: "Dogma has been the fundamental principle of my religion ... Religion, as a mere sentiment, is to me a dream and a mockery. As well can there be filial love without the fact of a father, as devotion without the fact of a Supreme Being. What I held in 1816, I held in 1833, and I hold in 1864. Please God, I shall hold it to the very end".[1] History has shown that he did.

The nature of the dogmatic principle is described by Newman in this remarkable passage: "The principle of dogma, that is, supernatural truths irrevocably committed to human language, imperfect because it is human, but definitive and necessary because given from above".[2] Christianity is therefore a dogmatic religion from the very nature of the case, being a communication from God to man in a medium that makes these truths accessible to man, while at the same time preserving their superhuman character.

It is this very quality that sets Christianity apart from every other religion. As a result, "the Church of God ever has had, and the rest of mankind never have had, authoritative documents of truth, and appointed channels of communication with Him".[3] As this revelation culminated in Christ Jesus and so closed with the death of his last Apostle, it is substantially complete by the end of the first century. It follows at once that if this definite and very real divine message is to remain in the world in its fullness, it must remain "one, absolute, integral, indissoluble,

---

[1] Ap, 150; see Dev, 359-60.
[2] Dev, 325.
[3] Ar, 80.

while the world lasts".[4] Newman therefore contends that the only consistent view of Christian revelation open to the genuine Christian is one which "holds that the Christian dogmas were in the Church from the times of the Apostles; that they were ever in substance what they are now".[5]

"Holy Scripture in its relation to the Catholic Creed"

We can take our consideration of his principle that Christianity is a religion of dogma, and not merely of sentiment, one step further by dwelling for a moment on one of the "Tracts for the Times", which he wrote in 1838, and in which he gives extended treatment to the ever controversial subject of the relationship between Scripture and Church doctrines.[6] When we recall the context of the "Tracts for the Times", we can reasonably expect to discover Newman at the height of his theological acumen. This expectation is borne out by investigation. And so we proceed to give an expository analysis of the Tract in terms of the difficulties and questions posed, and our author's answers.

The first difficulty arose from the standpoint of the Latitudinarians. Their cardinal principle was that Christianity is not based on any definite truths, least of all a system of doctrines, that propose to speak with authority about God, man, or man's destiny. It is therefore impossible to tell which interpretation of Scripture is true and correct: all one needs to do is to be sincere in one's own interpretation, and respectful towards other interpretations. There are, then, neither definite doctrines expressed in the pages of Holy Scripture, nor any ground at all for Church doctrines or a doctrinal interpretation of Christianity.

Newman's answer to this position is typically forthright. It is, he says, "maintainable supposing God had given us no Revelation". But the fact is that God has spoken, that He has broken the silence surrounding His ineffable Being. "Revelation implies a something revealed, and what is revealed is imperative on our faith, because it is revealed. Revelation implies imperativeness; it limits in its very notion our liberty of thought, because it limits our liberty of error, for error is one kind of thought." If God speaks as He most surely has spoken, then He says something.

---

[4] OUS, 317.
[5] TTE, 333.
[6] "Holy Scripture in its Relation to the Catholic Creed", DA, 109-253.

His Word shall not pass away. This anticipation is even shared by the commonsense view of mankind, who, weighed down by sin and the darkness of the world, "ask for something to lean on, something external to themselves. It will not do to tell them that whatever they at present hold as true, is enough. They want to be assured that what seems to them true, is true ... They will never be content with a religion without doctrines. The common sense of mankind decides against it. Religion cannot but be dogmatic: it ever has been".[7] This antecedent probability is confirmed by the manifold evidence which a perusal of the sacred volume supplies. Sacred Scripture itself claims to have a message, a "Gospel" for all men. Besides, this scriptural testimony is corroborated by the witness of ancient history that one, and one only, system of Christian belief prevailed in the orbis terrarum.

The second position that clashed with Newman's personal position (at this stage, the High Church party of the Oxford Movement) was that represented by the Protestant party. According to them, Christian revelation did have doctrines, but these lay clearly on top of its surface and could be recovered from it by a careful reading. Therefore, no doctrine was tenable in subsequent history which could not be clearly proven from the pages of Holy Writ, which taught all doctrines systematically.

Newman replies that this Protestant position is tenable if it is a fact that Holy Scripture is systematic, methodic and complete in its exposition of the divine message. However, this is both antecedently improbable and, upon investigation, discovered not to be the case. It is antecedently unlikely in that the Bible is a collection of writings, the works of inspired authors, who, at different times and to meet particular needs or counteract specific problems, wrote their inspired texts to convey some part of what they had learned through being "introduced into a knowledge of the unseen world". This anticipation is verified in fact through a study of "some instances of the unstudied and therefore perplexed character of Scripture, as regards its relation of facts".[8] Newman observes, for example, that St. Paul, in writing to the Corinthians, only reminds them of the Holy Eucharist, adding: "the rest will I set in order when I come".[9] Newman's comment

---

[7] DA, 130, 132, 133-4.
[8] Ibid., 147, 153.
[9] I Cor. 11 : 34.

is luminous: "when then we find the Church has always considered the Holy Sacrament to be not only a feast or supper, but in its fullness to contain a sacrifice, and to require a certain liturgical form, how does this contradict the inspired text, which plainly signifies that something else is to come besides what it has said itself? So far from its being strange that the Church brings out and fills up St. Paul's outline, it would be very strange if it did not".

It is now very much to our purpose to summarise briefly the conclusions and principles our author establishes in his study. Firstly, the Christian religion is of its very nature dogmatic in that "it will profess important information about the next world, it will have points of faith, it will have dogmatism, it will have anathemas. Christianity, therefore, will ever be looked on by the multitude, what it really is, as a rule of faith as well as of conduct".[10] Next, there are some doctrines clearly "on the surface" of the New Testament, "such as the divinity of Christ, the unity of God, the supremacy of divine grace, our election in Christ, the resurrection of the body, and eternal life or death to the righteous or sinners". Thirdly, to contend that only these scriptural doctrines were valid in "the time of the Church" was to develop "an impossible position", which proved too much: the method of scriptural proof for these same scriptural doctrines implied, of necessity, a "method of inferences" which in turn would "prove" and ground, in the course of the centuries other Church doctrines that all the while lay "under the surface of Scripture"; conversely, denial of this "method of inferences" of Church doctrines from under the surface of Holy Writ implied a principle that would ultimately work against the so-called scriptural doctrines.[11]

> On the whole then, I ask on how many special or palmary texts do any of the doctrines or rites which we hold depend? What doctrines or rites would be left to us if we demanded the clearest and fullest evidence, before we believed anything? What would the Gospel consist of? Would there be any Revelation at all left? Some all important doctrines at first sight certainly would remain in the New Testament ... Shall we give up the divinity of the Holy Ghost, original sin, the Atonement, the inspiration of the New Testament, united worship, the Sacraments, and Infant Baptism? Let us do so! Well, I will venture to say, we shall go

---

[10] DA, 161, 134.
[11] Ibid., 124, 145, 117, 152, 145.

on to find difficulties as regards those other doctrines, as the divinity of Christ, which at first sight seem to be in Scripture certainly, they are only more clearly there than the others, not so clearly stated as to be secured from specious objections.[12]

All this implies a further methodological doctrine about the derivation of Church doctrines from Scripture. In 1838, Newman put forward the Anglican position that every article of the Church's faith is so contained in Holy Scripture that it may thence be proved, provided there be added the illustrations and compensations supplied by Tradition.[13] Finally, as "Scripture is a deep book ... peculiar doctrines concerning the Church ... are in its depths". In fact, in the early Church, Christians esteeemed it as a book of divine Mysteries, and, like the Bible, did themselves conceal doctrines, such as the Blessed Trinity and Holy Eucharist, by means of the Economy and the Disciplina Arcani. Something more than text collecting or logical deduction will be necessary to plumb these depths in order to unfold their hidden riches of Revelation.[14]

Development of Newman's own idea of Doctrine

Some idea, perhaps, of what the Cardinal meant by doctrines and dogmas is beginning to emerge. Can we be more explicit and precise? We think it is possible to be so at this stage of our inquiry. In the famous sermon on "The Theory of Developments in Religious Doctrine", he says: "Theological dogmas are propositions expressive of the judgements which the mind forms, or the impressions which it receives, of revealed truth".[15] Another definition is given in the Grammar: "We are now able to determine what a dogma of Faith is, and what it is to believe it. A dogma is a proposition; it stands for a notion or for a thing".[16] In the last great work of his life, *A Letter addressed to His Grace, the Duke of Norfolk*, Newman wrote: "Now I am to speak of the Vatican definition, by which the doctrine of the Pope's infallibility has become de fide, that is, a truth necessary to be believed, as being included in the original divine revelation, for those terms,

---

[12] Ibid., 124.
[13] Diff, II, 11-14.
[14] DA, 194, 195, 237.
[15] OUS, 320.
[16] GA, 95.

revelation, depositum, dogma, and de fide, are correlatives".[17]
By analysing each text individually, and correlating the results, we
can discover for ourselves a preliminary idea of what our author
meant by doctrine or dogma.

The first common element that emerges is that dogmas are all
derived from one unique source, Revelation, which is called now
a "depositum", now an "original divine Revelation", now a "Revealed Truth". Dogmas therefore all start with the Truth, a "Divine Fact", in the words of the Sermon on Developments. The
second outstanding factor is that every dogma is a judgement
(expressed by the believer's mind or the community's mind).
The third fact is that the content of that judgement is derived
from the original "Divine Fact" and is included therein. It follows,
fourthly, that every dogma is an articulation of the original idea-
impression produced by the "great sight" of the "Revealed Truth".
Finally, the judgement itself, which constitutes a dogma, expresses a truth, in fact, a divine truth, in human language. As
the original divine revelation constitutes the "Divine Fact", so
a dogma articulates a particular fact contained in the original
revelation.

Newman had an instinctive sense of the real and the genuine
and the factual. And as he continually appealed to his contemporaries that they resign themselves to what is so, submitting
themselves to it rather than quarrelling with it, so he likewise
felt about all religious life.[18] To the objection that doctrines are
mere matters of opinion, he replied: "The doctrines of the Church
are after all not mere matters of opinion; they were not in early
times mere ideas in the mind to which no one could appeal, each
individual having his own, but they were external facts".[19] Like
facts, they were stubborn. A short time after writing these words
Newman found himself in controversy again, this time with the
liberal attitude to doctrines, as exemplified in Sir Robert Peel and
Lord Brougham: "Many a man will live and die upon a dogma: no
man will be a martyr for a conclusion. A conclusion is but an
opinion; it is not a thing which is, but which we are 'certain about'
... No one, I say, will die for his own calculations; he dies for

---

[17] Diff, II, 320; see Jfc, 316.
[18] DA, 141.
[19] Ibid., 241.

realities".[20] Doctrines, then, were realities on which one could stake one's life, even to the ultimate witness of martyrdom.

Newman, however, was aware that a school of thought existed, which held the view that, while doctrines could be tolerated, they told us little or nothing about the "Divine Fact". The revealed mysteries so transcended the dogmas that the human language, in which our dogmas are expressed, differs more from, than it conforms to, the heavenly realities. Dogmas, then were useless and inane. Quoting I Corinthians, 13:12 ("For now we see in a mirror dimly but then face to face"), Newman answers that our doctrinal expressions must necessarily be defective in our present earthly state. However, they give us a real and genuine knowledge of the "heavenly realities". The knowledge was real because it was communicated from above by the One who was not only the "Creator of all things, visible and invisible", but also the Revealer; it was defective only because man is not God, but is finite and limited. Like Beethoven's music which, though composed from the notes of the scale, produced musical masterpieces, "the outpourings of eternal harmony in the medium of created sound ... echoes from our home",[21] the Christian dogmas, though expressed in human language, were real expressions of eternal mysteries in a created medium, and real visions of our divine homeland.

Dogmas and their Formulations

From his engrossing studies of the early Christian centuries Newman was keenly conscious that a scientific language was a very late arrival in the field of Christian doctrine. In 1858, he wrote a tract for the Atlantis magazine on "St. Cyril's Formula, μία φύσις σεσαρκωμένη", in which he gives a good treatment of dogmas and their formulations.[22] As any human science only slowly develops clear concepts, accurate language and trustworthy formulae, so the first Christian writers used a common-sense language expression. Newman makes the point very well:

Since they (the Catholic doctrines of the Trinity and Incarnation) are from the nature of the case above our intellectual reach, and

---

[20] Ibid., 293.
[21] OUS, 347.
[22] Later incorporated in TTE, 329-82: a superlative contribution to Christology.

were unknown until the preaching of Christianity, they required on their first promulgation new words, or words used in new senses, for their due enunciation; and, since these were not definitely supplied by Scripture or Tradition, nor for centuries by ecclesiastical authority, variety in the use, and confusion in the apprehension of them, were unavoidable in the interval.[23]

Further, there existed a high regard for the apostolic language of the holy Scriptures. In fact, "the very confidence felt that Apostolic truth would never fail, would indispose Christians to define it, till definition became an imperative duty". Again, it might be expected that the variety and confusion prevailing in the current phraseology would lead to heterodoxy here and there. Thus "the word person, used in the doctrine of the Holy Trinity, would on first hearing suggest Tritheism to one who made the word synonymous with individual; and Unitarianism to another, who accepted it in the classical sense of a mask or character".[24]

It is easy to understand, therefore, how successful the Arian party was in getting Catholics to accept the "propriety of confining their statement of doctrine to the language of Scripture, and of rejecting ὑπόστασις, οὐσία, and similar terms, which, when once used in a definite sense, that is, scientifically, in Christian teaching, would become the protection and record of orthodoxy". Were the Christians careless about dogma, then? In no way. They enjoyed their independence of a set and rigid phraseology, while at the same time displaying a remarkable commitment to clear and definite dogmatic positions, as is instanced in the case of St. Ignatius of Antioch, whose Epistles belong to the Apostolic Age. In short, the Christians of the first four centuries of the Christian era "had not yet got it deeply fixed into their minds, as a sort of first principle, that to abandon the formula was to betray the faith". Again, Newman suggests St. Athanasius as the one who, more than all others, stands out for his bold independence of a rigid terminology, together with an equal fervour in sustaining, expounding and defending the Church's dogmas. "No one surely can read his work without being struck with the force and exactness with which he lays down the outlines and fills up the details of the Catholic dogma, as it has been defined since

[23] TTE, 335.
[24] Ibid., 336, 335: compare with what K. Rahner says on the same subject in his Theological Investigations, IV, London, 1966, 91-102.

the controversies with Nestorius and Eutyches, who lived in the following century; yet the word θεοτόκος, which had come down to him, like ὁμοούσιος by tradition, is nearly the only one among those, which he uses, which would now be recognized as dogmatic".[25] Finally, Newman states as a fact that, though the dogmas existed before the formulas were publicy adopted, they were defined with the passage of time. Such formulas were sanctioned by the appropriate ecclesiastical acts and so are vital now for the faith of Catholics, as enjoying a dogmatic authority.

The Dogmatic Principle as a Constitutive "First Principle" of Christianity

Newman, however, was at pains to justify not only doctrines, but also the principle of doctrine, or what he preferred to call the "dogmatic principle". Christianity in fact, is based on a "first principle" of being a definite divine message for all men of all times and places. It is, then, imperative for us to recall to mind our discussion of "first principles" in the previous chapter. "First principles", we saw, were the very inner constitution of the man. In the light of them he views events, deeds, persons, lines of conduct, aims, moral qualities, religions. They guide our thinking, our judging, our decisions, and our actions. Though absolute monarchs they are not tyrannical and may be detected, and then either retained or eliminated.[26]

We are now in a position to understand Newman's insistence that the "dogmatic principle" is essential to Christianity. As first principles constitute the man, so Christianity, that divine creation in a human medium, may be expected to be constituted by its own particular principles. It, too, will have its own pattern of constitutive principles that determine its identity, guide its activity, and control its growth. In terms of these same principles, we can understand the historical reality of the Christian Fact more fully. Among such constitutive First Principles, Newman sees the principle of dogma as most outstanding of all, in fact the source whence the others may be derived.

From the pages of the New Testament, and in his studies of the Greek Fathers, especially St. Athanasius, it was crystal clear to Newman that the Incarnation of the Second Person of the

---

[25] TTE, 338, 338, 339-40.
[26] GA, 57-70; Jfc, 333-4; Prepos, 271-314.

Blessed Trinity was not only a central doctrine of the Apostolic and Patristic Church, but was the source doctrine of Christianity and the ground of its other principles:

> I will consider the Incarnation the central truth of the Gospel, and the source whence we are to draw its principles. This great doctrine is unequivocally announced in numberless passages of the New Testament, especially by St. John and St. Paul, as is familiar to us all. "The Word became flesh and dwelt among us, full of grace and truth" (John 1 : 14). "That which was from the beginning, which we have heard, which we have seen with our eyes, which we have looked upon, and our hands have handled, of the Word of Life, that declare we to you" (1 John 1 : 1). "For ye know the grace of our Lord Jesus Christ, that, though He was rich, yet for your sakes He became poor, that ye through His poverty might be rich" (2 Corinthians 8 : 9). "Not I, but Christ liveth in me, and the life which I now live in the flesh, I live by the faith of the Son of God, who loved me and gave Himself for me."[27]

It is true, of course, that the Incarnation itself is a doctrine, but it is so central, as Newman ably shows by the foregoing phalanx of Scripture quotations, that it becomes a principle, a "law", from which, and on which, the other principles of the Faith are derived and interrelated.[28] Accordingly, Newman proceeds:

> In such passages as these we have
> 1. The principle of dogma . . .
> 2. The principle of faith, which is the correlative of dogma, being the absolute acceptance of the divine Word with an internal assent, in opposition to the informations, if such, of sight and reason.
> 3. Faith, being an act of the intellect, opens a way for inquiry, comparison and inference, that is, for science in religion, in subservience to itself; this is the principle of theology.
> 4. The doctrine of the Incarnation is the announcement of a divine gift conveyed in a material and visible medium, it being thus that heaven and earth are in the Incarnation united. That is, it establishes in the very idea of Christianity the sacramental principle as its characteristic.
> 5. Another principle involved in the doctrine of the Incarnation, viewed as taught or as dogmatic, is the necessary use of language, for example, of the text of Scripture, in a second or mystical sense. Words must be made to express new ideas, and are invested with sacramental office.
> 6. It is our Lord's intention in His Incarnation to make us what

---

[27] Dev, 324-5.
[28] Ibid., 178.

He is Himself; this is the principle of Grace, which is not only holy but sanctifying.

7. It cannot elevate and change us without mortifying our lower nature—here is the principle of Asceticism.

8. And, involved in this death of the natural man, is necessarily a revelation of the malignity of sin, in corroboration of the forebodings of conscience.

9. Also by the fact of an Incarnation we are taught that matter is an essential part, and, as well as mind, is capable of sanctification.[29]

The unusual length of this quotation is justified because of its usefulness. It helps us distinguish between principles and doctrines, and is effective in discriminating between true and false doctrines, and in evaluating good theology.

Firstly, then, doctrines can be seen to be distinct, though not separate, from principles. Dogmatic truths are as many expressions of the one principle, dogma: Christological truths, for example, are facets of the central fact of the Incarnation. Again, the various doctrines in the field of the Sacraments will be the expansion of the Sacramental principle. If it should happen in the course of history that these same sacramental dogmas increase they can never be more than their directive and grounding principle. Newman further clarifies the point in terms of a mathematical analogy: "doctrines stand to principles, as the definitions to the axioms and postulates of mathematics. Thus the fifteenth and seventeenth propositions of Euclid's Book I are developments, not of the first three axioms, which are required in the proof, but of the definitions of a right angle". Principles are abstract and general and permanent, while doctrines relate to facts that are concrete and particular. "The life of doctrines may be said to consist in the principle which they embody." [30]

Secondly, a principle puts into our hands a ready-made and powerful tool to discriminate between true and false doctrines. Thus Newman saw how St. Athanasius could masterfully employ the primary principle of the New Testament's teaching on the Incarnation to justify the dogmatic homoousion of Nicaea and reveal the falsehood of the Arian position.[31] Rather than merely

---

[29] Ibid., 325-6: in later editions Newman adds in the development of doctrine as a tenth "first Principle".

[30] Dev, 179, 178.

[31] Ath, II, 56, 86.

restate the authoritative teaching of that great Council, St. Athanasius preferred to oppose Arius with the weapons supplied by the guiding principle of the New Testament's teaching on the matter. St. Athanasius thus laid the foundation of all theology and "has impressed an image on the Church, which through God's mercy, shall not be effaced while time lasts".[32] As long as time lasts whatever is proposed as pastorally effective, spiritually fruitful, theologically original, or religiously valuable, can be effectively evaluated and tested in terms of the Incarnation.

The Critical Grounding of Dogmas

A doctrine or a dogma (the terms are interchangeable) is a proposition. This simple statement has hidden significance, which we must now explore. We will see how Newman has given a critical grounding to dogmatic definitions of the Church and to revealed truths through his treatment and articulation of the role of the mental act of judgement in our knowledge process. But we have already dealt with our actual cognitional structure as Newman saw it: that was our concern in Chapter II, where we analysed the *Grammar*, his formal exposition of the subject. It will be sufficient then, to recall briefly what we discovered and set forth there, emphasising such points as may be particularly helpful in our present inquiry.

"What struck Newman was the unconditional character of judgement." [33] This unconditionality was a fact for him, as much so as his own very existence, and to its consideration he devoted two whole chapters. And besides, this unconditional assent was given to concrete issues or things. In these cases the philosophers of the school of John Locke denied its possibility as well as its existence, but on "a priori, theoretical and unreal" grounds, as Newman was quick to point out. It was Newman's task, then, to explain how one reaches this absolute in concrete judgements. The problem seemed aggravated by the equally certain fact that all inference, be it syllogistic, informal or natural, was capable only of reaching a conditional or probable conclusion. Newman's solution is described partially at the conclusion of the chapter on Inferences, and fully in the next chapter on the Illative Sense.

---

[32] OUS, 97.
[33] F. E. Crowe, "Intuition", NCE, VII, 600.

The Illative Sense is an extraordinary name for a very ordinary mental faculty, judgement. There is a strange appropriateness, perhaps, in the fact that he gave this basic mental faculty such a distinctive name: Newman was the man, perhaps the only man, in his century to be fully aware of its decisive role in all our knowing, and, in bringing it out into the clear light of day, he gave it the distinction of a special name. In a century which was the victim of totalitarian and "prepared positions" in the field of ethics, philosophy and theology, it will be for ever to Newman's glory that he liberated the human mind, "more versatile and vigorous than any of its works",[34] from its tyrannical captors.

The Illative Sense is defined by Newman as "the regulating principle of all reasoning in the concrete", being the mind's "power of judging about truth and error in concrete matters". Besides, "the sole and final judgement on the validity of an inference in concrete matter ... is committed to a mental faculty, which I have called the Illative Sense". It is the bridge between probability or conditionality, and certitude or unconditionality. It is the faculty whose act makes that margin disappear which intervenes between verbal argumentation and conclusions in the concrete. In fact, the mind "determines what science cannot determine, the limit of converging probabilities, and the reasons sufficient for a proof". And it constructs the bridge between the conditional and the unconditional not by invincible syllogisms or brilliant intuitions, but "by objections overcome, by adverse theories neutralized, by difficulties gradually clearing up, by exceptions proving the rule, by unlooked-for correlations found for received truths ... by all these ways, and many others", until, in the end, a conclusion is so clearly grasped "that it is proved interpretative".[35]

The Illative Sense, then, is the power of judging "what is so", and of reaching the really existent. Newman claimed that its scope is in the difficult domain of matters of fact, of the "concrete", which is his equivalent for Aristotle's "contingent matter", to which he makes reference.[36] It is the faculty we use to reach the concrete in which we attain truth, what is simply true independently of our likes and dislikes, hopes and fears, though,

---

[34] GA, 346.
[35] Ibid., 354, 338, 346, 314, 316.
[36] Nicomachaean Ethics, VI, 3 and 4.

of course, its correct operation is much influenced by these moral dispositions. He still further illustrates its operation in terms of a comparison with Aristotle's phronesis, or faculty of moral judgement, and then with Newton's mathematical process of taking the limit. Having already dwelt upon the second comparison, we can omit it here and go on to the comparison he makes between the Illative Sense and Aristotle's phronesis.

Though an ethical system may supply laws, suggest principles to govern behaviour, and indicate the golden mean to be attained in one's actual living, yet in the final analysis the person is solitary and independent, and his assessment of a situation and actual response to it in conduct is worked out in terms of a personal moral faculty, which Aristotle calls phronesis. It is the same with the Illative Sense; it may not be fitted into rules of operation, or be guided by carefully selected methods of inference. Being in and of the person, it transcends such artificial treatment. What the moral guiding faculty phronesis is to the individual's moral life, the Illative Sense is to his intellectual life.[37] Let us listen again to Newman at this point: "in no class of concrete reasonings, whether in experimental science, historical research, or theology, is there any ultimate test of truth and error in our inferences besides the trustworthiness of the Illative Sense that gives them its sanction".[38] Fr. Bernard Lonergan said on several occasions that he read sections of the *Grammar* six times while in Heythrop.[39] Fr. Dessain, we feel, is correct, when in his unpublished paper, "Cardinal Newman and Bernard J. F. Lonergan, S.J.", which was written for, and delivered at, the 1970 Lonergan Congress in Miami, he claims that, although Lonergan does not use the term Illative Sense (in his great philosophical work, Insight), he "describes this purely intellectual faculty, when he speaks of how acts of understanding must be made invulnerable".[40]

The *Grammar*, we remember, was written as an extended Essay in answer to William Froude's contention that it was impossible to reach certitude in a concrete matter of fact. For Froude the

---

[37] See M. Novak, "Bernard Lonergan: A new Approach to Natural Law", Proceedings of the American Catholic Philosophical Association, 1967, 249.

[38] GA, 352.

[39] Quoted in D. Tracy, The Achievement of Bernard Lonergan, New York, 1970, 91-2.

[40] C. S. Dessain, "Cardinal Newman and Bernard Lonergan, S.J.", Miami, 1970, 6.

Christian dogmas, therefore, could never be assented to with certitude. Having appropriated his own cognitional structure, especially the role of judgement, Newman was in a powerful position to meet Froude's difficulty in particular, and ground the Catholic dogmas critically. And so we come to our next subject.

"On Consulting the Faithful in Matters of Doctrine": *an instance of critical grounding*

Shortly after Newman's entry into the Catholic Church the dogma of Our Lady's Immaculate Conception was defined by Pope Pius IX. It was the year 1854. We may consider this dogma as a test case for Newman. We can investigate how he set about its theological vindication and critical grounding. Where was the evidence for the dogma?

In the July, 1859 number of *The Rambler*, Newman wrote his famous article "On Consulting the Faithful in Matters of Doctrine".[41] If the definition of five years previously is the basic reason for the article, the immediate reason was a statement occurring in *The Rambler* of the previous May. The statement ran thus: "In preparation of a dogmatic definition, the faithful are consulted, as lately in the instance of the Immaculate Conception".[42] This sentiment provided Newman with an opening for his exposition on the subject: "Then follows the question, why? and the answer is plain, viz. because the body of the Faithful is one of the witnesses to the fact of the tradition of revealed doctrine, and because their consensus through Christendom is the voice of the Infallible Church".[43]

We have seen how Newman, as an Anglican, considered Marian dogma in the Roman Church a corruption of the original Faith, and how, on the breakdown of the Via Media and Anglican synthesis, he was forced to consider seriously the Roman claims, how that consideration led to the writing of *An Essay on the Development of Christian Doctrine*, in which he accounted for the specifically Catholic dogmas in terms of his carefully nuanced hypothesis of divinely guided dogmatic development, and how he

---

[41] The text is to be found in J. Guitton, The Church and the Laity, New York, 1968, 63-111; see also Ar, 445-68.

[42] The Rambler, May 1959, 122.

[43] On Consulting, 73.

verified his hypothesis historically and theologically. In this way of antecedent probability, coupled with verification, Newman "had been accustomed to account for the supposed phenomena" of new definitions. This was in 1845. But now in 1859 he says he has discovered "another way"!

What was the other way? Newman tells us: the way of a concrete judgement made by the body of the faithful. Such a consensus of the faithful was nothing more and nothing less than an expression of the Holy Ghost's phronesis, or Illative Sense, deep in the bosom of Christ's Church. It was clear to Newman that certain portions of the defined doctrine of the Church were not to be found in many of the Fathers, and the evidence of Scripture was equally scanty. Again, it was not easy to deduce such a doctrine as the Immaculate Conception by formal implication from another. How, then, could the definition be justified? Newman answered: a sensus fidelium, which became a consensus fidelium, is a "sign" for the Bishops and Pope that a right judgement, and therefore a dogmatic truth, has been reached in the Church. Having shown the existence of the sensus fidelium in Christian tradition, he goes on to draw out, with wonderful erudition, the precise nature of this consensus fidelium in five points.[44]

What the Illative Sense achieves on the natural plane in the individual, the supernatural Illative Sense, or the "phronesis" of the Holy Ghost, does in the supernaturally higher context of the Spirit-filled Christian community. If the Illative Sense can lift a theory to the level of fact, "by objections overcome, by adverse theories neutralized, by difficulties gradually clearing up ... by all these ways and many others",[45] it follows, mutatis mutandis, that the theory of Our Lady's Immaculate Conception could be, in fact has been, lifted to the level of certitude by an ongoing, centuries-long process in which objections are overcome, adverse theories neutralized, and difficulties are cleared up, until there comes a time when all the probabilities of past times converge on the certitude that Our Lady is immaculately conceived. As the Illative Sense terminates the reasoning process that leads us to give an unconditional assent to the proposition that "Great Britain is an island", so too the supernatural Illative

---

[44] Ibid., 74, 82-4.
[45] GA, 314.

Sense of that community, which is Christ's Mystical Body, may, in the Holy Spirit's good time, "determine what science cannot determine, the limits of converging probabilities and the reasons sufficient for a proof".[46]

It becomes clear at this stage, then, that for Newman, a dogmatic statement is an absolute truth, supernaturally higher than, though analogous to, a natural certitude. And as it is unreal and theoretical for some to maintain that we are immoral in having and living by certitudes in ordinary life, so a Christianity that does not have doctrines, that is, statements of fact and of "what is so", is equally "theoretical" and "unreal", indeed "a dream and a mockery".[47]

Nicaea and Doctrine

The first work of Newman's incredible literary career was his study of the First General Council of the Church of Nicaea, in which the dogma of the Incarnation was solemnly defined. That work he called *The Arians*, and it was more concerned with the historical context of the definition of Our Lord's consubstantiality with his Father than with the definition itself. The last work of his career was a defence of the twentieth General Council of the Church, which in 1869-1870 took place in the Vatican, and which defined the ex cathedra infallibility of the Pope. The defence, which was occasioned by Gladstone's expostulation against the definition, was addressed to the Duke of Norfolk.[48] By putting both of these works of his together we get a balanced insight into his thought on the permanence, development and historicity of dogmatic teaching.

The first Ecumenical Council, however, had the more decisive influence on his mind. In his study of it he came across the great school of Alexandria, founded by Clement. He encountered its "great theologian", St. Athanasius, whose treatise against the Arians he studied, and later translated into English between the years 1841-1844. Whereas it was the theological school of Alexandria that made possible the victory of the orthodox party over the Arian party at Nicaea, it was St. Athanasius who became the

---

[46] Ibid., 346: compare with Vatican II, Dogmatic Constitution on the Church, N. 12.

[47] See Ap, 150; Diff, II, 323, 312-3; GA, 157.

[48] The text is in Diff, II, 171-378.

champion of the teaching of the homoousion during the trouble-
some decades that followed. In Athanasius he detected the very
type and model of the orthodox Church that was the only heir
to the Church of the Apostles. He saw in Athanasius a man "who
spent his long years in fighting against kings for a theological
term",[49] the homoousion of Nicaea.

It was not, however, so much the term as the doctrine it expressed that preoccupied the great doctor. In our treatment of
dogmatic formulations earlier in this chapter, we saw that Athanasius, though the tenacious exponent of the doctrine contained
in the homoousion, was rather liberal in his actual use of the term
itself, for, as Newman explains, the Bishops of the day "had not
yet got it deeply fixed into their minds, as a sort of first principle, that to abandon the formula was to betray the faith".[50]

Newman was quick to detect what was actually happening
at Nicaea. Confronted by the Arian peril, the Church discovered
and appropriated her power to teach in the name of Christ. Though
this power had been hers all along, and though "it could not be
otherwise if Christianity was to teach divine truth in contrast
to the vague opinions and unstable conjectures of human philosophers",[51] Nicaea was the moment of truth. While hitherto the
Church's consciousness of her teaching authority was implicit,
now it had become explicit. He saw, besides, that the teaching
of Nicaea was not only a defence of the central principle of the
Christian Faith, the Incarnation, but was also an instance in
which a formal dogmatic statement of the Church was the result
of the clash of the viewpoints represented by the Christology of
Antioch and the Christology of Alexandria. Fr. Walgrave's comment is illuminating:

> From the beginning, and independently of any philosophy, New-
> man read in the facts themselves the dialectical structure of the
> history of ideas. In his first great work, The Arians, he described
> how the Christological controversy had its origin in the opposition
> between two theological schools, Antioch and Alexandria. The
> former considered Christ mainly from the point of view of the
> Synoptic Gospels, and saw in Christ a man, just like ourselves,
> upon whom the gift of divinity had been bestowed . . . The latter
> looked at Christ in the light of St. John's Gospel, and saw in Him

---

[49] ECH, II, 75.
[50] TTE, 338.
[51] Ath, II, 82.

the eternal Word who took flesh. In both positions the truth of Christ was endangered.[52]

The lesson was clear: the dialectic of positions and schools, as well as the opposition of heretics like Arius, could be the occasion of a dogmatic statement, which would determine for ever the truth of the portion of Revelation in dispute. In fact, this seems to be the basic sense of the whole section "The Assimilating Power of Dogmatic Truth" in the *Essay on Development*.[53]

Newman observed, further, a dramatic significance in Nicaea's employing the non-scriptural word, homoousion. To halt the evasiveness of the Arian party, it was useless to use Scripture terminology with disputants who had lost reverence for the transcendent meaning of Scripture. The homoousion had a definite meaning, which acts as a "point of convergence", as the "limit", of the scriptural data and the Christological data of the centuries preceding Nicaea. Newman notices that Athanasius only used the term once in his *Contra Arianos*, "and then rather in a formal statement of doctrine than in the flow of his discussion", and that the "doctrine which it upholds is never out of his thoughts".[54] In fact, "there are passages of his Orations in which he omits it, when it was the natural word to use". In one such passage St. Athanasius explains the meaning to the doctrine, and therefore of the term, in words which Newman translates: "The same things are said of the Son, which are said of the Father, except His being said to be Father".[55] If anything was clear to Newman it was that this proposition was an attempt on the part of St. Athanasius to apprehend the truth of Christ, not in experiential, imaginative, "real" terms, but in theological, notional terms, which related Him to His Father consubstantially. Arius and his party might use an unending series of scriptural terms, all of which evaded the issue at stake. But with St. Athanasius a decisive step has been taken. Systematic meaning had been employed effectively for the first time.

But the drama did not cease with the declaration of the great Council. It raged on for about thirty-five years. Finally, on the basis of the Son's consubstantiality, the Holy Spirit's consub-

---

[52] J. Walgrave, Unfolding Revelation, London, 1972, 309.
[53] Dev, 357-68.
[54] TTE, 337; Ath, II, 56.
[55] Ath, I, 361: PG 26:329A.

stantiality was defined in the Second Ecumenical Council at Constantinople in 381. But the Christological issue came up again. The Council of Ephesus had to affirm that He who was born of the Virgin Mary in time, was the one who was born of the Father before time began, so that our Lady was theotokos. This was in 431. Twenty years later it had to be defined against the Mono-physites that one and the same could be both God and man, per-fect in divinity and perfect in humanity, because He had two natures. With these Councils a series of new terms came into Church doctrines: besides homoousion, there were hypostasis, ousia, theotokos, to name a few of the more important. In this way, the Council of Nicaea was still further systematized and its teaching explained, or as Newman put it, the third and fourth Councils "interpret the Creed" of Nicaea.[56]

Fifthly, Newman noticed a doctrinal context emerging, within which it was possible to apprehend what was being said at each Council. With reference to the Councils of Ephesus and Chalcedon, he writes: "The dogmas relative to the Trinity and the Incar-nation were not struck off all at once, but piecemeal—one Council did one thing, another a second, and so the whole dogma was built up. And the first portion of it looked extreme, and contro-versies rose upon it, and these controversies led to a second and third Council, and they did not reverse the first, but explained and completed what was first done".[57] The great Greek Councils became a context, a definite horizon. There might be some ex-cuse for doubt as to what was affirmed and taught in Nicaea, especially as the term homoousion had been disowned as being inconsistent with orthodoxy at the provincial Councils of Antioch during the period 264-272. But after Constantinople, Ephesus and Chalcedon, the teaching of Nicaea had been interpreted, explained and completed. The shift from Scripture to Creed, which started at Nicaea, was an effort to bring some more system and order into what Christians during the first three Christian centuries had been saying and writing about the fundamental truths of Revelation. Perhaps Newman's mind is well expressed in the following quotation: "I must explain myself, when I say, that we depend for the Canon and Creed upon the fourth and fifth centuries ... we see in them an ever-growing tendency and ap-

---

[56] Ath, II, 86-7.
[57] Ward, II, 379; see Diff, II, 305-19.

proximation to that full agreement which we find in the fifth. The testimony given at the latter date is the limit to which all that has been before given converges".[58] The substantial nature of what had been going forward is highlighted by the fact that in this same fifth century the Christians of Europe, Africa and Asia were united in their acceptance of common doctrines that grounded their Christian living.

Transition from the Patristic to the Scholastic Doctrinal Context

But still further shifts were to take place. Newman gives an outline of these in a wonderful historical sketch of the work of the Benedictine schools in the Middle Ages.[59] The great merit of these Schools was that they consolidated the achievements of the Patristic age by "a careful review and catalogue of them". Theirs was a loyal adherence to the teaching of the past, a faithful inculcation of it, and an anxious transmission of it to the next generation. In other words, they were docile pupils of the Fathers, and so became effective teachers of their own age. But unlike the Fathers, they were not engaged in the answering of novel questions, in the resolution of new problems, or in the production of original works. But a time was coming when it would no longer be adequate for the Church's need merely to continue such a labour. "As the new Christian society which Charlemagne inaugurated grew, its intellect grew with it, and at last began to ask questions, and propose difficulties which catenae and commentaries could not solve. Hard-headed objectors were not to be subdued by their reverence for antiquity and the amenities of polite literature; and when the controversies arose, the Benedictines found themselves, from the necessity of the times, called to duties which were as uncongenial to the spirit of their founder as the political engagements of St. Dunstan or St. Bernard." [60]

Newman notices that, just as the Arian lack of reverence for holy Scripture operated the shift to a more systematic expression of the New Testament message about Christ's relationship to His heavenly Father in terms of the homoousion of Nicaea, a similar dissatisfaction began to arise in the eleventh and twelfth cen-

---

[58] DA, 237.
[59] "The Benedictine Schools", HS, II, 431-87.
[60] Ibid., 476-7, 478.

turies with the systematic statements, formulated by the Greek Councils and the Fathers, and transmitted by the Benedictine Schools. The new and original questions would require new and original answers. A "new theology was making its way into Christendom".[61]

This new theology finally emerged as the great work of Scholasticism. "Scholastic theology ... involved a creative action of intellect; that this is the case as regards the Schoolmen need not be proved." This "creative action of the intellect", though parallel to the Patristic achievement, yet was such "in a different way".[62] The new shift was basically the introduction of the Aristotelian philosophy, with its logic, ethics, psychology and metaphysics, into Christian reflection on the Patristic heritage in an effort to meet the demands of the new mentality. Newman had written of Aristotle that he was called the Bishop of the Arians, who used his logic.[63] But now St. Thomas took up Aristotle's metaphysics and employed them in his systematic treatment of the Christian heritage. In the words of Newman, St. Thomas made of Aristotle "a hewer of wood and drawer of water to the Church" after the manner of a "strong slave"![64] The originality of the Patristic period lay in its logical, systematic meaning: the originality of the Scholastic labour was its metaphysical context.

Dogmas to be Apprehended in their Historical Contexts

Newman, then, was high in his praise of the labours of the Scholastics. However, win as they did Newman's admiration and appreciation, the Scholastics did not win his discipleship. He did not imitate their methods. In his famous letter to Pusey, he writes that he preferred the Fathers' more elegant and fruitful teaching to the contentious and subtle theology of the Schola.[65] We can only wonder why. It is true that Newman grew up in the Anglican Church and had been immersed from the start in the Fathers. But in Rome in 1847, he came in contact with Scholastic theologians in the persons of Fathers Passaglia and Perrone,

---

[61] Ibid., 486.
[62] Ibid., 475.
[63] Ar, 31, 335, note 1; 29.
[64] Idea, 470.
[65] Diff, II, 24.

S.J. Our answer to the difficulty is that Newman could not conceive of truth, including revealed Truth, apart from the categories of history and the personal state of the inquirer. In other words, Newman prefers to have a method capable of dealing with the historical complexity of the contexts of the dogmas of the Church, and allowing for the fact that no man is a rational animal only, but a "seeing, feeling, contemplating, acting animal". That our solution is correct is substantiated by evidence from the corpus of Newman's writing.

In his *Lectures on the Present Position of Catholics in England*, which were delivered in 1851, there is a very revealing passage: "The legitimate instruments for deciding on the truth of a religion are these two, fact and reason, or in other words, the way of history and the way of science". In short, sound theological inquiry could in no way dispense with history. So true was this that, although "Catholics reasoned profoundly upon doctrine, Catholics also investigated rigidly the religious state of other times and places".[66] Further, Newman was of the conviction that this historico-theological character of Catholic inquiry was distinctive and set it apart from Protestant theology as he knew it. His defence of Papal Infallibility in his *Letter to the Duke of Norfolk* provides a classical instance of such Catholic inquiry.

In the claims of the See of Rome Newman recognized "the distinctive doctrine of the Catholic Religion". Gladstone vigorously rejected the teaching, (as he might be expected to, not being a Catholic) but his chief reason was a historical one. He viewed the Definition of Papal Infallibility of the Vatican Council as a "repudiating of ancient history" of the Church. Newman made his reply fit the objection, in giving an eminently historico-theological exposition of the new dogma. It was his method, he explained, in treating the "essential points" of the debate, to "go back a great way, and be allowed to speak of the ancient Catholic Church". Having drawn out the profile of "the ancient Catholic Church", he sees the feature of her "tradition of Apostolic Independence and freedom of speech" as outstanding. She was a Church conscious of her rights, privileges, prerogatives, and duties, as much during her time of trial under the persecuting Emperors as during her ascendancy after the time of Constantine. "As

---

[66] Prepos, 57, 59.

she (the Church) resisted and defied her persecutors, so she ruled her convert people." But where, one may ask, is such a Church to be found today? In particular, where is the Church to be seen today with such a "self-consciousness" of her mandate to teach? Newman replies that "the Pope is historically the heir", so that the belief of Catholics in "the Pope and his attributes, which seems so monstrous to Protestants, is bound up with our being Catholics at all".[67]

Does this mean that ecclesiastical history is an adequate ground for Papal Infallibility? He gives us a very definite negative to the query and goes on to explain his answer in a passage that is worthy of being cited, as it gives his final view on the indispensable, though limited, role of history in the apprehension of the Church's dogmas:

> For myself, I would simply confess that no doctrine of the Church can be rigorously proved by historical evidence: but at the same time that no doctrine can be simply disproved by it. Historical evidence reaches a certain way, more or less, towards a proof of the Catholic doctrines ... In all cases there is a margin left for the exercise of faith in the word of the Church. He who believes the dogmas of the Church only because he has reasoned them out of History, is scarcely a Catholic. It is the Church's dogmatic use of history in which the Catholic believes; and she uses other informants also, Scripture, Tradition, the ecclesiastical sense or φρόνημα, and a subtle ratiocinative power, which in its origins is a divine gift.[68]

Now prescinding from the expressly apologetical context of that passage, we can still conclude, and with good reason, that doctrines for Newman can only be apprehended properly within the flow of ecclesiastical history. To attempt to leave aside that history is to become "dry, uncertain, theoretical, and unreal", and is to misapprehend the great dogmas of the Church. In short dogmas possess, as an inalienable quality, an historicity. This in no way makes the dogmas mere relative statements: Newman saw very clearly that what was actually affirmed at the Vatican Council was a revealed truth of God, so that the meaning of the Council's statement was eternally true: "What has the long history of the contest for and against the Pope's infallibility been but a growing insight through the centuries into the meaning of

---

[67] Diff, II, 206, 195, 194, 197, 201, 206, 208.
[68] Ibid., 312-3.

those three texts, to which I just now referred, (Matthew 16: 16-19; John 21:15-17; Luke 22:32), ending at length by the Church's definitive recognition of the doctrine thus gradually manifested to her?" [69]

Newman rose above all traces of historicism. But having a deep sense of the "real", he wished to do justice to the reality of Christ incarnated in history, and not tend towards any kind of Monophysite disregard for the complexities of that historicity. He could write: "As the Church is a sacred and divine creation, so in like manner her history".[70] As he loved the Church, how could he but love her history as well? Fr. Walgrave in his new book on Christian tradition defends Newman's position admirably: "The history of dogma is not merely the object of an independent auxiliary science, useful perhaps for dogmatic theology as a quarry of possible arguments but not necessary to it. It is a living dimension of dogma itself in its present state and, if it is ignored, attempts at systematization will be like imaginary castles floating in the void".[71]

We have seen how Newman's method of theology in *An Essay on the Development of Christian Doctrine* opened up a new way of doing theology in terms of historical, experiential and personal categories. We have seen, too, how he took the method therein used a step further in the Grammar, which set out an Organon Investigandi for theological inquiry. And there is evidence to suggest that in the *Grammar* Newman was conscious that he was contributing, however modestly, to a method which would reinvigorate modern theology, by bringing out in full, and in terms accessible to our contemporaries, the thrilling mysteries of Christ's Kingdom.[72]

Apprehension of Dogmas Related to the Religious State of the Theologian

The historical dimension of the Church's dogmas led Newman to prefer a theological method that was not scholastic. He now realised that the Scholastic method, even if he had known it from the beginning would not have helped him solve the spiritual and

---

[69] Ibid., 319.
[70] Ibid., 309.
[71] Unfolding Revelation, 4.
[72] See Chapters, II, III; Ward, II, 275-78.

theological crisis of 1841-1845. But there was another reason for his going beyond the Patristic and Scholastic methodologies. "The rays of truth," he wrote, "stream in upon us through the medium of our moral as well as our intellectual being." The conversion of the theologian was as vital to the doing of theology as erudition, brains, ingenuity or industry. The reality of the theologian was a factor of no small importance in his reflections on the reality of his Faith. Abstract reasoning or formal logic, though useful, could never supply for this lack of conversion. Newman therefore preferred a theology that took into account the state of the theologian. This interiority he called conversion and to its role in theology we have devoted the chapter on conversion. The basic and most obvious articulation of such conversion was religious conversion. In fact, it is the second reason why Newman preferred to go beyond the Scholastic method, which he considered had come at an epoch in Christian history in which the turn to the interior had not yet been fully effected.

The Permanence and Development of Doctrines

So far we have only spoken of the development of doctrines incidentally. Still, we have been considering the phenomenon of recently defined dogmas, such as Our Blessed Lady's Immaculate Conception, and Papal Infallibility. Earlier we saw how Nicaea set in motion a series of Councils, which interacted to "interpret, explain, and complete" their respective dogmatic pronouncements. But more important still, we have been just now engaged in an investigation of the great shifts from the Apostolic times into the more systematic period of the great Greek Councils, from the creative achievement of Patristic Theology into the original synthesis of Scholasticism, and finally, the emergence of the need for history and interiority in dealing with the riches of Tradition. All this went a long way towards explaining why doctrinal developments occur.

At the outset of the Oxford University sermon on developments in religious doctrine Newman had attributed development to the discursiveness of the believer's mind, and saw Our Lady as the model of such reflection.[73] In his work on doctrinal developments, he was struck by the fact that in first Christian centuries,

---

[73] OUS, 312-4.

the most august Christian mysteries had only gradually been shaped in the mind of the Church, so that "it was necessary to qualify the Vincentian Canon ('what has been believed everywhere, always and by all') in such a way that the sameness of faith in the course of history was not to be conceived as a static immutability but as a dynamic continuity".[74] In fact, he saw that "from the nature of the human mind, time is necessary for the full comprehension and perfection of great ideas".[75] Convinced that the supreme test of any Christian Church of today was her identity with the Apostolic and Patristic Church, he saw that the only doctrinal developments admissible would be such as could be reconciled with the Church's "originating experience", which is recorded in the holy Scriptures and immemorial tradition.

The question, then, was whether the specifically Catholic doctrines, regarded by other Churches as "corruptions", were genuine developments of the doctrines of Antiquity. The upshot of the matter was that Newman eventually discovered them to be such, in fact, to be nothing but the very continuation of that principle on which alone the undeniable doctrinal developments of the fourth and fifth centuries could be justified. "The decrees of the later Councils, or what Anglicans call the Roman corruptions, were but instances of that very same doctrinal law which was to be found in the history of the early Church; and that in the sense in which the dogmatic truth of the prerogatives of the Blessed Virgin may be said, in the lapse of the centuries, to have grown upon the consciousness of the faithful, in the same sense, did in the first age, the mystery of the Blessed Trinity also gradually shine out and manifest itself more completely before their minds." [76] So obvious was this "doctrinal law" through the whole sweep of the history of the Catholic Church's teaching, that Newman, in the 1878 edition of his work on Development, added in development as the tenth "first principle" of Christianity.

It was a fact that there was an ongoing doctrinal development of the original deposit of Faith. And in showing that Newman judged this to be the case, we have gone quite a distance in showing the actual process of development. Newman wished to submit his views to the judgement of Fr. Perrone, S.J., of the Gregorian

---

[74] J. Walgrave, Unfolding Revelation, 298.
[75] Dev, 29.
[76] Diff, I, 395.

University.[77] In short, development took place during the unfolding of Christian history and within the Christian consciousness, between two poles: on the one hand, the unique Revelation in Christ Jesus, the "Verbum Dei Objectivum", and, on the other hand, the open, ongoing objectification of this in doctrinal form: the "Verbum Dei per Ecclesiam Manifestatum".[78]

But the most valuable section of this little work is the final one, in which he gives a summary, in twelve theses, of the laws and principle of development.[79] The final import of this work is the showing forth of the dynamic growth of God's one and only Self-Gift in Jesus Christ through the Holy Spirit. The Catholic Faith is a dynamic harmony between growth and permanence, between energetic life and enduring truth. Today it does not exist in a "static immutability", but in a "dynamic continuity", with the Faith of the Apostles. Fr. Walgrave gives a splendid description of the developmental process itself in words that might come from the pen of Newman:

> The process of development is a process of reasoning. However, reasoning for Newman is a manifold, subtle, and intricate activity. It covers the whole realm of discursive thought, including not only deductions but also that kind of induction by which the concrete is determined by seeing the convergence of independent probabilities, as well as other processes, too subtle to be noticed, which are at work in the living out of the mind under the guidance of the Illative Sense, which controls the whole process per modum unius.[80]

The Need for an Infallible Developing Authority

As there are true judgements, so also there are false ones. Considering the human situation, the complexity of society, and the inevitable absence to some extent of intellectual, moral and religious conversions, both false judgements and corruptions were far from being beyond the limits of possibility. There would be need for a criterion of discrimination between true and false Faith-judgements. It was reasoning of this nature which led Newman to anticipate the need for the actual existence of such a principle of doctrinal discrimination in the *Essay on the Development*

---

[77] De Catholici Dogmatis Evolutione (Newman-Perrone Paper), ed. T. Lynch, Greg, 16 (1935), 402-47.

[78] Ibid., 407-17.

[79] Ibid., 417-47.

[80] J. Walgrave, Unfolding Revelation, 304.

of Christian Doctrine. The Illative Sense, or faculty of judgement, which operates in the individual, is "supernaturalised" by the presence of the Holy Spirit in the Catholic Communion, and, in the final analysis, is coincident with the authoritative and infallible statement of Pope or of Council. In fact, the dogmatic statements of Councils and Popes are nothing less than this supernatural illative sense reaching certitude in a matter of Faith or morals within the believing community. It terminates a process from a first stage of confusion through an increasing clarity, then a consensus of faithful and theologians, until, in the end, a certainty is reached.[81]

[81] See Dev, 75-92; Diff, II, 319.

CHAPTER SEVEN

THE MEANING OF THE CHRISTIAN MYSTERIES

The Objective of the Chapter

When Newman was only twenty-eight years of age he wrote an article on Aristotle's idea of poetry for the "London Review", the newly-founded magazine of his friend, Blanco White.[1] The article dealt with the object of Poetry, which is "the beautiful", and not with its function, "moving the affections through the imagination". Accordingly, the author's principal objective was the treatment of poetry as an inner spiritual activity of the person, and not so much as the external and verbal expression of this activity. Poetry "is originality energizing in the world of beauty; the originality of grace, purity, refinement and good feeling". The inner state of the person is therefore vital to his poetry and "a right moral state of heart is the formal and scientific condition of a poetical mind".[2] At this point in his reflections, it seems that a deep insight struck him as to how he might further illustrate his main contention.

According to the above theory, Revealed Religion should be especially poetical, and it is so in fact. While its disclosures have an originality in them to engage the intellect, they have a beauty to satisfy the moral nature. It presents us with those ideal forms of excellence in which a poetical mind delights, and with which all grace and harmony are associated. It brings us into a new world— a world of overpowering interest, of the sublimest views, and the tenderest and purest feelings. The peculiar grace of mind of the New Testament writers is as striking as the actual effect produced upon the hearts of those who have imbibed their spirit ... With Christians a poetical view of things is a duty, we are bid to colour all things with hues of Faith, to see a divine meaning in every event, and a superhuman tendency. Even our friends around are invested with unearthly brightness—no longer imperfect men, but

---

[1] "Poetry with reference to Aristotle's Potiecs", ECH, I, 1-29: see excellent study of this article by G. Tillotson, "Newman's Essay on Poetry", John Henry Newman: Centenary Essays, London, 1945, 178-200.
[2] ECH, I, 21.

beings taken into Divine favour, stamped with His seal, and in training for future happiness.[3]

If the ordinary Christian, who tries to "lead a life worthy of the calling to which he has been called" reflects on the Faith, on its doctrines and content, he will come into the presence of a great sight that holds him. The theologian, however, does this professionally and scientifically. His whole being must breathe in response to this "new world of overpowering interest", which is filled with realities and facts, which "no eye has seen, nor ear heard, nor the heart of man conceived".[4] "As philosophers of this world bury themselves in museums and laboratories, descend into mines, or wander among woods or on the sea-shore, so the inquirer into heavenly truths dwells in the cell and the oratory, pouring forth his heart in prayer, collecting his thoughts in meditation, dwelling on the idea of Jesus, or of Mary, or of Grace, or of eternity, and pondering the words of holy men who have gone before him till before his mental sight arises the hidden wisdom of the perfect, 'which God predestined before the world unto our glory' and which He 'reveals unto them by His Spirit'." [5]

If anything was clear to Newman it was the riches with which this "new world" abounded for the present world, which so often cuts itself off from the world to which it pointed. If the Christian had the privilege of being a citizen of this new world, the theologian had the duty of drawing out new things and old from among the "unfathomable riches of Christ" the Head of this new world, and of making these available to his brothers, both those who had already entered this new world of meaning, and those who might. The world might pretend it had all treasures, but the Church had with her, Newman wrote, "the very archetypes of which paganism attempted the shadows".[6] She was able to bring in all the riches of the Gentiles, and, without denying their intrinsic worth, situate them in the world to which they belonged and in which alone they can be seen in their proper perspective.

---

[3] Ibid., 23: compare with (i) K. Rahner, "Priest and Poet", Theological Investigations III, London, 1967, 294-317, and ((ii) H. Urs von Balthasar, "Offenbarung und Schönheit", Hochland, 51 (1959), 401-14; and Glaubhaft ist nur Liebe, Einsiedeln, 1963.

[4] Ephesians 4 : 1, I Corinthians 2 : 9.

[5] Mix, 343.

[6] Dev, 372; see sections om assimilative power of Christian doctrine 185-9; 355-82.

What is to be Apprehended: the Mysteries of Faith

The reality and objective nature of this new world has already been firmly established. This was the purpose of doctrines and dogmas, which occupied us in the last chapter. Doctrines and dogmas are in the context of religion what facts and truths are in the context of life. And as "facts are stubborn", so doctrines do not pass away. The author of the *Essay on the Development of Christian Doctrine* knew only too well that doctrines grew and that dogmas developed in the course of the Church's history. But it was growth, not reversal; development, and not change. Doctrines remain as windows on the great world brought before us by Christian Revelation.

Doctrines are the facts of this world, and without them this new world becomes a kind of dreamland, and no longer is the world of the "blessed vision of peace". He who rejects doctrines will be found to "throw back unthankfully again into the infinite abyss any of the jewels which God has vouchsafed to bring us".[7] We desperately need these treasures. Each one of us "has a depth within him unfathomable, an infinite abyss of existence", to which the divine jewels can minister, if only we accept them in faith and ponder over them in a spirit of love.

Newman's treatment of doctrines was both thorough and critical. It was thorough because the vital personal decisions of his spiritual odyssey turned on the truthfulness or not of the doctrines of the Catholic Church; it was critical in so far as he analysed and personally appropriated the vital role played by assent, or judgement, in the process of human knowing, and so also in human activity and life.

With his clairvoyant vision of the supernatural it was then an easy task to lift this whole exercise in critical psychology on to the level of a supernaturally higher context, such as the life of the Church, in which the one and only gift of Revelation is received and authoritatively taught. This reception and transmission of God's timeless Self-communication, which is what Revelation is, necessarily involves faith-judgements, or doctrines, which are made by the community, whose head is the infallible Teacher, the Pope. If we could reasonably enjoy certainties and correspond-

---

[7] ECH, I, 55; see LG, 68: "Revelation . . . being the abyss of God's counsels".

ing certitudes of mind, about so many facts and realities of every-day life, how much more right had we to be confident in the certainties proposed by God in holy Scripture and Tradition, and taught to us by His mouthpiece and organ, the infallible Head of an infallible Church?

Even before entering the Catholic fold Newman had demonstrated time and time again a forceful and tormented dissatisfaction and impatience with Evangelicalism, which proposed to dispense with Creeds altogether in the name of the purity of the Gospel. As early as 1836 he wrote: "the Church Catholic has ever taught, as in her Creeds, that there are facts revealed to us, not of this world, not of time, but of eternity, and that absolutely and independently ... primary objects of our Faith, and essential in themselves".[8] He displayed a similar antagonism to Evangelicalism's philosophical expression, which even denied all meaning to the Creeds. "My battle was with liberalism; by liberalism I meant the antidogmatic principle and its developments." [9]

"Colouring all Things with Hues of Faith"

While it was an unquestioned assumption among the liberal Theologians of the day that doctrines were devoid of all significance, being merely verbal formularies, Newman on the contrary saw them as full of meaning, luminous stars reflecting their precious light on an otherwise nonsensical world.[10] The meaning of the mysteries of faith was his constant preoccupation, the shedding of their light on the myriad aspects of human life his great concern. He used his consummate skill as a controversialist and apologist to defend a doctrinal Christianity, and his considerable psychological and philosophical acumen to ground critical doctrines; but he did not stop there. He went on to show the wonderfully rich meaning of doctrines. All his life long he had been devoted to meaning and to understanding. In the article on poetry which we considered at the very outset of this chapter, he gave expression to his love of the search for understanding: "Christians ... are bid to colour all things with hues of Faith, to see a divine meaning in every event and a superhuman tendency". Shortly after he wrote these words (1829), he undertook a study of the

---

8 ECH, I, 69-70.
9 Ap, 150; see ECH, II, 186-248.
10 See ECH, I, 97; PPS, VI, 82; Diff, I, 290.

Council of Nicaea, which turned out in the event to be more a study of St. Athanasius and the Alexandrian Church. Here he discovered both a devotion to doctrine on the one hand, and an intellectual hunger and search for meaning and apprehension, on the other.[11]

The very range and depth of the inquirer's difficulties, problems or objections only stimulated Clement and Origen, the founders of this theological school, to greater heights in their search for intelligibility and understanding of the mysteries of the Faith. These mysteries might infinitely exceed the capacity of the finite mind, but it was precisely this quality of theirs which made them the inxhaustible fountainheads of light and life. A good question might be the occasion of an original answer. In Alexandria, there was no room for obscurantism, but there was room for an "intellectus Fidei". How tragic, then, for Newman to see many of his contemporaries give up vital portions of revealed truth! In 1833, at the beginning of the Oxford Movement, he wrote a letter that perfectly reveals his state of mind on the matter: "The most religiously minded men are ready to give up important doctrinal truths because they do not understand their value. A cry is raised that the Creeds are unnecessarily minute, and even those who would defend them, through ignorance, cannot ... What is most painful is that the clergy are so utterly ignorant on the subject. We have no theological education".[12]

As early as 1841, Newman had given some idea as to how he would go about giving an original "intellectus fidei" in a sermon entitled "The Cross of Christ the Measure of the World". The opening of this sermon is worth quoting, as it is very much to the point under consideration.

> A great number of men live and die without reflecting at all upon the state of things in which they find themselves. They take things as they come, and follow their inclinations as far as they have the opportunity. They are guided mainly by pleasure and pain, not by reason, principle, or conscience; and they do not attempt to interpret this world, to determine what it means... How are we to look at things? This is the question which all persons of observation ask themselves, and answer each in his own way... Now,

---

[11] See Ap, 127-9; Ar, 39-99; M. Novak, "Newman on Nicaea", TS, 21 (1960), 444-53; J. Artz, Newman-Lexicon, Mainz, 1975, 608-11, 763, 14, 75-9.

[12] Anne Mozley, editor, Letters and Correspondence, II, 129-30.

let me ask, what is the real key, what is the Christian interpretation of this world? What is given us by revelation to estimate and
measure this world by? The event of this season—the Crucifixion
of the Son of God.[13]

The thought structure of this passage is significant. First, there
is the mystery of life, with its manifold problems, and countless
phenomena. Next, this forces the believer to inquire about its
meaning, to interpret it. Thirdly, as a believer he has been given
Revelation with which to estimate and measure this heart-rending
spectacle, which is the world, and so to the mysteries of his faith
he now turns in inquiry. Lastly, the mystery of life is solved by
the Crucifixion of Our Lord. We may observe that Newman has
thereby shed some more light on life from the Christian Mystery
and Doctrine that the God-Man suffered and died on the Cross
for all men, and this he has done by relating the mysteries of
our holy Faith to the great problems of the world, of history and
of mankind. And we may observe in conclusion on the method of
Newman's "intellectus fidei" exhibited here, that it is characterized far more by a quest for apprehension and the discovery
of hidden meaning in the doctrines than is "thesis theology",
whose model is the syllogistic deduction of conclusions from the
dogmas of Faith.

We have already had occasion to consider Newman's autobio-
graphy, the *Apologia,* in which he gave "the true key" to his
"meaning". But that work has a structure which is particulary
interesting in our present preoccupation with Newman's method
of gaining an "intellectus Fidei". After two introductory parts
on Kingsley's method of disputation and on the true mode of
meeting his attack, Newman gives, in four consecutive parts,
the history of his own itinerary into the fullness of Catholic meaning.
During this itinerary, "the most toilsome, but also the greatest,
the most meaningful, the most conclusive that human thought
ever travelled during the last century",[14] he gradually assembled
the elements and the doctrines of the Catholic Church, which he
recognized to be the one true interpreter of the voice of Revelation.
However, Newman considered it insufficient to show what that
Faith was, which he had accepted and embraced as divine. He

---

[13] PPS, VI, 83-4.
[14] Pope Paul VI, Address at the Beatification of Blessed Dominic Barberi, C.P., l'Osservatore Romano, 28 October, 1963, 1, col. 7.

had indeed come into harbour after turbulent waters, but this in no way precluded further reflections on theological subjects. In fact, it only invigorated his efforts to give some inkling of the meaning and sense of these very mysteries. This desire produced Part VII, the most original expression of the Faith he ever uttered, and that because he wanted to show to his adversary the wealth of meaning in the doctrines which constituted the bedrock of the Catholic Church. In this section he is no longer simply narrating the stages of his ascent into the Church. He does not appeal to authorities, but he does try to give some degree of understanding of the mysteries of Faith by indicating how it could be that the doctrinal facts are what they are.[15] In this way, Newman hoped that Kingsley and the many others, whose attitudes to Catholic doctrines Kingsley exemplified, might learn to "understand the value" of the Catholic Creed. We shall have to return to this section VII later in this chapter.

The Need for Originality of Apprehension

Furthermore, the understanding of the mysteries which Newman sought would have to be original. His quest for Christian meaning was a genuine "fides quaerens intellectum". "Originality may perhaps be defined the power of abstracting for one's self, and is in thought what strength of mind is in action ... minds of original talent feel a continual propensity to investigate subjects, and strike out views for themselves; so that even old, and estabished truths do not escape modification and accidental change when subjected to this process of mental digestion," [16] wrote Newman in 1829. In fact, Newman was convinced that both Patristic and Scholastic theology were the results of the genius of the patristic age and of the scholastic age.

> Patristic and scholastic theology each involved a creative action of intellect; that this is the case as regards the Schoolmen need not be proved here: nor is it less true, though in a different way, of the theology of the Fathers. Origen, Tertullian, Athanasius, Chrysostom, Augustine, Jerome, Leo, are authors of powerful, original minds, and engaged in the production of original works. There is no greater mistake, surely, than to suppose that a revealed truth precludes originality in the treatment of it.[17]

---

[15] Ap, 331-72; compare with St. Thomas, Summa Theologica, Ia, Q, 32, Art 1, ad 2; B. Lonergan, Method in Theology, 346f.

[16] ECH, I, 20.

[17] HS, II, 475.

We recall that, as far back as 1836, Newman had expressed the need for such an "original treatment" of the truths of Revelation in a letter to James Stephen: "Christianity needed to be developed to meet the age". In fact this objective occupied Newman all during his life. Fr. Dessain, in his excellent biography, has shown how at Oxford it was Newman's abiding concern to recapture the rhapsody of the Christian truth of Antiquity in its external entirety and its internal harmony:

> He elaborated the Christian truths, not like a theologian in his lecture hall or his study, but as a pastor who wished his hearers and readers to build their Christian lives on the foundations laid in the New Testament. He wished to provide for them a complete and balanced doctrine, derived from Scripture and the Fathers . . . The late Abbot Vonier used to sigh for a classical theology, where every truth of revelation would be stated in its proper proportion and balance, and not, as is so often inevitable, distorted, or exaggerated, or obscured by reaction against heresy . . . And so it comes about that, especially in these later Anglican writings, we find a classical, a truly Catholic Catholicism.[18]

Wilfrid Ward, in his classical biography reports an interchange of letters between Newman and a friend, on the subject of the *Grammar*, which appeared in 1870, and which Newman frankly, but perhaps too humbly, admits to his correspondent to be a mere effort at supplying a clue as to how a Baconian "Novum Organon" might be worked out for a contemporary theology, which could then do for our times what Patristic and Scholastic theology did for their times! [19]

The Integration of Natural and Revealed Theology

An outstanding characteristic of Newman's reflection on Christian Revelation as preserved and maintained in the Catholic Church, and on man and his history in the light of these realities, was his dynamic integration of Natural and Revealed Religion. This quality of his theology sharply contrasts with the procedure that has come to be accepted and practised in recent centuries among Catholics. The outstanding statement of this integration is to be had in a discourse given in 1850 on the "Mysteries of Nature and Grace", while the defence of this integration is given rather accidentally in the final chapter of the *Grammar*.[20]

---

[18] C. S. Dessain, John Henry Newman, 44.
[19] Ward, II, 275-8; see HS, II, 476-7.
[20] Mix, 260-83; GA, 379-485.

In his discourse Newman put forward his thesis boldly: "It is quite as difficult, and quite as easy to believe that there is God in Heaven as to believe that the Catholic Church is His oracle and minister on earth ... And I consider that when once a man has a real hold of the great doctrine that there is a God, ... he will be led on without an effort, as by a natural continuation of that belief, to believe also in the Catholic Church".[21] In other words, it is just as easy, or as difficult, to be naturally as to be supernaturally religious in the order in which we find ourselves in this world. Newman is thinking of man as we actually find him, in his ambivalent world in which he may, or may not, possess religious, moral and intellectual conversion. Having inherited this view of natural and revealed theology from the Fathers, and having seen it practised by the great Anglican divines of the sixteenth and seventeenth centuries, he was reluctant to abandon it. In accepting the mystery of God's Being, "in spite of the darkness which surrounds Him, the Creator, Witness and Judge of men", one is called upon to come out of oneself, to triumph over oneself, and to eradicate that "great obstacle to Faith in Revealed Religion, a proud self-sufficient spirit". He does not discuss the question if it is possible for an individual, in his concrete situation, to arrive at the certitude of God's existence, independently of God's help in Grace. What he does discuss is the implication of a man's state of intellect, heart, and soul for revealed religion. For Newman, the man who has assented to the Being of God, "has passed a line; that has happened to him which cannot happen twice; he has bent his stiff neck".[22]

The ground for this integration is expounded with confident clarity in the *Grammar*. Christianity does not substitute for nature. On the contrary, it is an addition to it. Christianity "recognises and depends on it, and that of necessity: for how possibly can it prove its claims except by an appeal to what men have already? ... for what would be the worth of evidences in favour of a revelation which denied the authority of that system of thought, and those courses of reasoning, out of which those evidences necessarily grew?" [23] Further, Newman concludes from the New Testament that Our Lord and His Apostles always treated their mes-

---

[21] Mix, 260-1; see Ward, II, 417-8; Idea, 66.
[22] Mix 274-5.
[23] GA, 383; see Diff, II, 254; GA, 479-80.

sage as the very completion and fulfilment of Natural Religion. Finally, the very "doctrines" of the latter point and orientate towards the doctrines of the former: problems that are raised and only partially solved in natural religion are completely resolved in supernatural religion, thus showing that revealed is the completion of natural religion. Consequently, only that theology that relates both organically, while being careful to distinguish the one from the other, is properly balanced.

The actual proof of the existence of God in Newman is implicit, more than formally exhibited, and has been the subject of much investigation in recent years.[24] In brief, while the evidences and arguments for God's existence were individually convincing and cumulatively powerful in his own case, he found it difficult to draw them out into a convincing argumentative shape.

Mystery and Understanding

But can there be an understanding of the transcedent mystery of God, "the infinite abyss", and "the Divine Being", whose mind is "an Infinite Mind", and "who is Himself Mystery", and who has spoken into history through his Self-Revelation? Newman answers this question in the negative: "There is some chance of our analysing nature, none of our comprehending God".[25] But does this mean then, that his Self-Revelation is meaningless for man? Newman is equally definite in answering again in the negative: "Considered as a Mystery, Revelation is a doctrine enunciated by inspiration, in human language, as the only possible medium of it, and suitably, according to the capacity of language; a doctrine lying hid in language, to be received in that language from the first by every mind, whatever be its separate power of understanding it; entered into more or less by this or that mind, as it may be; and admitting of being apprehended more and more perfectly according to the diligence of this mind and that. It is one and the same, independent and real, of depth unfathomable, and illimitable in its extent".[26] This means that, though God in Himself is not understood, the mysteries in which he speaks and

---

[24] A. J. Boekraad, The argument from Conscience to the Existence of God, Louvain, 1961; more recently, M. Sharkey, On Affirming the Existence of God, according to Newman, Rome, 1973 (unpublished).

[25] ECH, I, 39.

[26] Ibid., I, 41.

communicates with us, have meaning for us, in fact, "unfathomable and illimitable" meaning. A revealed mystery is in no way a series of "words which make nonsense".[27]

Newman is careful to point out that, whereas full understanding of any revealed mysteries of Faith is not to be had, we can have, and ought to have, an apprehension of the mysteries of Faith. "A Mystery is a proposition conveying incompatible notions, or is a statement of the inconceivable. Now we can assent to Propositions (and a Mystery is a proposition) provided we can apprehend them; therefore we can assent to a Mystery, for, unless we apprehended it, we should not recognise it to be Mystery, that is, a statement uniting incompatible notions. The same act which enables us to discern that the words of the proposition express a mystery, capacitates us for assenting to it." [28]

Theology has the task of gaining an apprehension of the Mysteries, which are "supernatural matters". However, it is nourished and supported in this task by God's gift of His illuminating Grace. "One of the defects which man incurred at his fall was ignorance, or spiritual blindness; and one of the gifts received on his restoration is a perception of things spiritual ... You ask, what it is you need, besides eyes, to see the truths of revelation: I will tell you at once: you need light. Not the keenest eyes can see in the dark. Now, though your mind be the eye, the Grace of God is the light." [29] Only the religiously converted can really do theology fruitfully, for the curiosity that excites and maintains that process whereby one ponders in one's heart the mysteries of God, is the fruit of deep faith and loving obedience. In a word, religious conversion is a prerequisite for the fruitful grasp of the meaning of the divine mysteries. No one was more aware than Newman that the pages of ecclesiastical history are strewn with the wrecks of theologians and theological schools, who either irreverently rejected mystery altogether, or else watered it down to fit it into man-made categories. There were the Arians and the semi-Arian Eusebians: the former "did not admit into their theology the notion of mystery", while the latter "are consistent in their hatred of the Sacred Mystery".[30]

---

[27] GA, 44; see Dev, 59-60.
[28] GA, 43-4.
[29] Mix, 169-70, 171.
[30] Ath, II, 44; Ar, 272.

But how different was the genuine Christian theological temper! In his own prototype, St. Athanasius, as well as in St. Augustine, Newman recognised that loving reflection on revealed truth, which both safeguarded its celestial content and penetrated its meaning.

> The Arians went ahead with logic for their directive principle, and so lost the truth; on the other hand, St. Augustine intimates that, if we attempt to find and tie together the ends of lines which run into infinity we shall succeed in contradicting ourselves, when, in his treatise on the Holy Trinity, he is unable to find the logical reason for not speaking of three Gods as well as of One, and of One Person in the Godhead, as well as Three . . . Accordingly, St. Augustine . . . does no more than simply lay it down that the statements in question are heretical, that is to say there are Three Gods is Tritheism, and to say there is but one Person, Sabellianism. That is, good sense and a large view of the truth are correctives of his logic.[31]

St. Augustine in his *De Trinitate* had given an original theology of the Blessed Trinity in terms of his "Psychological Analogy", which in the 1,500 years that have since passed, has been improved on, but not replaced. Newman knew this. In fact, in 1836 he wrote in an article already alluded to: "The utmost reason does is by some faint analogies to show it is not inconceivable".[32] Analogy, then, would be the chief method whereby Newman would gain access to a fruitful grasp of the "jewels of God's infinite abyss" which constitute the "new world" of Christian Revelation. We will proceed to consider how Newman was to explore and use a theological analogy which enabled him reach a rich apprehension of the Faith.

Analogy

Newman's predilection for the Fathers is one of the great aspects of his theology. Among the many factors which won this affection from him, the Fathers' use of analogy in their theological labours is not least. "The battle of Arianism was fought in Alexandria; Athanasius, the champion of the truth, was Bishop of Alexandria; and in his writings he refers to the great religious names of the earlier date, to Origen, Dionysius, and others who were

---

[31] Diff, II, 81-2; see Ar, 273; SN, 282, 297, 289.
[32] ECH, I, 43.

the glory of its see, or of its school. The broad philosophy of Clement and Origen carried me away." [33]

What was that "broad philosophy" that exerted such an influence on Newman? Basically, it was the Alexandrine use of analogy in the light of which Newman could write in 1841:

All that exist or happens visible, conceals and yet suggests, and above all subserves, a system of persons, facts, and events beyond itself . . . All that is seen—the world, the Bible, the Church, the civil polity, and man himself—are types, and, in their degree and place, representatives and organs of an unseen world, truer and higher than themselves. The only difference between them is that some things bear their supernatural character upon their surface, are historically creations of the supernatural system or are perceptibly instrumental, or obviously symbolical: while others rather seem to be complete in themselves, or run counter to the unseen system which they really subserve, and thereby make demands upon our faith.[34]

Though Platonic in inspiration and in its philosophical derivation, the Alexandrine idea of analogy was based on the theological datum of the similarity that exists between the various orders and economies of the Creator's work in the universe and in the Church. The beautiful harmony between the various works of the One God facilitated reflection on individual works. The "analogy" between them allowed the great school of Alexandria, the school founded by Clement, made famous by Origen, and glorious by the "great theologian", Athanasius, to produce a theology that was characterized by its creativity, devotion to meaning, and an ongoing search for understanding.[35] Thus, for Newman, "nature was a parable: Scripture was an allegory: pagan literature, philosophy and mythology, properly understood, were but a preparation for the Gospel. The Greek poets and sages were, in a certain sense, prophets".[36]

In the study of Joseph Butler's *Analogy*, which was "an era in his religious opinions", Newman found an Anglican divine, who had been inspired by Origen, whom Butler actually quotes in the introduction to his great work. As Athanasius was his "great theologian", Butler was now his "great philosopher". From his

---

[33] Ap, 127-8.
[34] ECH, II, 192, 193.
[35] See Ar, 39-99; M Novak, "Newman on Nicaea" TS, 21 (1960), 444-53.
[36] Ap, 128.

reading of his two masters, Newman refined his notion of analogy in terms of two derived principles, which, he confesses, form "the underlying principles of a great portion of my teaching".[37] Klaus Dick, in his illuminating study of our author's idea and application of analogy, states these two principles as, firstly, the principle of Sacramental Representation or Economy, and secondly, the principle that Probability is the guide to life.[38] While the latter principle has an apologetical rather than an interpretative function (and as such has been the object of a study), the former principle is highly significant in our present context. This principle provided him with the tools to reflect on the great dogmatic truths that had indelibly imprinted themselves on his inner being in his conversion experience at the age of fifteen. It is responsible for such statements as the following one, in which Newman gives us a rare insight into his theological method of gaining access to the revealed mysteries: "Holy Church in her Sacraments and her hierarchical appointments, will remain, even to the end of the world, only a symbol of those heavenly facts which fill eternity".[39]

An Outline of Newman's Idea and Use of Analogy

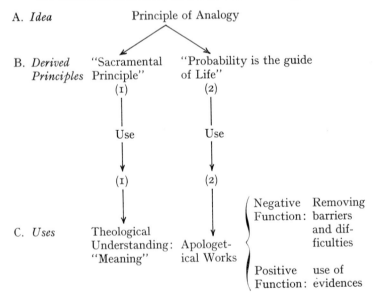

A. *Idea*   Principle of Analogy

B. *Derived*   "Sacramental   "Probability is the guide
   Principles   Principle"   of Life"
                      (1)   (2)

                      Use   Use

                      (1)   (2)

C. *Uses*   Theological   Negative   Removing
                 Understanding: Apologet-   Function: barriers
                 "Meaning"   ical Works   and dif-
                                                                  ficulties

                                                      Positive   use of
                                                      Function: evidences

---

[37] Ibid., 113.
[38] K. Dick, Das Analogieprinzip, Newman Studien, V Folge, Nürnberg, 1962, 9-228, especially 122-3.
[39] Ap, 128-9.

Newman's idea, and consequently his use, of analogy differs considerably from that of St. Thomas, who derived his idea of analogy from Aristotle's analogy of attribution, though with the Platonic modification of the notion of participation in being. In Sillem's judgement, Newman's idea of analogy is ultimately a metaphysical doctrine concerning the eternity and the unchangeableness of being in its ultimate perfections, whereas the Thomist notion is the logical counterpart of his metaphysical doctrine of participation in being. Besides, Newman's type of analogy enjoyed far greater flexibility and so it could be used as a tool to solve many problems which a narrower, more rigid tool would have found beyond its range.[40] In fact, we have already had occasion to notice a case in point. Newman's great sermon, "The Cross of Christ the Measure of the World", is a good example of how he used analogy to shed the light of the mysteries of faith on the darkness of life, in this case, the light that comes from the Crucified Saviour to the sinful and chaotic world of man: Christ is thus not only any way, but the way of understanding our human existence—He is the "Concretum Universale", and so Catholic dogmatic statements are seen to have real substance.[41]

The Value of Analogy

Although the idea of analogy was always with him, Newman applied it, as we might have expected, according to, and only according to, the special needs of his day. These needs, then, determine his actual practice, or application of analogy, in his reflection on the content of Faith. The needs may be summarized under two headings:

(a) the need to meet the liberals' contention that the mysteries were meaningless: the mysteria Fidei must be shown to be radiant with light and luminous with meaning.

(b) the need to give a deeper "realisation" of the facts of the new world to the faithful, many of whom had a mere glib or notional apprehension of the realities of this "unseen world", and all of whom needed to realise more vividly the

---

[40] See PN, I, 171, 172.
[41] See W. Kasper, The Methods of Dogmatic Theology, Shannon-Ireland, 1969, 59; PPS, VI, 83-93; H. Urs von Balthasar, "Christlicher Universalismus" Verbum Caro: Skizzen Zur Theologie, I, Einsiedeln 1960, 260-75.

electrifying power of these realities for the living of the Christian life.

(a) *The Meaning of the Mysteries: Newman's Answer to the Liberals*

As one who had immersed himself in the theology of the Fathers, especially in the spirit of the great Alexandrian School, who had a long personal spiritual itinerary, and had finally discovered the fulfilment of the abyss of his own existence in the infinite abyss of the God of the Catholic Church, Newman clearly saw that the doctrines of the Church answered the great problems of history, uplifted man's nature while safeguarding his freedom and dignity, and answered his great question about the meaning of life and the mystery of death. In 1851, Newman quoted with approval "an impartial writer, neither Catholic nor Protestant", who wrote: "Few even of educated Englishmen have any suspicion of the depth and solidity of the Catholic dogma, its wide and various adaptation to wants ineffaceable from the human heart, its wonderful fusion of the supernatural into the natural life, its vast resources for a powerful hold upon the conscience".[42]

1. The doctrines of the Church answered the great questions of history. In part VII of the *Apologia*, he tackles the problem which has eternally bewildered mankind, the problem of evil. "The sight of the world fills me with unspeakable distress, and is nothing else than the prophet's scroll, full of lamentations, and mourning, and woe". It seems to give the lie to the great and primary truth of the existence of the divine Creator and Moral Governor. It impresses itself upon the mind with reason-bewildering force and cuts into the heart with heart-piercing power: it looks for a solution and demands an explanation. To refuse to meet the problem is to be obscurantist. Newman gives his answer, thus: "If there be a God, since there is a God, the human race is implicated in some terrible aboriginal calamity. It is out of joint with the purpose of its Creator. This is a fact, a fact as true as the fact of its existence; and thus the doctrine of what is theologically called original sin becomes to me almost as certain as that the world exists, and as the existence of God". The doctrine of original sin stands the test of history's questions: in fact, it

---

[42] Prepos, 331-2; see GA, 300-1 where he quotes Pascal's Pensées.

gains in meaning and in depth once related to these very questions. We have already seen how, in his sermon on Our Lord's Crucifixion, he used an identical approach: starting from the context of human existence and its accompanying miseries, evils and sin, he asked the question of its meaning and of its possible interpretation, and found this meaning and interpretation fully given in the "great and awful doctrine of the Crucifixion of the Son of God", the second Adam, who undid the original sin of the first Adam.[43]

It was only then a short step to the derivation of some particulary striking analogies for the understanding of the Church's mission in the world at large. For example, what conscience is in the individual the Church is in the world, and as the development of the conscience develops the individual human being, so too the progress and success of the Church in the world leads to the improvement of the world.[44]

2. Next, the mysteries of faith are able to meet the questions posed by man about the sense and purpose of his own existence, with its manifold problems connected with freedom, and death, and the satisfaction of the great yearnings for unlimited fulfilment in knowledge and love. Now the history of the world and of civilizations and peoples is the history of man himself. It seems that man is obviously under the control of a mighty adversary, who has possession of him. Historically and practically speaking, man is fallen, and his actions and past performance are adequate proof and evidence of his condition. His nature and his intellect have been deeply wounded and injured. Wounded in his nature, man's actions have necessarily borne the imprint of his sinful condition.

Is there any medicine for man's nature? Newman answers affirmatively:

> She (the Church) does not teach that human nature is irreclaimable, else wherefore should she be sent? not that it is to be shattered and reversed, but to be extricated, purified, and restored; not that it is a mere mass of evil, but that it has the promise upon it of great things, and even now, in its present state of disorder and excess, has a virtue and a praise proper to itself. But in the next place she knows and she preaches that such a restoration, as she

---

[43] Ap, 339-40.
[44] See Dev, 361; GA, 379f; Ap, 337f.

aims at effecting in it, must be brought about, not simply through certain outward provisions of preaching and teaching, even though they be her own, but from an inward spiritual power or grace imparted directly from above, and which is in her keeping. She had it in charge to rescue human nature from its misery, but not simply by restoring it on its own level, but by lifting it up to a higher level than its own . . . And thus the distinctions between nature and grace, and between outward and inward religion, become two further articles in what I have called the preamble of her divine commission.[45]

Grace is precisely the medicine for man's nature, sickened by evil and weighed down by the burden of sin. It leads to man's rebirth. The splendid faculty of intellect is equally contaminated. Though "one of the greatest of our natural gifts", its natural tendency is "towards a simple unbelief, in matters of religion". It is driven by a "fierce energy of passion and that all-corroding, all-dissolving scepticism in religious inquiries" and tends "to suicidal excesses". If the Creator should will to enter the human scene and come on the stage of man's dramatic existence, such an entry should have to have an in-built protective against the wild antagonism of intellect. Newman makes this point in these terms:

When I find that this is the very claim of the Catholic Church, not only do I feel no difficulty in admitting the idea, but there is a fitness in it which recommends it to my mind. And thus I am brought to speak of the Church's infallibility, as a provision, adapted by the mercy of the Creator, to preserve religion in the world, and to restrain that freedom of thought, which of course in itself is one of our greatest natural gifts, and to rescue it from its own suicidal excesses.

What the reality of Grace does for human nature, infallibility does for the human intellect. However, Newman is well aware that it could be objected, that such a divine prerogative might easily be availed of to repress the intellect utterly to its detriment and to the advantage of a religous absolutism. Basing himself on the history of the Church, Newman shows that the contrary is true, in fact, and that infallibility has saved the Christian from the excesses of both Fideism and Rationalism. But perhaps it is better to listen to his words:

---

[45] Ap, 339-40.

Catholic Christendom is no simple exhibition of religious absolutism, but presents a continuous picture of Authority and Private Judgment, alternately advancing and retreating as the ebb and flow of the tide—it is the vast assemblage of human beings with wilful intellects and wild passions, brought together into one by the beauty and majesty of a Superhuman Power, into what may be called a large reformatory or training-school, not as if into a hospital or into a prison . . . brought together as if into some moral factory, for the melting, refining, and moulding, by an incessant, noisy process, of the raw material of human nature, so excellent, so dangerous, so capable of divine purposes.[46]

In one of the lectures, which make up the first volume of *The Difficulties of Anglicans*, Newman replies to the objection of Anglicans that Catholic countries display "a hard, irreverent, extravagant tone in religion". He reminds them that this "is the very phenomenon which must necessarily result from a revelation of divine truth falling upon the human mind in its existing state of ignorance and moral feebleness". Not only does Newman accept the fact used in the objection, but he shows how this fact can be used to highlight the sense in the Catholic doctrine of a real distinction between the substantive reality of Faith on the one hand, and Hope and Love, on the other: because they are distinct, one can have real faith in Catholic doctrine without being in love with the objects of these realities perceived in the light of Faith. The spectacle of Catholic countries, then, "is the spectacle of supernatural faith acting upon the multitudinous mind of a people; of a divine principle dwelling in that myriad of characters, good, bad and intermediate, into which the old stock of Adam grafted into Christ has developed". In this way Newman turns a question and a difficulty into a means and method of getting hold of the real meaning of specifically Catholic doctrines.[47]

3. And finally, the doctrines revealed a wonderful intelligibility and deep sense by being interrelated with one another. We have seen how the Essay on the Development of Christian Doctrine con tituted for Newman a theological self-appropriation of his life in Christ, worked out in terms of an encounter with, and personal appropriation of, the labyrinthine diversity

---

[46] Ap, 335-6, 337, 344; see P. Murray, Newman the Oratorian, Dublin, 1971, 272-81.
[47] Diff, I, 268, 277; 270-1.

of Christian history.[48] The historical and personal formulation of this self-appropriation is to be found in the *Apologia*, while its philosophical grounding is to be had in the *Grammar*. What took place in Newman's inner life and theological consciousness in this personal, theological, historical and philosophical self-appropriation was a vivid "realisation" of the organic structure and "beautiful harmony" of the mysteries of faith among themselves. His interiorisation and realisation of the Church's natural and supernatural history resulted in a vivid grasp of her gradual growth in understanding of the once-for-all fact of revelation in Christ. Given the fact that Newman's personal spiritual odyssey was co-extensive with this very development, his knowledge of the fides credenda also provided him with a clue to their interrelation, which in turn provided him with a ready-made method of historical anaolgy, and consequently, historical understanding. Kasper makes an interesting comment, illuminating at this point of our considerations: "This method of historical dialectics (we have called it 'historical self-appropriation') was worked out by B. Pascal, J. E. Kuhn, J. H. Newman (in particular), and, more recently, by B. Welte. It bears a relation to the approach of contemporary hermeneutic inquiry as exemplified by H. G. Gadamer".[49]

None realised more vividly than Newman that the Church was an historical reality, the fruit of an historical event, the Incarnation, and the expression of the inner vitality of that same reality for all men in all places and all times, such that she resembles a "stream which is carrying them down to eternity". That "blessed Vision of peace" had gained his intellectual assent, won his discipleship, and captivated his heart by a love of the "world unseen". It mediated a world of "overpowering interest, of the sublimest views", which then became the key to his personal history and to world history, on condition that he had come out of himself and triumphed over himself in terms of an intellectual, moral and religious transformation.[50]

In his work, *The Modernity of St. Augustine*, Jean Guitton shows how the spiritual order and the historical order illuminated and

---

[48] See Diff, I Lecture XII, Ecclesiastical History no Prejudice to the Apostolicity of the Church, 363-400.

[49] W. Kasper, The Methods of Dogmatic Theology, 40-1.

[50] See Chapter IV.

strengthened one another in Newman, in such a way that Newman "deserves the name given to him by Father Przywara, of Augustinus Redivivus, Augustine come back to earth".[51] In Guitton's opinion, both Augustine and Newman wrote the treatises on Grace (Augustine's *Confessions* and Newman's *Apologia*) and on Church (Augustine's *The City of God* and Newman's *An Essay on the Development of Christian Doctrine*) in eminently personal and historical categories.[52]

The locus classicus for Newman's use of the interrelation of the mysteries, as a tool for disclosing their meaning, is the final section of his *Discourses to Mixed Congregations*, which were delivered in 1850, and which take as their subjects the Immaculate Conception and the Assumption of Our Lady. He immediately declares the intentions which are to guide his treatment of the doctrines: "I am not proving then what you already receive, but I am showing you the beauty and the harmony . . . of the Church's teaching; which are so well adapted as they are divinely intended, . . . to endear it to her children". And how does he a-chieve his objective in regard to the doctrine in question? The opening of the final discourse gives us the answer:

> You may recollect, my brethren, Our Lord's words when on the day of His resurrection, He had joined the two disciples on their way to Emmaus, and found them sad and perplexed in consequence of his death. He said: "Ought not Christ to suffer these things and so enter into His glory?" He appealed to the fitness and congruity which existed between this otherwise surprising event and the other truths which had been revealed concerning the divine purpose of saving the world. And so, too, St. Paul, in speaking of the same wonderful appointment of God: "It became Him", he says, "for whom are all things, and through whom are all things, who had brought many sons unto glory, to consummate the Author of their salvation by suffering". Elsewhere, speaking of prophesying, or the exposition of what is latent in divine truth, he bids his brethren exercise the gift "according to the analogy, or rule of faith"; that is, so that the doctrine preached may correspond and fit into what is already received . . . This great principle which is exemplified so variously in the structure and history of Catholic doctrine, which will receive more and more illustrations the more carefully and minutely we examine the subject, is brought before

---

[51] J. Guitton, The Modernity of St. Augustine, London, 1959, 65.
[52] Ibid., 65.

us especially at this season, when we are celebrating the Assumption of Our Blessed Lady, the Mother of God, into Heaven.[53]

There follows a brilliant account of the "fitness" and "harmony" of Our Lady's prerogatives in terms of the analogy of faith, or their splendid compatibility with the other mysteries of faith, especially that of the Incarnation. Newman shows how to resolve all the various doctrines of Mariology into the doctrines of Christology, and both of these in turn into the unique mystery of God. The analogy of Faith is, then, an indispensable principle of theological appreciation, or understanding, and is one other instance of Newman's breakthrough against the stifling overlay of conceptualism and Kantian scientism. As such it is surely one of Newman's greatest claims to that originality which he extolled.

Professor Coulson comes nearer than most in his determination of what is going forward all the while in Newman. His view is worth quoting.

> We may, therefore, conclude that there exist certain models of intelligibility other than that of exact science, equally good at co-ordinating experiences ... For the Christian, those specific models are the concept of a personal God, an interpretation of the life and death of Our Lord, and the activity of the Holy Spirit. If you say: "These help me to relate together many of the most precious experiences and feelings", you have started where the scientist starts when he tries to develop a scientific theory.[54]

In addition to the strict analogia fidei, there was also the theological analogy derived from ecclesiastical history and in particular from the history of the development of Christian and Catholic doctrines, and which seems to be but another formulation of the analogy of faith, the only difference being that the latter is in terms of the doctrines themselves, whereas the former is in terms of doctrinal history. The historical analogy was the fruit of "his mind working on history". In his great *Letter to the Duke of Norfolk*, Newman indicates how the teaching of the First Vatican Council on Papal infallibility could be better grasped once related to the history of the first four Councils (Nicaea, Constantinople, Ephesus, and Chalcedon), which dealt with the doctrines of the Trinity and the Incarnation.[55]

---

[53] Mix, 356, 360 (Lk 24 : 26, Heb 2 : 10, Rom 12 : 6).
[54] C. A. Coulson, Christianity in an Age of Science, London, 1953, 25.
[55] Diff, II, 305-8.

Shortly after the Vatican Council Newman wrote to a friend: "The dogmas relative to the Holy Trinity and the Incarnation were not struck off at once, but piecemeal—one Council did one thing, another a second, and so the whole dogma was built up. And the first portion of it looked extreme, and controversies led to a second and third council, and they did not reverse the first, but explained and completed what was first done. So it will be now. Future Popes will explain and in a sense limit their own power".[56] In other words, what Chalcedon was to Ephesus in Christology, some future council will be to the First Vatican in Ecclesiology. Perhaps, the Second Vatican Council provided such a "completion" and "explanation" of Papal infallibility by its teaching on Collegiality? [57]

(b) *Method of Gaining Real Apprehension of the "Unseen World"*

In our study of Newman's treatment of cognitional structure we noticed how he posited the mental act of apprehension between experience and assent, and that he was at pains to distinguish between real and notional apprehension. Apprehension, which was an intelligent perception of an object or of a proposition, was not conceived by him as being identical with understanding. However, the two modes of apprehension could be more vividly appreciated in terms of a contrast and distinction systematically formulated in terms of (a) presence or absence of reality or value; (b) direction of attention; and (c) quality of content. The whole thing is present to us in real apprehension, as a unity-identity-whole, while a mere aspect, or aspects of a number of things in mutual relation, are present in notional apprehension. Our attention, secondly, is focused on the whole, concrete, individual thing in real apprehension, on only an aspect in notional. Thirdly, the content of what engages the mind in real apprehension has superior power for influencing us more deeply than the object of notional. In real apprehension a whole object impresses itself upon the imagination so indelibly that it perpetuates itself vividly in the memory and becomes the source of what moves us most and spurs us furthest.[58]

The relevance of this distinction for theology is at once obvious.

---

[56] Ward, II, 379.
[57] Dogmatic Constitution Lumen Gentium, nn. 22-5.
[58] See GA, 31-3; PPS, IV, 201-3.

Is it possible to have a real apprehension (and consequently a real assent, for assent follows upon the apprehension of an object and, though essentially unconditional, varies in power from strong to weak in strict proportion to the strength or weakness of the antecedent apprehension) of the "facts of the new world", the mysteries of revelation? "Can I believe as if I saw?", Newman asks. That is the question and Newman answers affirmatively. And he does us the great service of showing us his method of gaining a real apprehension of the objects of our faith in Chapter 5 of the *Grammar*, which is significantly headed: "Religious Assents in Religious Matters", and in which he considers three cardinal doctrines of Christian Revelation: belief in One God; belief in the Holy Trinity; and belief in Dogmatic Theology.[59]

As regards a real apprehension of the Being of God, Conscience is, as we might have anticipated, the medium through which "a picture of a Supreme Governor, a Judge" falls upon the mind. Conscience, as really one of our mental acts "as the action of memory, of reasoning, of imagination, or as the sense of the beautiful", is "a voice, imperative and constraining, like no other dictate in the whole of our experience", and so provides us with a range of "characteristic phenomena", which in turn become the raw material for a real apprehension of the Being of God. The office which the senses fulfil as regards the external world devolves indirectly on certain of our mental phenomena as regards the Maker of the world. "Those phenomena are found in the sense of moral obligation," one of the aspects of conscience. His approach to the subject is summarized, perhaps, in the following passage: "If, as is the case, we feel responsibility, are ashamed, are frightened, at transgressing the voice of conscience, this implies that there is one to whom we are responsible, before whom we are ashamed. If, on doing wrong, we feel the same tearful, broken-hearted sorrow which overwhelms us on hurting a mother; if, on doing right, we enjoy the same sunny serenity of mind, the same soothing, satisfactory delight which follows on our receiving praise from a father, we certainly have within us the image of some person ... These feelings in us are such as require for their exciting cause an Intelligent Being".[60] Though very valid as a method of getting a real apprehension of God's Being, Newman is

---

[59] GA, 99; 95-149.
[60] Ibic., 107, 102, 104, 105, 106.

convinced that this approach will not avail, as a method, with others, who do not start from the same principles. C. S. Dessain, however, is of the opinion that Newman's approach is universally valid as a method.[61]

The great doctrine of the Blessed Trinity is similarly capable of a real apprehension, though only in terms of the different propositions that compose the mystery when the believer dwells singly on each proposition. Nine propositions make up the mystery. One by one they admit of a real apprehension, as they contain no scientific terms, but only popular, practical words, like Person, Nature, He, Three, One, God, Father, Son, Holy Spirit. It is not the mystery, as such, nor, what is the same, the doctrine viewed as a whole, which is put forward by the Church as the direct object of religious faith. It is only when we relate the propositions "per modum unius" that we run into a mystery, which does not admit of a real apprehension.[62] An ongoing developing dogmatic theology is to be expected from the very nature of the case, on account of the discursiveness of the human mind and the unfathomable riches of the Christian Fact.[63]

This is the source of the objection, often levelled against the Church, that she imposes an intolerable burden on the souls of the faithful by the endless succession of dogmatic propositions each demanding the assent of Faith. Far from a real apprehension, it is claimed, the faithful can merely attain an intellectual enslavement to these new truths. But "the difficulty is removed by the Dogma of the Church's infallibility, and the consequent duty of 'implicit faith' in her word. The 'One, Holy, Catholic and Apostolic Church' is an article of the Creed, and an article, which, inclusive of her infallibility, all men, high and low, can easily master and accept with a real and operative assent",[64] and therefore, we conclude, with a "real and operative" apprehension also, for apprehension must always precede assent. In other words, dogmatic pronouncements of the Church occur during her history in this world below, but they can then be resolved into a central doctrine of the Nicene Creed, namely, the infallibility of the One,

---

[61] C. S. Dessain, Cardinal Newman and Bernard J. F. Lonergan, S.J. unpublished lecture, Miami, 1970, 15-6.

[62] GA, 118-37.

[63] Ibid., 138-49.

[64] Ibid., 146.

Holy, Catholic and Apostolic Church. Of this doctrine a real apprehension may be had, inclusive, by implication, of all the Church's infallible pronouncements. These pronouncements are central to dogmatic theology and are manifestations of the "dogmatic principle" and the "doctrinal law".

Religion and Scientific Theology

The distinction between real and notional apprehension grounds the distinction between theology and religion. A quotation from Newman will help to indicate his carefully nuanced position:

> Without a proposition or thesis there can be no assent, no belief, at all; any more than there can be an inference without a conclusion. The proposition that "there is one Personal and Present God" may be held . . . either as a theological truth, or as a religious fact or reality. The notion and the reality assented to are represented by one and the same proposition, but serve as distinct interpretations of it. When the proposition is apprehended for the purposes of proof, analysis, comparison, and the like intellectual exercises, it is used as the expression of a notion; when for the purposes of devotion, it is the image of a reality. Theology, properly and directly, deals with notional apprehension; religion with imaginative.[65]

If we allow for the flexibility everywhere present in Newman's philosophical and theological terminology, it is only a short step to the conclusion that our author is here proposing the distinction in terms of the distinction between "thing-to-us" categories and "things-between-themselves" categories. The former are experiential, personal, and therefore self-involving categories, while the latter are explanatory, scientific and non-involving categories. As real and notional apprehension are not in opposition but rather complementary, so too "religious" and "scientific" theology are mutually complementary. Religious theology, which is clearly exemplified in the New Testament with its accent on the I-Thou order, gives depth, but not breadth, of vision, and is the principle of stability, permanence and spiritual influence in our reflection on the Faith. Scientific Theology, on the other hand, gives a broad vision of the world of Faith and its realities, but is superficial. It is, however, the principle of doctrinal developments and theological advancement.

---

[65] Ibid., 115-6.

Here we see once more Newman's genuine devotion to meaning and his conviction that the role of understanding in all human knowledge is central. Without an attempt at understanding, there is no meaning. A theology which dispenses with understanding runs down the abyss of conceptualism, imprisons itself within a set of capriciously, often dishonestly, chosen theological tools and so becomes "theoretical and unreal". This was Newman's great condemnation of the Liberal philosophers and theologians, who imprisoned themselves within the fortress of the syllogism and then said they were free to proclaim the faith and defend it! This was the great bone of contention between Athanasius and Arius: in his denial of the Incarnation, Arius had enough erudition about holy Scripture to keep on escaping the real issue at stake: Is Christ God? St. Athanasius made him face the issue by forcing him to leave aside the ready-made scriptural concepts, which Arius irreverently, though skilfully employed, and by coining the non-scriptural homoousion, as an understanding of the New Testament's teaching on the matter, which he then proceeded to embody in a proposition or judgement: "eadem de Filio, quae de Patre dicuntur, excepto Patris nomine".[66] And as for the future, theology would have to go in search of ever deepening meaning through its penetration and appreciation of the gifts of the "jewels of His infinite abyss".

Some Conclusions

Before we terminate this chapter, some conclusions are in order. Those conclusions have emerged from our deliberations on Newman's method of disclosing the meaning of the mysteries of Christianity. The gradualness of their emergences has only impressed them more deeply on our mind.

To begin, Newman has worked out ways of understanding the Church's doctrines that are very close to the ways of the First Vatican Council. In fact, in this respect it is no exaggeration to say that he anticipated that Council. The relevant teaching of the Council is to be found in a paragraph of its Dogmatic Decree, *Dei Filius*. The paragraph speaks of an "intelligentia fructuosissima" which can be had of the "mysteria Fidei". It proceeds immediately to indicate three variations of analogy useful in the

---

[66] St. Athanasius, PG 26, 329A.

pursuit of such an understanding. The three variations are: (a) "ex eorum, quae naturaliter cognoscit, analogia", (b) "e nexu cum fine hominis ultimo", and (c) "e mysteriorum ipsorum nexu inter se".[67] The mysteries disclose their meaning by being related to the great questions of history, of which they can be seen to be the answers and fulfilment. Again, the articles of faith are capable of perfecting man's nature, improving his powers, safeguarding his dignity, and answering his anxieties about the meaning of life and his questions about the stark fact of death. And finally, the articles of faith are fruitfully apprehended by being interrelated and reduced, Christologically and eschatologically, into the one ineffable mystery of God.[68]

In earlier pages we were at pains to discover Newman's method of apprehending the faith. We saw how he did so by confronting the dogmas of faith with the great questions of history, and the problems of man, as he finds himself in this world of sin and death. He further illustrated the rich sense of the mysteries of Faith by showing their "harmony", "consistency" and "fitness" among themselves. In these ways he was able to disclose to others the claims of the faith on their acceptance and its boundless relevance to the problems of their days, as well as to their personal and particular needs and problems. Christ, the centre of all these mysteries, was the "concretum universale", "the way, the truth and the life". Those who followed Him would never walk in darkness.

In the second place, Newman's high regard for the spirit and philosophy of the great School of Alexandria, and its "great theologian", St. Athanasius, led him to restore to the Catholic Communion what was valuable in the Patristic way of doing theology. In particular, he repatriated the Alexandrians' quest for meaning, their conviction that all obscurantism was a denial of faith in the "unsearchable riches of Christ", and their dialogue with all comers, whose needs, they felt, could only be met by Christ. It was his fortune to have come via the Fathers into the Catholic Church. In his own original mind he gradually refined the Alexandrian method into a tool useful for his own problematic.

It follows, thirdly, that though Newman and the First Vatican Council rediscovered the idea of understanding, they did so from different sources and different viewpoints. Newman's sources

---

[67] DS, 3016.
[68] See W. Kasper, The Methods of Dogmatic Theology, 62-5.

were Patristic, empirical, and personal. Just as he refined the Alexandrian methods of Clement, Origen and Athanasius, so too he refined Locke and Hume. But the personal source was preeminent. He might use Butler's *Analogy* to powerful effect, but it was ultimately the self-appropriation of his own progressive understanding of the Christian Fact in history, that gave him his deep love for, and devotion to, the quest for an "intelligentia Fidei". The Council, however, recovered the notion of understanding from the conceptualism that had been in the ascendancy since the advent of "dogmatic theology".[69]

In the fourth place, Newman's procedure in apprehending the meaning of the mysteries of the Faith, has been further highlighted in the Second Vatican Council. For example, the Council's Decree on Priestly Formation, *Optatam Totius*, speaks of "the mystery of Christ, that mystery which affects the whole history of the human race, influences the Church continuously". It proceeds to encourage the student of Theology to search for solutions to human problems with the light of revelation, to apply eternal truths to the changing conditions of human affairs, and to communicate such truths in a manner suited to contemporary man.[70] In its Pastoral Constitution on the Church in the Modern World, *Gaudium et Spes*, the Council views the Church and the world as mutually related, in such a way that the former provides the answer to the latter's questions, which then clarify and deepen our actual grasp of the mysteries of Faith. And the Council envisages this dialogue as necessary and beneficial, both to the Church's deposit of truth, whose meaning it deepens, and to the world and mankind, whose needs it uncovers, articulates and answers.[71] In other words, dogmatic theology in future will be far less thesis and more quaestio. It will be a "fides quaerens intellectum".

To appreciate the novelty of this approach, and so to grasp the originality of Newman's method in penetrating into the heart of the Christian mystery, it is necessary to turn back the hands of the clock, as it were, to the origin of the discipline of dogmatic theology as such. The dogmatic theology, that has been taught for centuries in the Church, assumed its form in the seventeenth

---

[69] Y. Congar, Théologie, DTC, XV/1, 432f; B. Lonergan, "Theology in its New Context", Collection, II, 55-67.

[70] Optatam Totius, nn. 14, 16.

[71] Gaudium et Spes, nn. 41, 40, 58, 76, 89.

century. In this century "people had grown tired of theological bickering, so they appealed to the teaching office of the Church, to dogma and the articles of the faith. The disputes raging between the different schools of thought were thrust aside as mere theological opinions. As a result, more and more emphasis was placed on the Church, or the Magisterium, and its normative function in matters of faith".[72] In the theological treatment of dogma it was inevitable that a methodology should emerge to express this authoritative viewpoint. That methodology involved three steps: 1. presentation of the Church's teaching; 2. an appeal to Scripture, the Fathers, the Councils, the theologians and Schola, to prove or support this teaching; 3. speculative exploration of it.[73] The resulting theology was set and arid. This aridity developed in proportion as the doctrines of the Church became separated from their life-giving source in Scripture and Tradition. Such a theology became a "thesis theology". It could not lead one further into the heart of the faith, for this was not its concern at all.[74] Fr. Lonergan makes the point very well:

> Dogmatic Theology replaced the inquiry of the quaestio by the pedagogy of the thesis. It demoted the quest of faith for understanding to a desirable, but secondary, and indeed, optional goal. It gave basic and central significance to the certitudes of faith, their presuppositions, and their consequences. It owed its mode of proof to Melchior Cano and, as that theologian was also a bishop and inquisitor, so the new dogmatic theology not only proved its theses, but also was supported by the teaching authority and the sanctions of the Church.[75]

The second Vatican Council reversed this order completely. It restored the priority of the quest of faith for understanding over the centuries-old "thesis theology".

All the time Newman had been the prophet of this approach. His personal history and disposition made him realise vividly that the most sacred facts of the Faith cannot even be proven to his satisfaction, that logic and the syllogism "do not fit the facts", and that, on the principle of the Incarnation, all Christian truth and value had been radically related to history in such a

---

[72] W. Kasper, The Methods of Dogmatic Theology, 23.
[73] Ibid., 11.
[74] Ibid., 22-32.
[75] B. Lonergan, Collection, II, 57.

way that only those who were docile to the history of doctrine could "realise" the thrilling and enlivening mysteries of God's Kingdom. And as we have seen, Newman certainly preferred "the inquiry of the quaestio to the pedagogy of the thesis". Perhaps this explains a sentiment he expressed in 1865 in his famous *Letter to the Duke of Norfolk* where he says he preferred their (that is, the great Fathers of the Church) more elegant and fruitful teaching to the contentious and subtle theology of the middle age.[76]

Finally, Newman furnishes a method of dogmatic theology that relates, dynamically, theology and spirituality. Indeed, every Christian should be a poet who contemplates his "Revealed Religion ... and its disclosures ... a new world—a world of overpowering interest".[77] Many a priest educated before the Second Vatican Council will testify to the spiritual barrenness of the dogma he was taught. Newman's great discourses on Our Lady's Immaculate Conception and Assumption are splendid instances of how he could exhibit the meaning of the Church's doctrine in such a way as "to endear it to her children". But the clinching evidences of his ability to do dogmatic theology fruitfully are his sermons, in which he so well achieves his goal of "cor ad cor loquitur". As one who listened to some of his *Parochial and plain Sermons* while an undergraduate in Oxford, Matthew Arnold wrote long afterwards: "Forty years ago Newman was in the very prime of his life; he was close at hand to us at Oxford; he was preaching in St. Mary's pulpit every Sunday; he seemed about to transform and renew what was for us the most national and natural institution in the world, the Church of England".[78]

Our present existence is one of profound mysteriousness. Each person has within him "a depth unfathomable, an infinite abyss of existence". But the mystery of our being is solved by Christ and His Truth in the Church. Still, the Church's Truth yields up its solution only to the inquirer, who is ready "to probe the wounds of our nature thoroughly as did Augustine ... to lay the foundation of our religous profession in the ground of our inner man". In the event of failure to do this? "Our religion, as non-interior, is hollow".[79]

---

[76] Diff, II, 24.

[77] ECH, I, 23.

[78] M. Arnold, Discourses in America, London, 1885.

[79] PPS, IV, 82-3; V, 127.

CHAPTER EIGHT

NEWMAN'S THEOLOGICAL METHOD AND TODAY

Newman: A Significant Theological Thinker

In the foreword which he wrote for Fr. David Tracy's *The Achievement of Bernard Lonergan*, Fr. Bernard Lonergan had this to say, among other things: "For over a century theologians have gradually been adapting their thought to the shift from the classicist culture, dominant up to the French Revolution, to the empirical and historical mindedness that constitutes its modern successor. During this long period there has been effected gradually an enormous change of climate. It crystallized, burst into the open, and startled the world at Vatican II. Earlier contributors to the movement made their mistakes and were denounced. Later contributors, despite their mistakes, not only are acclaimed but even have books written about them".[1] Cardinal Newman was one such contributor to the early part of the movement. He wanted Christianity developed to meet the age in which he lived. He laboured to bring out its incomparable splendour and to reveal its hidden riches for his contemporaries. But Newman, especially after the affair of his article "On consulting the faithful in matters of Doctrine" in 1859, had been regarded as "the most dangerous man in England". "It is perfectly true," continued Mgr Talbot, the convert papal chamberlain, in the same letter, written in 1866 to Archbishop Manning of Westminster, "that a cloud has been hanging over Dr. Newman in Rome ever since the Bishop of Newport deleted him to Rome for heresy in his article in the 'Rambler'." [2] That cloud tended to hang there in the minds of many, until in 1908 Pope St. Pius X exonerated him from every suspicion of Modernism in a letter to Bishop O'Dwyer of Limerick: "Profecto in tanta lucubrationum ejus copia, quidpiam reperiri potest, quod ab usitate theologorum ratione alienum videatur, nihil potest quod de ipsius fide suspicionem afferat".[3]

---

[1] D. Tracy, The Achievement of Bernard Lonergan, New York, 1970, xi.

[2] Letter of Mgr. Talbot, quoted in C. S. Dessain, John Henry Newman, London, 1966, 117.

[3] St. Pius X, Letter "Tuum illud Opusculum" ad Romanum Episcopum Limiricensem, March 10, 1908, quoted in J. Guitton, The Church and the Laity, New York, 1964, 10.

It was not until the Second Vatican Council that Newman's full significance dawned on the mind of the Catholic Church. The Council represents the full vindication of what Newman prayed, suffered and laboured for, namely, a new way of saying old truths,[4] a novel method of engaging the forms of contemporary culture, and an effective style of communicating the eternal truths to our times. That he was successful in this enterprise can be seen in the influence he still exerts in our own day. According to Werner Becker, "German theology at present is concerned with the same questions which preoccupied Newman. It wants to help the Christian to see himself as God sees him; and—with Newman—it asks what are the grounds for our Christian belief. It considers the Church realistically as on pilgrimage, or as a diaspora in the pluralistic world of today. It no longer conceives grace and nature as two floors, one above the other, but as permeating each other. Like Newman—if not always with the Englishman's sense of practical reality—German theology turns to the concrete, the individual, and the historical".[5] To take only one witness to Newman's influence during the deliberations of the Vatican Council, Archbishop Robert J. Dwyer of Reno, Nevada, has this to say: "Half way along the course of the Second Vatican Council this writer set down certain reflections on the influence of Cardinal Newman on the development of the thinking of the Fathers. So decisive was this influence, in his opinion, that the Council might well be described as the flowering of the Cardinal's whole philosophy of religion".[6] More recently Pope Paul VI singled out Newman as a "beacon for all who are seeking an informed orientation and sure guidance amid the uncertainties of the modern world". The Pope continued: "Many of the problems which he treated with wisdom—although he himself was frequently misunderstood and misinterpreted in his own time—were the subjects of the discussion and study of the Fathers of the Second Vatican Council, as, for example, the question of ecumenism, the relationship between Christianity and the world, the emphasis on the role of the laity in the Church and the relationship of the Church to non-Christian religions. Not only this Council but also

---

[4] HS, II, 476.

[5] W. Becker, "Newman's influence in Germany" Red, 188.

[6] R. J. Dwyer, "Newman's influence at the Council", Twin-Circle, The National Catholic Press, December 3, 1967, 7.

the present time may be considered in a special way as Newman's hour, in which, with confidence in divine providence, he placed his great hopes and expectations: 'Perhaps my name is to be turned to account as a sanction and outset by which others who agree with me in opinion should write and publish instead of me, and thus begin the transmission of views in religious and intellectual matters congenial with my own, to the generation after me' ".[7] And it is precisely the present moment that suggests, in a particularly pressing and persuasive way, the study and diffusion of Newman's thought. As his "philosophy of religion" has been the object of the present study, it is now our purpose to conclude by an effort to sum up his theological method. We can show his relevance for theology today by bringing his view of the subject into contact with current theory and practice in theological thinking.

Relative Context and Horizon

Looking back on his long life Newman could clearly see in it the finger of God's gracious dealings with him. Already in 1837 in a Sermon he could write: "Let a person who trusts he is on the whole serving God acceptably, look back upon his past life, and he will find how critical were moments and acts, which at the time seemed most indifferent: as for instance, the school he was sent to as a child, the occasion of his falling in with those persons who have most benefited him, the accidents which determined his calling or prospects whatever they were. God's hand is ever over his own and he leads them forward by ways they know not of".[8] Newman must have noticed, in his later years, the prophetical character of that statement in his own case. It was the turn of providence which largely determined the actual context of Newman's life, religious, historical, philosophical and cultural. We now propose to summarize, as briefly, and as accurately as possible, the determining factors of providence in an effort to describe the relative horizon, within which Newman lived and worked and wrote. We can bring together what follows under the following headings: (a) The religious context that was determined

---

[7] Pope Paul VI, Address to Newman Symposium, Rome, Easter 1975, l'Osservatore Romano, April 17, 1975, 1, 3; quote from Newman in Ward, II, 202.

[8] PS, IV, 261.

by the conversion of 1816; (b) the historical context which brought him into contact with a renewed interest in History, especially the history of the Church of the Great Fathers; and (c) the philosophical and cultural context which he diagnosed as largely under the influence of an ever more powerful Liberalism.

(a) *The Religious Context*

The religious conversion which Newman underwent while still a schoolboy had its lasting effect.[9] Falling under the influence of a definite creed, and receiving into the intellect impressions of dogma, which through God's mercy, were never effaced or obscured, Newman henceforth lived under the great dome of transcendence. About ten years later he could write: "We begin, by degrees, to perceive that there are but two beings in the whole universe, our own soul, and the God who made it. Sublime, unlooked for doctrine, yet most true! To every one of us there are but two beings in the world, himself and God".[10] That initial and vital conversion was followed by two further "conversions", the one in 1828 away from the tentacles of an incipient Liberalism, and the other in 1845 into the fullness of truth in the Catholic Church.

In our chapter on Newman's view of proper theological foundations we tried to show how Newman appropriated his own conversion processes in their meanings for his life and, in particular, in their significance for his theology. Like St. Augustine before him, he wrote and preached and reflected on the Faith as one who had become somebody new because of conversion. As that conversion was to a God who had communicated knowledge of himself in terms of a "definite Creed", the conversion involved at the same time the acceptance of a Creed which in turn excited the intellectual activity of theology. That theology would then be, in fact could only be, the theology of a converted believer. Newman's theological concern, then, is directed from the outset to what Fr. Karl Rahner calls "the turn to the subjective at the beginning of modern times".[11] But that "subjective" Newman preferred to call "conscience".

---

[9] C. S. Dessain, "Newman's First Conversion", Newman-Studien, III, Nürnberg, 1957, 37-53.

[10] PS, I, 10.

[11] K. Rahner, Theological Investigations, IV, London and Baltimore, 324.

(b) *The Historical Context*

In the *Rediscovery of Newman: an Oxford Symposium* there is a lengthy section devoted to the sources of Newman's power. Prominent among these sources was Newman's devotion to the Fathers, and to the Patristic age generally. Once the Oxford Movement had been launched, Newman's great concern was the revitalisation of the Church of England along the pattern he saw outlined in the history of the first centuries. History supplied the model and the archetype; his was the task of "realising" the model in his own day. However, it was no kind of "museum Christianity" he sought to revive. "Some persons", he writes, "speak of Christianity as if it were a thing of history, with only indirect bearings upon modern times; I cannot allow that it is a mere historical religion. Certainly it has its foundations in past and glorious memories, but its power is in the present. It is no dreary matter of antiquarianism; we do not contemplate it in conclusions drawn from dumb documents and dead events, but by faith exercised in ever-living objects, and by the appropriation and use of ever-recurring gifts".[12] He was concerned with the pale distant fact of ancient Christianity as seen in the more recent light of Anglicanism which was neither Rome nor Protestantism. He sought a Via Media. Still he wondered if it could be reached. "Protestantism and Popery", he wrote, "are real religions; no one can doubt about them; they have furnished the mould in which nations have been cast; but the Via Media, viewed as an integral system, has never existed, except on paper".[13] All the works that appeared in this period (1833-1845) had the overriding scope of "commencing a system of theology on the Anglican idea". His hope was to "bring out in substantive form, a living Church of England in a position proper to herself, and founded on distinct principles".[14] With the other leaders of the Movement he shared the objective of intruding into the Anglican Church "the principles of St. Athanasius and St. Ambrose", "which were the principles of Apostles, Martyrs, Evangelists, and Doctors".[15] Once his allegiance to the Via Media idea was pulverized in

---

[12] GA, 480.
[13] Via Media, I, 13; quoted, in part. in Ap, 168.
[14] Ap, 165, 171.
[15] Diff, I, 43-48.

1841, Newman began a search for the genuine heir to the Church of the Fathers. That search was conducted through the annals of ecclesiastical history and yielded an insight into that history's meaning. In terms of an ever more carefully nuanced hypothesis of doctrinal development, he began to see that the great idea of Christianity articulated itself in history, progressively issued forth in statements and finally in doctrines, and preserved unity of type and continuity of principle down the arches of the centuries. But far from permitting his theory of development to be used to dismiss inconvenient facts of history, "Newman was prepared for the logical possibility of its empirical refutation ... Newman vigorously rejected the dishonest distortion of history for the sake of some gratuitous theory".[16] The final fruit of his research was the monumental *The Development of Christian Doctrine*, which was mainly instrumental in his acceptance of Rome as the heir to the Church of the Fathers, whose doctrines, principles, ethos, and mission it alone upheld and continued in full.[17] Does this mean that history is adequate evidence of the truthfulness of Church doctrines? We have already encountered Newman's answer to the question: "For myself, I would simply confess that no doctrine of the Church can be rigorously proved by historical evidence: but at the same time that no doctrine can be simply disproved by it".[18] Thus we can appreciate to the full how much Newman anticipated the modern accent on the respect the theologian must have for "the labyrinthine diversity of tradition, as it has taken shape in history".[19]

The final influence of this way of doing theology on Newman was twofold: a very definite historical approach, and a sense of deep responsibility for his own decisions, actions and standpoints. Accordingly, when he had to discuss the role of the laity and their "sensus Fidei" in "On Consulting", he could take up the history of their performance in the fifty troubled years after Nicaea. At the close of his lecture on the difficulties of Anglicans, there is a lecture whose title explains its thematic: "Ecclesiastical his-

---

[16] J. D. Holmes, "A note on Newman's Historical Method", Red, 97-8; the author refers to HS, II, 342.

[17] See Chapter III.

[18] Diff, II, 312.

[19] W. Kasper, The Methods of Dogmatic Theology, Shannon-Ireland, 1968, 38.

tory no prejudice to the Apostolicity of the Church". Perhaps the most outstanding instance of all in his treatment of the theology of the history-dogma relationship is to be found in his brilliant *Letter to the Duke of Norfolk*,[20] which we have already had occasion to consider in our chapter on doctrine. Newman's sense of responsibility is described mildly in the *Apologia*. It consisted essentially of a deepening consciousness of his mission in life in terms of a call from God to do a work in England.[21] In the future drama of the Church of England, he saw himself as an actor, and not as a mere spectator.

(c) *The Cultural Context*

The popular thinking and philosophy that was in the ascendancy in Newman's age was the result of the convergence of scientific and philosophical currents, which had been developing momentum in the previous centuries. In our opening chapter we discussed the origin, growth and application of the New Philosophy. It produced a mentality and philosophical ethos which Newman chose to describe in one word, Liberalism. The position established by the champions of this approach was attacked by Newman in no uncertain terms. It was the occasion of the stimulus he always needed to write.[22] It was responsible for forcing Newman to bring out what he held and what he did not hold, with a richness of explanation. At the same time as he established his own positions he set about reversing the "prepared positions" of his rivals. The beginning of this labour was heralded in by the *Oxford University Sermons*, and culminated in the *Grammar*, to the study of which we devoted our second chapter. As already indicated in our first chapter, Newman added a note to the 1865 edition of the Apologia in which he outlined eighteen propositions fundamental to the liberal view of theological science.[23] In the early propositions we have the nucleus of the liberal position, which Newman assailed. The diagram below may be of some help in summarising the respective positions and counter-positions of Newman and the Liberals.

---

[20] Diff, II, 171-378, especially 195, 206, 314-5.
[21] C. S. Dessain, John Henry Newman, 32-4.
[22] Ward, Life, II, 400.
[23] Ap, Note A, 491-502.

A. *LIBERAL COUNTER-POSITIONS*	B. *FALSE PRE-SUPPOSITIONS OF LIBERAL COUNTER-POSITIONS*	C. *NEWMAN'S POSITION*
"2. No one can believe what he does not understand." "Therefore, for example, there are no mysteries in true religion".	Human mind is the measure of all truth whatsoever.	We can have a "real apprehension" of the Mysteries of Faith (See Chapter VII)
"3. No theological doctrine is anything more than an opinion which happens to be held by bodies of men." "Therefore, for example, no creed is necessary for salvation."	In matters of fact certitude is impossible	Doctrines of Faith are concrete judgements of Faith (See Chapters II and VI)
"4. It is dishonest in a man to make an act of faith in what he has not had brought home to him by actual proof." "Therefore, for example, the mass of men ought not absolutely to believe in the divine authority of the Bible."	All proof is reducible to formal demonstration.	The Catholic faith can be proven, not syllogistically, but by a convergence and cumulation of probability (See Chapter V)
"5. It is immoral in a man to believe more than he can spontaneously receive as being congenial to his moral and mental nature." "Therefore, for example, a given individual is not bound to believe in eternal punishment."	Religion must leave "natural man" unconverted.	Conversion of our being to God enables us to accept all of what God reveals. (See Chapter IV)
	Basic Presupposition of Liberals: Man is the centre of Universe	*Basic Position of Newman:* God is the centre of the Universe

Basic Horizon and New Worlds of Meaning

The supreme benefit of Newman's contest with Liberalism was that he was driven from the relative context and horizon, which we have just described, into a basic context and horizon within which he was expected to defend his positions and authenticity. Though we have already spoken of Newman's "conversions", he only articulated fully that conversion in his *Apologia* in reply to Kingsley's question, What then does Dr. Newman mean? Kingsley's very question, Newman noted, "pointed in the very same direction as that into which my musings had turned me already. He asks what I mean; not about my words, but about my arguments, not about my actions, as his ultimate point, but about the living intelligence, by which I write, and argue, and act. He asks about my mind".[24] The *Apologia* is the record of his meaning, of the meaning that had developed for him, and into which he had grown, as a result of his conversions. The Apologia, then, stands as the account of his praxis of historical self-appropriation of his authenticity in Christ. The theoretical side of such self-appropriation had been dealt with already in the *Essay on the Development of Christian Doctrine*, in which he had discovered the "permanent structure of method ... the same general process of experience, of hypothesis, and of verification".[25]

Still, the philosophical grounding of his great decisions and the justification of the new worlds of meaning he entered, first the Anglican in virtue of the conversions of 1816 and 1828 and, finally, the Roman Catholic, come only in the *Grammar*. This great work had as a further objective the exposition of a method which could be used by the educated layman to self-appropriate his own "being in Christ". It was meant to be a "Novum Organon Investigandi", a "popular, practical and personal" way of giving an account of one's faith. The final result of this historical, theological and philosophical self-appropriation was an entry into the "unseen world", as revealed in Scripture and mediated in Christian tradition, which Newman sought to "realise" ever more vividly, both for himself and for others.

The *Grammar*, however, had a further value. It provided an articulation of cognitional structure which brought to light our

---

[24] Ap, 99.
[25] B. Lonergan, Collection, I, London, 1967, 151, 150.

faculty of judgement, the vital faculty by which we reach the existent, that which is so.[26] It was this level of cognition that engaged Newman's attention "at great and laborious lengths",[27] in an attempt to communicate a highly theoretic discovery in a palatable and permanent form. In our chapter on doctrines we saw how serviceable this discovery was in Newman's handling of a doctrinal Christianity, such as Catholicism. Furthermore, on the level of "apprehension", Newman articulated the differences between "real" and "notional" apprehension. The former commits the assenting person personally and in the fulness of his being, intellectual, moral, and spiritual, in contrast to the latter, which is engaged with the explanatory relationships of objects among themselves. Our chapter on meaning underlined the value of this distinction.

Newman effected a synthesis between the underlying but often undetected method of the positive sciences and theological method. In the conclusion to our third chapter we spoke of this similarity as their isomorphism. In this way he supplied a model for concrete, historical and practical inquiry.[28]

The importance of this achievement ought to be fully appreciated. Aristotelian science had been the master of all ratiocination until with Bacon, Newton, Descartes and Galileo a breakthrough had been effected. But Aristotelian science was capable of dealing only with the certain, the necessary and the universal. It was powerless in the domain of the probable, the contingent and the particular. But the science that began in the sixteenth century and developed powerfully in the succeeding centuries, was studied by Newman during his years at Oxford and was never out of his mind. It is significant that in the *Grammar* he illustrated the functioning of the illative sense by comparing it with the parallel ethical faculty of Aristotle's *Ethics*, the phronesis. It seems that the reason why Newman preferred the Aristotle of the Ethics and Poetics to the Aristotle of the Metaphysics was because he saw in the former a principle of wisdom for the practical field (the phronesis), which he wished to expand into the speculative field.[29] It is the contention of this study that,

---

[26] Chapter II.

[27] D. Tracy, The Achievement of Bernard Lonergan, 127.

[28] Dev, 122-3; GA, 311-316; Ward, II, 586-9.

[29] GA, 347-352: the illative sense "is the instrument of induction from particulars", GA, 354; see F. E. Crowe, TS, 23 (1962), 639.

in terms of his illative sense, Newman has worked out a highly original and unique model for concrete, speculative inquiry.[30] "Now it is notorious that many central mysteries of the faith are particular and contingent events, or even developing processes; they seem to demand a theology modelled more on modern science than on ancient." [31] Again it is our view that Newman has supplied exactly such a model for theology. The most contingent and most particular of all the Christian mysteries is the one which Newman considered to be "the central truth of the Gospel", the Incarnation "in those days when a decree went out from Caesar Augustus that all the world should be enrolled".[32] The Incarnation being lodged in history, became a developing process through and in that history; in fact, it became a history.

The Development of Christian Doctrine represents an effective handling of the multitudinous detail, stout ramification and multidimensional appearance of that sacred history, in terms of a solid scientific method, which discovered, first a tentative probable intelligibility, and then verified and raised the probable understanding, thus attained, to the level of certitude. No wonder Newman could compare his theological method to the basic method of the positive sciences, properly understood, when in 1879 he wrote his famous letter to the scientist, William Froude.[33] Günther Rombold has, in our estimation, accurately described Newman's method as being an "illative Methode".[34] It is not, in the ultimate analysis, an inductive method, as Wilfrid Ward contends, an empirical-psychological method, as Przywara described it, or a merely phenomenological method according to Boekraad.[35]

---

[30] M. Novak, "Bernard Lonergan: a New Approach to Natural Law", Proceedings of the American Catholic Philosophical Association, Washington, 1967, 249; see B. Lonergan, Verbum: Word and Idea in Aquinas, London, 1968, 47.

[31] F. E. Crowe, TS, 23 (1962), 637.

[32] Dev, 324; Luke 2 : 1 (RSV).

[33] Ward, II, 586-9.

[34] G. Rombold, "Das Wesen der Person nach John Henry Newman", Newman-Studien, Volume IV, Nürnberg, 1960, 19; compare with Hans Urs von Balthasar, Herrlichkeit: eine theologische Ästhetik, III, 2, 2, Einsiedeln, 1969, 15-16.

[35] Ward, II, 275; E. Przywara, Religionsbegründung, Freiburg, 1923, 286; A. J. Boekraad, The Personal Conquest of Truth, Louvain, 1955, 137-140.

The Modernity of this Method

The thorough modernity of Newman is at once obvious. He noticed the various areas in which theology was being influenced in his day and he developed his way of thinking on the faith to meet these new demands and sensitivities. The main sources of influence lay in the fields of science, philosophy and history.[36] Newman incorporated much of the method of the new positive sciences, having first purified it of its totalitarian ambitions and having exposed its misuse in the hands of the liberal logicians. In philosophy he shook off the shackles of the school of the day that imposed on all an a priori way of studying philosophy which Newman recognised as "theoretical and unreal". In its place he put forward an eminently personal style of philosophical thought in terms of highlighting the various stages of the cognitional process. And finally, as regards history, he has substituted, as basically relevant categories for Christian thinking, "the principles of history and historical appreciation ... indeed it can be argued that historical categories are more apt for a religion of incarnation than are those of Greek idealism".[37] These same influences continue to affect theology, even more intensely today. It follows that Newman's insights into theological method are of permanent value for present-day theology. This has been, in fact, the case, as we will proceed to show by a brief treatment of his influence today.

In Germany Newman is recognized as an original theologian, the source of seminal ideas, and the harbinger of new approaches in theology. Amidst the ruins of an afterwar Cologne the reality of the International Newman Conference was born. Under the guidance of such outstanding theologians as Heinrich Fries, Gottfried Söhngen and Werner Becker, the papers of successive Conferences have appeared as the Newman Studien. In his Cologne lecture Söhngen pinpoints the aspect of Newman which contemporary theologians find most attractive and helpful: "Newman finds his place, so to speak, in the prolegomena to dogmatics, he is far more a philosopher of religion and a fundamental theologian than, in the strictest sense, a dogmatist".[38]

---

[36] Compare with B. Lonergan's similar analysis of the influences on theology today, "Theology and Man's Future", in Collection, II, London, 1974, 135-148.

[37] B. C. Butler, "Newman and the Second Vatican Council", Red, 240.

[38] Quoted in Red, 184.

In 1967 there appeared the first volume of a new work on dogmatics, *Mysterium Salutis*. From the index of the first volume
one can gather that of all the authors of the nineteenth century,
or even of the entire period since Thomas Aquinas, Newman is
the most quoted. Trütsch, one of the contributors, remarks on
a new aspect of Newman's influence on the theological thinking
of today. He suggests that Newman "helped Catholics in France
and in Germany to adopt and develop methods of thought which
have appeared (in German philosophy especially) only *after*
his death".[39] What is common to these various compliments to
Newman is the fact that present-day theologians see Newman's
relevance in his theological method. N. Lash speaks of "the genius
of his methodological insights". Perhaps one of these experts
summarises this agreement: B. D. Dupuy, speaking at the First
Oxford Symposium on Newman in 1966, locates the source of
his influence in "his religious philosophy ... quite certainly it
is the aspect of his influence which holds the most promise; it
could inspire the renewal of contemporary theology".[40] A theologian who candidly admits the inspiration he has received from
Newman is Bernard Lonergan, S.J.

The Interest and Attention of Bernard Lonergan, S.J.

In our view Lonergan has both taken up and developed some
aspects of what Newman himself worked out gradually and tor-
tuously through his theological labours.

Firstly, Lonergan has taken up certain insights of Newman
into the correct way of doing theology. Although St. Thomas
has exerted a vital influence on Lonergan, yet the Newmanian
influence came earlier and may have been providentially responsible for the direction Lonergan later took. "Now it is true that
I spent a great deal of time in the study of St. Thomas and that
I know I owe a great deal to him. I just add, however, that my
interest in Aquinas came late. As a student in the philosophy
course at Heythrop College in the twenties, I shared the common
view that held the manuals in little esteem, though I went through
the main parts of Newman's Grammar of Assent six times".[41]

---

[39] Quoted in Red, 185.

[40] B. D. Dupuy, "Newman's Influence in France", Red, 173.

[41] B. Lonergan, Proceedings of the American Catholic Philosophical
Society, Washington, 1967, 257; see J. Coulson, "Front-line theology: a
marginal comment on Newman and Lonergan", P. Corcoran, editor, Looking
at Lonergan's Method, Dublin, 1975, 187-193.

The influence therefore was considerable. Fr. F. Crowe, S.J., one of Lonergan's best commentators, claims for Newman's work "a profound influence on Lonergan's developing epistemology".[42]

The actual influence has been carefully analysed by Fr. C. S. Dessain of the Birmingham Oratory, who "notices certain fundamental themes in which they (that is, Lonergan and Newman) appear to be in substantial agreement".[41] The fundamental themes include an empirical starting point in working out the actual intellectual operations that constitute our cognitional structure, that judgement is the decisive moment in knowledge, and that "moral dispositions are indispensable for gaining truth in religious matters".[44] By drawing out, thematizing and explaining our cognitional and ethical structures, Lonergan supplied himself with a basis for explaining what one is doing when doing Theology, and for giving a notion of theological method as "a normative pattern of recurrent and related operations yielding cumulative and progressive results".[45] But Newman's work was only a beginning, and so Lonergan had to go beyond him considerably. This he did by an analysis of our knowing structures that was more explanatory than descriptive. From here Lonergan could go on to explain decisively, and not merely describe, "the whole theological enterprise as a dynamic and ordered set of eight functional specialties". The closest approach Newman makes to a clear grasp of any branch of theology as a "functional specialty", in the Lonergan sense, is his critical grounding of doctrines and a doctrinal Christianity in terms of a supernaturalized illative sense in the Christian man and his society. This fact emerged clearly in our chapter on doctrines.

And so we have come to the end of the present study. Studying Newman's thought was like sailing on a sea with currents innumerable. His interests were many, his concerns deep, his labours varied, and his personal history a great spiritual and intellectual itinerary. Down the length of this journey we have fol-

---

[42] F. E. Crowe, Introduction to B. Lonergan, Collection, I, IX; see same author's article, "Intuition", NCE, VII, 700 where Fr. Crowe claims that "Newman's path was followed by B. Lonergan"; and again "The Exigent Mind", Spirit as Inquiry, Continuum, 2 (1964), 320.

[43] C. S. Dessain, "Cardinal Newman and Bernard J. Lonergan, S.J.", unpublished paper for Lonergan Congress, Miami, 1970.

[44] Ibid., 2, 3, 6-7, 11.

[45] B. Lonergan, Method in Theology, London, 1972, 316, 5, 133-6.

lowed him looking for his theological method. In 1879 he wrote something, which, in retrospect, sounds like a summary of his labours and sufferings: "What I trust that I may claim all through what I have written, is this: an honest intention, an absence of private ends, a temper of obedience, a willingness to be corrected, a dread of error, a desire to serve Holy Church, and, through Divine Mercy, a fair measure of success. And I rejoice to say, to one great mischief I have from the first opposed myself. For thirty, forty, fifty years I have resisted to the best of my powers the spirit of liberalism in religion. Never did Holy Church need champions against it more sorely than now, when, alas, it is an error over-spreading, as a snare, the whole earth".[46]

In our judgement he is such a champion, not in any narrow or merely defensive manner, but as one who has effectively related the future of the Church and the future of man. That future, we feel, cannot but be richer if Newman's theological method is brought into play. "To speak the word evoking order and peace," Newman once wrote, "and to restore the multitude of men to themselves and to each other, by a reassertion of what is old with a luminousness of explanation which is new, is a gift inferior only to that of revelation itself." [47] His method in theology is capable of furthering this high goal.

---

[46] Cam, 394-5.
[47] HS, II, 476.

INDEX OF PROPER NAMES